Frances,
Countess Lloyd George:
More than a Mistress

Acknowledgements

My profound thanks are owed to my mother, Jennifer Longford, not only for delving into her memory but for her constant help with so many points, also to John Grigg who advised and encouraged me. My sister, Catherine Longford, devoted hours of her time to checking my spelling and compiling the index and her husband, Thor Beverley, helped to alleviate our guilt by keeping our children happy. Suzy Turner, our volunteer PA, organised us wonderfully. Finally, I must say how grateful I am to my husband, Andrew Nixon, for his unfailing support.

Frances,
Countess Lloyd George:
More than a Mistress

Ruth Longford

First published in 1996

Gracewing
Fowler Wright Books
2 Southern Ave, Leominster
Herefordshire HR6 0QF

ISBN 085244 324 2

Typesetting by Action Typesetting Ltd,
Gloucester, GL1 1SP

Printed by Cromwell Press,
Broughton Gifford, Wiltshire SN12 8PH

Contents

Chapter One

A Greater Freedom

On a bright June Sunday in 1911, the Welsh Baptist Chapel near Oxford Circus in London, rang to a rousing peroration in Welsh spoken by the Chancellor of the Exchequer, David Lloyd George. Amid the congregation, unable to understand a single word, but nevertheless responding to the passion in the tone was twenty-three year old Frances Stevenson.

Despite a yearning for greater adventure, Frances had become a teacher in a small girls' private school in Wimbledon, because having graduated in classics in 1910, she found there was little else she was qualified to do. When the Welsh housemistress invited Frances to accompany her to see the famed Chancellor, Frances seized the opportunity even though the service would be in Welsh. She was later to record that she 'instantly fell under the sway of his electric personality.'

Frances had read *Ann Veronica* and found that Wells described the twenty-one year old heroine in such terms as made her feel he was describing herself: 'her manner was one of quiet reserve, and behind this mask she was wildly discontented and eager for freedom and life.' This summed up her own feelings exactly. No wonder a quiet, restrained existence in the wholly female environment of a girls' school struck her as a gloomy destination.

The struggle to provide girls with a good education had achieved great things in a relatively short space of time, but the progress women had made demanded a great deal of commitment from the women involved. Many of them accepted that by educating girls and providing them with opportunities to advance, they were choosing a vocation that could well preclude marriage. During term time there were very few opportunities for meeting men and the academic environment was not conducive to frivolity or any great excitement.

In the summer of 1911 Frances was fortunate enough to be available when her former headmistress at Clapham High School was approached and asked to recommend a teacher who would go to Wales and help Megan Lloyd George reach the standards she would find at school. It was felt that a knowledge of French was an important requirement and Frances had been brought up in a household with her French grandmother and spoke French fluently.

1

Olwen, Lloyd George's elder daughter remembered that two girls attended an interview and the other candidate was Swiss: Olwen thought she was the better candidate, but described how Frances 'wore a little flowered hat for the interview and looked very sweet. She was certainly prettier than the Swiss girl.'[1]

Frances was not a classic beauty, but she was always much sought after as a partner. Janet, her next sister was only fourteen months younger, had thick golden hair and more classic features, but lacked animation. For Frances, bursting with vitality and excitement, life was really something of a riot – especially since her gentle and demure appearance meant her mischievous wit often came as a delightful surprise.

She had her father's Celtic colouring. Her ash blonde hair was thick and wavy, escaping into tendrils around her face. Her blue grey eyes sparkled with good humour and her complexion was clear. She had little dress sense as a very young woman, but she was pretty and bubbling with fun.

In the enclosed all female environment of a small school she came in for some spiteful banter from some members of the staff, particularly the ones who were opposed to women's suffrage. Frances attended meetings at Queen's Hall and the Albert Hall to hear the Pankhursts speak and felt very passionately that women should have the vote. The middle-aged staff seemed very narrow to her and before the end of a year she was looking around for some alternative means of making a living. She visited various newspapers to see if they would employ her a journalist. Since she had no experience of writing for any kind of magazine or paper she was turned down, but kindly, and it was suggested to her that she ought to learn shorthand. In the evenings she began to teach herself the basic arts of shorthand and typing which were to be of such great value to her as a secretary.

Even though she was away from the lively political discussions that had always resounded around her parents' home in Wallington, and immersed in the concerns of a girls' school, Frances could not fail to be aware of Lloyd George. He had become Chancellor of the Exchequer in 1908 and he was not the sort of Chancellor the public could miss – even a preoccupied final year undergraduate. The year Frances graduated Lloyd George had been engrossed in his fight for the People's Budget. His provocative speeches and the repercussions of the budget were affecting everyone and causing discussion everywhere. Apart from this with her concern for woman's suffrage, Frances would have noticed Lloyd George's lack of involvement in an issue so dear to her heart.

In the opinion of the Women's Social and Political Union, the fact that

[1] *Lloyd George Was My Father* – Autobiography by Olwen Carey Evans, Gomer Press

Lloyd George claimed he was sympathetic to their aspiration for votes for women and yet failed to do anything about it, made him a worse villain than Asquith, who openly admitted he did not agree with their aims. Lloyd George, as an acknowledged radical leader, was felt to be letting the suffragettes down badly.

Frances's closest friend at the school when she first arrived was a young teacher named Sian, who shared her sense of frustration. She was, sadly for Frances, already planning to leave at the end of the year and go and work in Paris. Many hours were spent together discussing their reading, gossiping, and complaining. They both agreed that Lloyd George should stop sitting on the fence, but Frances was also disgusted by female acts of aggression and thus not wholly antagonistic to the Chancellor. Moreover his fight for a pension scheme was to be admired, although the arrangement for paying insurance stamps made an impact on her new salary. That was a bit of a personal blow as Frances always had plans for spending at least twice what she earned.

Although Frances was not thrilled by teaching, she was very thrilled by the idea of working for the Chancellor of the Exchequer. As well as his increasing reputation for achievement, his immediate impact struck her as equally exciting. She later described that 'there was something more even than this which distinguished him from all other men I had ever met... a magnetism which made my heart leap and swept aside my judgement.' [2] He had a high forehead and forceful eyebrows over eyes which one minute could beam with good humour, or change to grave perception. Unquestionably he was a very attractive man in his late forties, still dark haired and with these remarkable eyes. Although short for a man (he was exactly the same height as Frances) he had breadth and stature so he never seemed very small.

Attracted to the soft little figure in the flower hat, enough at least to give her the job, Lloyd George also asked her to come to lunch before she went down to Wales. Her first introduction to the lively circles surrounding Lloyd George enthralled her: 'I had never before listened to such witty and stimulating conversation'.

Lloyd George liked women, and enjoyed exercising his charm. In reaction to the hypocrisy prevailing in the nineteenth century it has been understood that Lloyd George was a Casanova seducing every available female. He did not come across as such to Frances at this time. There were libidinous periods later when he might alarm a young typist, but there is little evidence that while he was in office he found the time or the need for as much sexual stimulation. Politics was usually enough and his behaviour to the young and innocent Frances would certainly not have aroused

[2] *The Days That Are Past* – Autobiography by Frances Lloyd George, Hutchinson

any comment in the first summer of their acquaintance. Indeed, Lloyd George was only with the family at the home in Criccieth for three weeks of the summer recess.

Those weeks were the high spot for Frances. When she recalled her time teaching Megan in Criccieth she said that Lloyd George's arrival meant that 'the tempo of the household was considerably enlivened.'[3]

He came and brought the Mastermans, and both Lucy Masterman and Frances later wrote recalling these idyllic days when Lloyd George transformed every day into a party. Lucy described their host as 'in the wildest of high spirits, enjoying himself like an inspired child'.[4]

Meal-times were flexible with luncheon especially random. Mrs Lloyd George understood that wonderful weather might impose its own distractions and some sort of meal would generally occur when everyone happened to turn up. Once, when supplies failed to arrive as appointed for a proposed picnic, Lloyd George organised a lunch hunt. Provisions secured, a fire was lit and Lloyd George set to work with his friend 'Charlie' Masterman to try and cook wild mushrooms. Frances found them inedible, but she was delighted by the high spirits of the party, and by Lloyd George in particular.

He was suffering from the minor irritation of having to sit still and inside for at least a couple of hours every day while Christopher Williams tried to paint his portrait. In order to make these sessions bearable, Lloyd George insisted that Megan and Frances come in and entertain him. Frances had to chat and amuse the Chancellor (of the Exchequer) while seeing him painted in his glorious court uniform and looking extremely impressive. If Mr Williams failed to contain Lloyd George, it meant that as the weather was too good for standing in sweltering robes he had escaped to the golf course, so Frances would take Megan swimming and join Lucy Masterman on the beach.

Politics was obviously much discussed and the recent confrontation with Germany over Morocco revealed certain alarms and prejudices throughout the party. Lloyd George said that the Germans as a nation filled him with respect, but he was made very nervous by the 'junker' class who struck him as militaristic and antagonistic. One evening he spent some time showing the party the possible line of advance by a hostile German army. Frances, with her French relations still bitter towards a victorious Prussian army, could quite accept Germany was an aggressive and potentially dangerous threat.

In spite of all these discussions, she did not return to England full of doom and despondency at the idea of possible war. Instead she had a new

[3] ibid

[4] *C.F.G. Masterman, A Biography* – Lucy Masterman, Nicolson & Watson

hero in her life and passionate love for those things she had tasted in Wales during the long summer days. She wrote of how she adored the Welsh countryside, Welsh hospitality and even described Megan as 'an enchanting child'. Plainly the two of them did get on as Megan asked to be allowed to go to Allenswood, the little school in Wimbledon where Frances was still teaching. Frances was delighted; it would mean that her friendship with the Lloyd Georges, all of them, would continue.

During that autumn term when she might have been expected to miss her friend Sian, she was able to write to her in Paris of the great excitements of her life. She was invited several times to tea at Number 11 Downing Street. Lloyd George had discovered in Wales that, like his greatly missed daughter Mair, Frances could play the piano. Her French grandmother had originally been a teacher and with her first born grandchild she had taken great trouble to attend, not only to her French, but also to her piano practice. Frances now found she was often expected to accompany them all in singing Welsh hymns.

Lloyd George plainly liked Miss Stevenson, but he had made no move that could be construed as even faintly amorous but Frances did assume that the tea invitations in London originated from him. She was quick to sense that Mrs Lloyd George only really felt mistress of the Welsh home, yet she did added that people who expected the Welsh minister's wife to be an uneducated peasant were greatly surprised by her intelligence and calm sense of dignity. In London it was Lloyd George who made most of the arrangements, but that was because he had certain needs there and Margaret was prepared to fit in. Lloyd George was not always at the tea parties and Frances seems to have enjoyed these occasions almost as much: 'the family were always less restrained in his absence.'

At this time Margaret was making an effort to give support to her husband in London, but she was not remotely in awe of his success. She regarded him, as she always had done, with love mixed with anger at his infidelities, and she had confidence in her own worth. Both had been adored as children and she had also been materially indulged. They shared a great sense of their own specialness, to a greater extent than Frances ever did. Margaret could not bring herself to worship David and tend to his every whim as he expected. She had far too strong a recollection of how she had taken a risk to marry the unknown and unproved David Lloyd George.

He never ceased to be the lad she had condescended to marry and she would not rush around and make herself uncomfortable to pander to him. Unlike Frances, she did not feel she should be self-effacing or care for this man's needs above her own. Particularly, she did not think she should put his demands above the needs of her children. As an indulged and adored child Lloyd George had enjoyed total attention and support. He respected his wife's independence but he never fully understood it, and he felt he needed a woman's cossetting to the exclusion of any other demands on her time. As he became increasingly successful, he came almost to regard it as a right and, no matter how loyal Margaret was, and however much they shared, she would never be able to give him the total commitment he demanded.

Nevertheless, their marriage had by no means drifted into a meaningless sham designed to placate the world as Frances later believed. From the vast number of letters which survive between the couple, one sees that Lloyd George remained fond of his 'Maggie bach' until she died. They had areas of experience he could share with no one else. Both understood Welsh ways, she remembered him in his youth and they had shared the pleasures and pains of a family. But his huge success had rather taken him away from being a family man even in the earliest days of their marriage, and Margaret had not seen any need to be with her young husband in London when she felt that it would be to her children's disadvantage.

When first an MP, Lloyd George had had very little money. His brother continued to run their legal practice and support his brother's family. It was therefore easier, and probably healthier, to keep the young Lloyd George children in Criccieth. These long separations put a strain on the marriage and meant that Margaret could not share her husband's early anxieties, hopes and successes. Lloyd George also felt resentful that she should put the children's needs first and saw no reason to reject the kind attentions of sympathetic and interested women.

Margaret was bitterly hurt and outraged by these affairs, but by the time Frances appeared on the scene such episodes had become part of history and the marriage had settled into a fairly satisfactory working arrangement. Margaret and David were able to talk to each other frankly, and he could count on Margaret's support in Wales. The two were fond of each other and Lloyd George had less need, or excuse, for turning to other women for solace as Margaret now spent most of her time in London. Nonetheless, he found himself more and more intrigued by the pretty and vivacious school mistress, and he could not fail to enjoy her blatant admiration.

Frances came to believe that the marriage was effectively over. Lloyd George told her that when his eldest daughter died in 1907, he and his wife drifted apart. 'They could not go to each other for sympathy and understanding when Mair died ... The gap of incompatibility which had always been there became emphasised and more difficult to bridge'.[5]

Naturally it suited Frances to believe what Lloyd George told her but it was not true. At the time of Mair's death, David and Margaret had clung

[5] F Lloyd George op cit

together. The death of a gentle and admiring daughter left a gap in Lloyd George's life which Frances was to fill. It was only then that the marriage suffered from Mair's death. In her diary Frances later wrote that Lloyd George told her she had 'taken the place somewhat of Mair' and that she 'made up for her loss a little'. It is telling that she did not mind being seen as a kind of substitute: her relationship was that of an admiring subordinate. It was clear that she considered him so important that any way she could serve him was good enough. Naturally he enjoyed that.

Over the winter of 1911 and 1912 Lloyd George began to acknowledge Frances's manifest attractions. Here was a soft, pretty woman with a gentle manner whose lively sense of humour appreciated his jokes, and who wanted to tend his every need. Megan once described her as 'like a thick pile carpet into which one's feet sank gratefully' and this some years after Megan had begun to loathe her.[6] Yet she recognised that especial quality of being responsive and easy to be with, while at the same time intelligent and well educated.

Frances found that giving pleasure was one of the things she enjoyed most in life. It was fortunate that during her youth, this coincided with passing exams, winning scholarships, doing translation for Grandmama and practising her piano. Her French improved, her piano playing delighted and she also acquired some knowledge of politics as her Grandmama liked to translate the French political magazines: *Journal des débuts* and *Revue des Deux Mondes*. She obtained a scholarship to Clapham High School where her great admiration for a certain Miss Trenerry propelled her towards success in Latin and Greek. She obtained a scholarship to London University. She had originally wanted to go to Girton like her admired Miss Trenerry, but the headmistress pointed out that a scholarship in the hand was probably worth a great deal more than a possible exhibition to Cambridge in the bush. Her parents' finances were never likely to make further education easy, though they were delighted at the prospect of Frances being able to continue at very little expense to themselves. Ultimately they hoped that Frances would make a happy marriage and live a secure and protected life, but they were both from a background that considered education enormously valuable. Confident that it could only improve Frances's chances for fulfilment and despite the financial drain provided by their four other children, they encouraged Frances to go on to University.

Frances herself did not regard education as a means to any specific career or goal. She also expected to marry and have many children, but academic distinction was a very satisfying reward for all her hard work and a good way of winning approval. Classics were easy to master and

[6] *Lloyd George from Peace to War 1912–1916* – John Grigg, Methuen

further study postponed the day when she would have to earn a living. In the autumn of 1907 Frances had gone up to Royal Holloway College to read classics and it was here she made some lifelong friends free from the rather dominating influence of her mother. They were being taught by women for whom education was a victory after a long drawn out battle against circumstances and Frances with her friends discussed and worried about social inequalities.

She became a suffragist, wanting the vote for women but very unwilling to involve herself with violent and strident campaigns. She once wrote that she thought that she would have been far more fervent as a suffragist if she had met and been personally inspired by Mrs Pankhurst. She felt that women tended to become devoted to a cause through individuals,

> I found the greatest difficulty in setting up any real genuine enthusiasm for the suffrage movement at college, keen as I am on votes for women, though I have no doubt that if I knew Mrs Pankhurst I should be devoted to her and through her to the cause.[7]

Her spirits could be engaged by a rousing talk or a well written book, but her deepest emotions were not yet caught up and her intellect did not persuade her to be consistently concerned. Also at heart, Frances had been brought up to believe men were of more importance than women. She knew she was as intelligent as many men and she considered that she should receive equal reward in pay for equal contribution in effort. She also felt that women could make a valuable and vitally needed contribution to politics if they were allowed the vote, but she was not so radical as to want to change the existing family structure. Men were the breadwinners, therefore their careers and their talents were more important. The vote would help women achieve justice and equal treatment and prevent them being forced into subjection to the wrong man. But her feelings about men were those of Wells' heroine, Ann Veronica: 'only God, who made the world, can alter things to prevent her being a slave to the right one.' Since she considered that men were the real achievers, women, however intelligent and independent should be supportive.

In the spring of 1912 Frances's friendship with Lloyd George deepened. He found she could provide him with a competent translation and summary of a book on land systems in France and possible reforms. The following summer extended his reliance on her. and the attraction was becoming dangerous. They even began to talk about it. Almost a year after

[7] Private papers retained by Frances Lloyd George and left to her granddaughter Ruth Longford henceforth referred to as FLG papers.

Frances had attended Number 11 for her interview, Lloyd George came down to an open day at the school on her request, having confessed to her that 'something serious was happening'.

Now Frances no longer worked for the Lloyd George family, but specifically for him. They were more and more alone, ostensibly because she was doing more work for the his planned land campaign, but in reality she was going to listen to him in the House of Commons, giving him her support and appreciation. Her evident admiration, and her idealistic desire to help meant a lot to him. He liked to see his ardent supporter in the Visitors' Gallery and talk over his performance with her afterwards. Her opinion was valuable too: she understood his aims and judged the effect with intelligence, though with the bias of admiration. Thus Lloyd George had the immense boost of praise backed by reason, and that from a pretty as well as an intelligent source. They corresponded almost every day, and when she could get up to hear him in debate he would try to take her out to dinner.

Frances realised the direction events were taking, but she had long since failed to find it possible to resist Lloyd George's charm. At school in the autumn term, her daily letters were handed over by a patently disapproving headmistress. She must have known that her feelings of intense attraction were in conflict with the rules of her upbringing. She had been brought up in a happy home by parents who complemented each other and she viewed marriage as a most desirable destiny. Her mother, Louise Augustine was intelligent, ambitious and mercurial. She enjoyed reading and discussing politics and literature. She liked music, art and the theatre and if she was going up to London to buy material in the sales she would always take one of the children and combine the outing with a visit to a gallery or a play. Her favourite author was E F Benson with his gentle satire of English society, but while Louise liked to laugh at English snobberies, she was very defensive of her own ability to fit in with them perfectly. Respectability mattered greatly to her.

Although from a slightly Bohemian artistic background Louise had been firmly grounded in French bourgeois principles by her mother. In addition, she knew that John Stevenson's Scottish family were upset when he chose to marry a French woman. Louise was not of a temperament to cope with possible criticism and she was highly defensive towards her husband's family. She joined the Church of England and determined to prove to the Stevensons that she could bring up respectable middle class children.

Despite her acquaintance with French art and literature and her own keen intelligence, it was of the utmost importance to her that her children should conform to standards followed by her neighbours and relatives. She was a strong woman and her volatile temper was awesome.

Open opposition was foolhardy. Cycle riding had been done in secret at first as Mama had not considered it respectable. She was hospitable and friends of her children might come to tea, and later they could enjoy exuberant musical parties, but they had to come from similar backgrounds. She had a certain arrogance and a conviction that she was anyone's equal and she would prove it. Her children were never remotely conscious of so-called 'humble origins'. If anything they were bestowed with a special confidence that they, at least, knew 'how to behave.'

Frances knew that her mother would have been appalled that she should even contemplate a relationship with a married man, but by now, however, she was fired with such ardent devotion that if her hero demonstrated a need for her services she felt wholly justified in providing them.

She would tell herself that Margaret neglected David. Margaret should come to the House and hear David speak. Margaret should provide him with comfortable little suppers and the admiration he needed to encourage him in his work. If she chose to neglect him, attending first to the interests of her children, and. having no interest in making her home comfortable, then she should expect him to find a soft shoulder to lean on, or at least a willing listener to talk to.

At first this was all she was, but it was becoming clear that she must decide if this was all she wished to remain. She was by now very much in love with him, and it was hard to resist his pressure to become his mistress. She could confide her dilemma to no one, not even to Sian to whom she wrote a long letter in the autumn. She admitted that Lloyd George had said he might be able to find work for her, but made no reference to the condition on which this work relied. Rather, the letter described parties and gaieties as though her private and personal life were still remote from Lloyd George.

This was a good test of what life would be like were she to submit. She would never be able to rejoice openly in her love and in the glorious feeling of being loved in return. She would never be able to bask in his reflected glory – at least she could not count on ever being able to do so. Quite apart from this, her parents would be devastated.

At this time she claimed to have 'completely renounced religion'.

I have been reading some of Anatole France's books lately and they make one fearfully cynical, but all the same it was not that that influenced me, as I had come to my conclusion long before I started on him.

Before Sian left Allenswood in the previous summer term they had agreed that they did not know whether there was a God, and this was a convenient conclusion for Frances to come to in the light of her desires. She did not want to acknowledge any possible moral barrier to what was becoming a tantalisingly attractive road.

As a child she had been rather disillusioned when despite her earnest prayers her grandfather had not recovered from his cancer. Prayers and attendance at the Anglican Church had been seen to by Louise, although John Stevenson was Presbyterian and Louise was nominally Catholic. The children were encouraged to be conventionally 'Christian', probably more because Louise did not want them to labour under the handicap of non-conformity, than because there were any strong convictions about it. Papa was easy-going and prepared to pray in any Church and Mama was not basically very religious. Once she had seen to it that her children were confirmed into the Anglican Church she left their religious observances to them. In the case of Muriel, her youngest child, she failed even to ensure confirmation.

Frances did receive such education in religion as was gained from regular attendance at Church and the extensive instruction still followed in all Anglican schools. She was able to question her own faith and decide for herself which way her natural inclinations took her. For most of her youth, they led her to enjoy the comfortable conviction that there probably was a God, and that he would be supportive and kind to those in need, particularly her own family. Like so many idealistic teenagers she did experience intense moments. On reading *Quo Vadis* she yearned to be a Christian martyr or missionary. A biography of St Catherine led to a short spell of believing that she should become a nun; a beautiful, romantic virtuous nun. But the practicalities involved did not appeal to her robust side, and for the most part she accepted and believed implicity that one day she would 'meet her fate' and marry him.

It says something for the strength of her upbringing that although she was trying to represent herself as a 'new woman' and free from social pressures, she held out against Lloyd George's charms for as long as she did. She went away to Scotland at Christmas, to try and decide what she should do.

Lloyd George plainly wanted her to become his mistress. He stressed his loneliness and need, and quite obviously did not talk to her of the bond his years with Margaret had forged. He was, however, honest enough to make it absolutely plain that he would not, or as he put it, could not, divorce Margaret and offer Frances marriage. For all she liked to imagine herself as an emancipated twentieth century woman, marriage and the prospect of children meant a great deal to her. Lloyd George did say that if he was ever free to do so he would marry her, but he gave her a book on Parnell to explain his position: 'by marrying Kitty O'Shea, Parnell had destroyed his own career and destroyed the Irish Party: and he held that no man has a right to imperil his political party and its objective for the sake of a woman'.

It may have seemed possible to become his secretary without the corollary of becoming his mistress; she had resigned from Allenswood at the end of the Christmas term in order to work for him full-time. Although she had not liked teaching she must have been quite competent. The headmistress was distressed at her resignation and told her she could have reached the top of her profession. No doubt her vivacity enlivened a classroom and she was full of jokes and challenges for the girls, but she did have problems, particularly with discipline. She found it very hard to distance herself from her pupils and her older students found it hard to see where the dividing line lay between her friendship and her authority. They called her 'Pussy' which Lloyd George was to deem appropriate in view of her softness and kittenish good humour.

Soft she may have been but she needed to think seriously about all the aspects of her future with Lloyd George and she then went to Scotland to decide. It is reasonable to assume that she realised the difficulty of resisting such a persuasive man when they planned to work in such close proximity.

While in Scotland, she gave serious consideration to the considerable counter attractions of marriage. She met again a young civil servant called Stuart Brown who had fallen in love with her the previous summer and who now asked her to marry him. His sister Dorothy was a close college friend, and the attention she received from this much admired older brother left her confused and by no means indifferent: 'He was in every way a desirable parti', highly intelligent, musical, a civil servant with a "future"'.[8] He was also witty, and slightly arrogant and it felt like something of a coup to persuade this rather imposing young man to fall in love with her.

She was flattered and also attracted to the idea of security, pleasing to her parents, a future with children and all the other attributes attached to being a married woman at the time. She wrote to tell Lloyd George that she was being tempted by the idea of marriage.

At first he replied saying he must honourably leave her to do as she saw best, but almost immediately afterwards he wrote again saying that something terrible had happened and that he 'needed' Frances. Thinking that she was needed caused Frances to rush straight back to London.

The 'terrible thing' was the Marconi scandal, but indications that this would cause trouble had first shown in the previous autumn and the real storm did not break until March 1913. It seems likely that Lloyd George was using the scandal as the clinching argument to sweep away Frances' doubts. If so it had the desired effect, because Frances not only rushed to his side, but also placed herself, as she puts it, 'in his hands unconditionally'.

[8] F Lloyd George op cit

It does not seem that she did this on a tidal wave of physical passion overthrowing her judgement. Sex never meant a great deal to her and she could easily endure long patches without it that occurred during their relationship. She admitted many years later that she thought sex was the cause of a great deal too much fuss. Maybe this was because Lloyd George was a selfish or older lover. Certainly she did not lack sensuality. In other areas she showed an ardent physical response: to beauty, to luxury, to pleasure in many forms, but when it came to sex she seems to have been driven by her desire to please the person she loved. She felt she was necessary to him and to his work which she considered so valuable; that Lloyd George had been lonely before and that she could change all that. She justified the step that she had been taught was immoral, by feeling that it was a great and glorious 'love' and she wrote that 'love justifies many audacities'.

Later she would see that not everything he did was infallible, and she came slowly to resent aspects of her servitude, but she never ceased to be his ardent admirer, always ready to put his interests above her own. The Marconi scandal was a foolish blunder for a Chancellor of the Exchequer to make and could easily have destroyed Lloyd George's career, but it did not disillusion or upset Frances. She was quite prepared to accept his perception of events. It was not very creditable to be revealed as guilty of insider dealing when Chancellor, and still less creditable to be caught out trying to evade the truth in parliament, yet Frances agreed that the whole blame must be laid on Rufus Isaacs, whose advice should have been trustworthy as the chief law officer of the crown.

For several weary days, Frances toured newspaper offices to look up past papers and find out whether there had been any public mention of the American Marconi shares, making them available to the general public. This would have exonerated the two men publicly, but was not in fact the case. She did all she could to comfort Lloyd George, talking to him and helping him 'to cross the raging torrent of political hatred which would gladly have compassed his downfall'. She described Isaacs as having a 'cafeteria mind – self service only.'

Lloyd George had won himself a dedicated and loyal servant as much as an attractive young mistress. Some years later Lloyd George's political adviser Thomas Tweed wrote a novel called *Rinehard* in England and *Gabriel over the White House* in the United States. The book described the relationship between the politician and his secretary, based on what he had observed between Frances and Lloyd George.

The great ones of the world, who are always so tiresomely in earnest about their country, or their politics, or their business or even shall I say their books and speeches, are all like spoilt children in one respect … they want to be praised.

You may call it vanity – perhaps it is – but it is a natural wholesome and quite understandable vanity. You will say to me: 'Surely the cheers of the crowd, the eulogies of the critics, the heads turned towards them in the restaurant and theatre, the gentle adoration glowing in the shy – but not wholly averted – eyes of the women – surely this is praise enough?' But no it is not. It is the private compliment, the personal and possessive adoration that they seek and find sweeter.

'But', you say, 'surely a man receives his mead of personal and private congratulations in his home, and his nostrils are filled with the incense burned in his honour by the wife of his bosom?'

My friend, you know little about husbands and wives if you believe this. A husband may admire his wife and she may still retain a romantic affection for the lover of her youth, but alas! propinquity and a long familiarity have made her realise that the great one who is her husband, whom the papers praise and the women run after, is to her mind something of a fraud.

She is proud to bask in the warm sun of his godlike reputation, but while the crowd is cheering and the band is playing, she looks out of the corner of her eyes at her middle aged mate and remembers how dreadful he looks in his striped pyjamas; how insufferable he is over the housekeeping accounts; how nothing can cure him of snoring when he is in bed.

To her he is a compound of baby and overgrown schoolboy, and she does not hesitate to let him know that this is her conception. Though she is pleased at the plaudits of the multitude she is a little jealous because the multitude is taking something away, is intruding upon her sense of possession and privacy. Every wife thinks it necessary for her self-respect to deflate the public's hero by the administration of a little common sense and a few home-truths. No man is a hero to his wife, but unless he is a hero to his private secretary she does not long remain his private secretary...

Whether he had made a good speech or a bad speech, whether there had been wild enthusiasm or marked coldness, Rinehard never quite relaxed from the tension of the nervous and mental strain until in the privacy of his room Pendie had said: You were brilliant tonight, my dear; I never knew you in better form ... easing 'jagged nerves' and soothing the pent up soul of the orator.'[9]

Compare this with a typical little note in Frances's writing: 'A really admirable little speech. You got into your stride again very soon after the interruption, were in excellent form. The House deeply interested and

[9] *Rinehard* T F Tweed published by Arthur Barker Ltd 1933

very pleased. I thought especially with the part about America!' signed P for Pussy and undated.[10] Compare it, too, with her own comments in her autobiography where she says: 'He used to receive such messages after a speech to reassure him. With the true temperament of the artist he was glad to receive praise for his work'. and quotes another one which said: 'First class. It was everything I could have wished. Every point however quietly made, went home, and you had the rapt attention of the House. It was a complete success. P'

In her role as private secretary, Frances found she was able to be almost constantly at his side in a way few wives can be. She could support him and encourage him in this fashion, supplying the admiration he failed to find at home where if familiarity did not exactly breed contempt, there was a certain degree of casualness.

As had been the case when she was at school, when inspired Frances had the intelligence to discipline her mind and stretch herself. Her passion to please LG and help him with his burdens made her an incomparable private secretary. She discreetly took up her new role and, competently set about putting his chaotic papers in order. She also attuned her mind to the political developments of the day and became a keen political observer and partisan on his behalf.

Lloyd George had acquired a young and efficient aide de camp with intelligence enough to follow his arguments and contribute opinions of her own. Her thoughts were more conventional than his, but her youth gave her a different standpoint, and her capacity for sensing what people thought, combined with her education and wit, provided him with a filter of public opinion much sweetened by her bias in his favour. She became a marvellous audience on which he could test his ideas.

There were risks to Lloyd George's career: the media might expose the affair and thus offend his supporters, but this was not a serious threat. To quote John Grigg,

> as long as no marriage was endangered public men were left to carry on their private affairs in private. The press did not take it upon themselves to publicise affairs unnecessarily except when marriages were in jeopardy and that was because 'marriage was an institution whose maintenance was in the public interest and... public men should therefore set an example by upholding it in their own lives.' [11]

While a mistress could be trusted to be discreet exposure was unlikely.

For Frances, the benefits were less obvious. A J P Taylor wrote that he

[10] FLG papers
[11] J Grigg op cit

admired Frances for the way she sacrificed all for love. He went on to call this seriously into doubt by printing a comment a friend of his made saying that for Frances 'the relationship was pure gain'.[12] The friend felt that Frances was lifted from her position as a teacher in an obscure school and placed at the heart of events where she mixed with kings and ministers, stayed in luxury hotels and could feel she was helping to make history.

Initially the novelty of these developments in her life may have reconciled Frances to a life of insecurity and subterfuge. There is no doubt that the life unfolding before her as secretary to one of the foremost of the great offices of state was a lot more exciting than the world she had known as a school mistress, but there were some serious sacrifices to be made.

If she were to accept that their love was for life, and her justification for it was that it would be, Frances had to face the likelihood that she would not be able to have children, certainly not openly and probably not at all. She loved children and she loved approval. She would have delighted in the public approbation marriage would have brought together with the security. It hurt her that she had to disappoint her parents so badly, and, foolishly perhaps, she told them of the arrangement, hoping to reconcile them to her choice, and perhaps deep down to find acceptance for it.

Naturally enough, considering how they had brought her up, they were very disappointed and upset. Until then their daughter had given them a great deal of cause for pride and they had been encouraged to envisage a happy and successful future for Frances. They did not cast her off, but they never ceased to condemn her choice bitterly and to try and persuade her to leave him.

Quite reasonably they feared she would sacrifice her youth and reputation for Lloyd George and find herself eventually bereft and disgraced. Her position was without security. While he had said that divorce was out of the question and assured her that marriage would follow in the event of his first wife's death, nothing was put on paper. Mrs Lloyd George was not old, or unwell, why should anyone presume that she would die first? Frances might have faith that Lloyd George would remain loyal but there were a great many examples of women badly let down in the past. Even if Frances was unaware of Lloyd George's eye for a pretty woman, what gave her the confidence that she could hold him? Nothing really, apart from her youthful optimism and a lack of bruising experiences that might have knocked some of the confidence from her. She simply believed that their love must be meant, that he needed her and that all was bound to

[12] *A Diary by Frances Stevenson* edited by A J P Taylor published Hutchinson 1971

work out for the best: – It was a confidence her parents could not share. Their grief upset her, but she was convinced, like H G Wells' heroine, Ann Veronica, that if this wonderful man had need of her then she was right to dedicate herself to him as his devoted slave. It made her an ideal partner for Lloyd George who twenty-four years earlier had written to Maggie,

> I am of the opinion that woman's function is to soothe and sympathize and not to amuse. Men's lives are a perpetual conflict. The life I have mapped out will be so especially – as lawyer and politician. Woman's function is to pour oil on the wounds – to heal the bruises of spirit received in past conflicts and to stimulate to renewed exertion.[13]

Where Maggie actually found his demands arduous and exacting in the extreme, Frances was content to fulfil them. She was also excited by the challenges of her new position. Unlike Maggie, she came from a political home and the people she met and the tasks she performed were made all the more fascinating because she had gained an inside knowledge of affairs she had always heard keenly discussed. 'I was more than excited – I was thrilled to find myself thus in the centre of the political scene and identified, in a very humble way with momentous events.'[14]

In a pamphlet describing the role of private secretary which she wrote later she said:

> There is perhaps no other profession in which there are so many occasions when a woman might let her employer down. Most of the time her views are understood to be his views: her opinions his opinions. If she makes a mistake, it is probably her employer who will suffer. She must essentially be in complete sympathy with her employer...
>
> You will see that some of these qualifications that I consider necessary imply a certain amount of unselfishness. It is self subordination without subservience that is required – a willingness to remain in the background rather than to share in the limelight. The limelight is not meant for secretaries. By this I do not mean to imply that one should become a doormat, far from it. That is not advisable for one's own sake or the sake of the person one is serving. One's own individuality must be preserved. But there is a fine mean between the two which is ideal and which we should strive to maintain.'

[13] Lloyd George Family Papers DLG to MLG (National Library of Wales)
[14] Autobiography FLG op cit p58

Frances did not consider herself a 'doormat' to Lloyd George and in fact believed that it was important for him that she should not become so. In private they sometimes argued and she could criticise him, and contribute her own views on politics and the people involved, but fundamentally she was his supporter and ally against the world. He knew that he could trust her with his most private thoughts and count on her sympathy in his aims. Self subordination indeed, and in time Frances did find that there were occasions when this did feel like self sacrifice.

In the beginning, however, it did not and on 21st January 1913, she made the final commitment to Lloyd George and showed that she had put thoughts of marriage and security away for the time being at least. They consummated their relationship at last and regarded this from then on as the date of their 'marriage'.

Chapter Two

'Marriage' and War

A very tempestuous and sometimes very lonely 'marriage' began for Frances. By 17th February there is a formal little note from her lover asking her to perform some small errands and revealing that, even so soon after their 'marriage', Lloyd George could enjoy a holiday apart from her. In this instance he was in the South of France with Rufus Isaacs, driving down to Nice and playing golf there with Bonar Law and Max Aitken.

The pattern was becoming established and Frances admits in her autobiography that the demands her new life placed upon her caused her to neglect her own friends: 'I worked early and late, as indeed LG expected everyone employed for him to do. I had no leisure: from now on I was dedicated to LG and his works. I saw less and less of my friends.'

The demands of her career and her lover saw to that, but she did make some new friends.

She was lucky in that she got on extremely well with her fellow private secretary, J. T. Davies, another Welshman. He had also been a school teacher and had only recently joined Lloyd George's staff as a private secretary when Frances began her role in the office. Yet he had been there long enough to have some experience and authority, and clearly did not feel threatened or critical when Frances received private little notes from Lloyd George or disappeared for quiet meals with him after work.

Frances also managed to become friends with Lloyd George's housekeeper, Sarah, a forceful woman who voiced her opinion that Margaret was a neglectful wife. She not only accepted and catered for Frances's visits to the house in Margaret's absence, but she also posted letters to Frances from Lloyd George when the family were out.

It was fortunate that two such closely involved people were sympathetic, as in other ways the affair was, at first, awkward to manage. Frances had returned to her parents when she left her rooms at Allenswood. Having left home at nineteen, at least during term time, to go back at twenty-four needed some adjustment. She had often found her mother's influence somewhat overwhelming, though they were fond of each other. Louise took no active steps to break up the affair, but her sarcastic comments and pained expressions were something of a strain. Nights

19

spent away, and working weekends when she missed family occasions often began with Frances tense and miserable, having left tension and anger at home.

In the early stages the couple did not have anywhere to go. Margaret was sometimes away from Downing Street, as for example in the summer, but there were long periods when she was there. Nor was the house there, swathed in dust sheets and deserted of staff, a very comfortable place and the conditions were hardly conducive to romance.

Sir George Riddell was building a house at Walton Heath, near the golf course, for Lloyd George to use as a country retreat not too far from London. However, on 19th February, while Lloyd George was still playing golf in the South of France, suffragettes planted several bombs there. Not all went off and there were no casualties, but progress was delayed.

There is no evidence as to what Frances thought of this drastic action on the part of the WSPU, but it did not affect her strong desire to see them win the vote for women. As well as the tension at home about her position, lively arguments were also taking place about women's suffrage. Her brother, now a rather pompous prefect, would come home from school very sure of his own opinions adamantly opposed to female emancipation in any form. No one ever revealed to him the full details of his sister's new job. He would have been appalled. Life at home was noisy and difficult, but as to take on a home of her own was bound to provoke even more disapproval and fury, Frances hesitated and hoped that Walton Heath might provide a cosy hideaway.

In fact it did nothing of the kind. It was furnished with left-overs from Lloyd George's former houses and it lacked comfort and adequate heating. The spare bedroom had no form of heating at all and used to get very damp. Housework was all done by one old Welsh woman who would produce simple meals on request, but when Frances suggested adding a drop of cream to enliven the food the woman replied that she 'could not include such extravagance in her account to Dame Margaret'.[1]

Nevertheless the house did provide a refuge in rural air where they could stomp off together into nearby heathland scented with gorse and bracken. Once it was finished they often escaped there, sometimes managing to spend entire weekend on the pretext of work.

This was not purely an excuse. They did accomplish a lot in the time, but they also enjoyed going for long walks together across the common. Lloyd George would tease and tell her stories of his youth. In the evenings they relaxed together after a simple shared meal, perhaps Lloyd George's favourite bacon and potatoes, or some delicatessen food acquired by

[1] F Lloyd George op cit

Frances before they came down, and she would play the piano.

There was much to be done. As well as the basic Treasury requirements, Lloyd George was trying to establish improved conditions in the country both for agricultural workers and land production. The subject was a vast one, immensely complicated and necessarily bordering on other areas. An agricultural report was produced in the summer of 1913 after extensive research but, without the urban report that was also being worked upon, it had certain weak points. Lloyd George spent the autumn of 1913 trying to stir up support for some kind of reform, but it did not get any very great response and gradually his own attention became distracted (he hoped only temporarily) from immediate land reform.

Over the winter months leading into 1914, Lloyd George found himself becoming increasingly involved in Irish problems. As Chancellor of the Exchequer it was not really his territory, but Asquith recognised that Lloyd George might be useful in this area since he was a renowned mediator with known Celtic sympathies.

The Home Rule bill was due to become law, despite the Lords' opposition, by the summer of 1914, but the defiance in Ulster was supported by many, including a very large element in the army expected to enforce home rule. Some kind of compromise seemed necessary if rebellion were to be avoided, and Lloyd George initiated the idea for an 'Amendment Bill' whereby the Ulster counties would retain an option to remain outside home rule for six years. At the end of this period they would automatically be included unless the government had voted differently in the interval. It was hoped that this proposed compromise would at least put the unionists in the wrong if they rejected it out of hand, but by March reinforcements were being sent to Ulster to deal with expected trouble, and Lloyd George was suffering with the throat trouble which always seemed to affect him at times of severe stress.

In this instance, stress was compounded by his work on another provocative budget. The year had begun with a struggle between Lloyd George and Churchill over naval estimates which Churchill had won. The budget now had to allow for greatly increased naval expenditure. More importantly, Lloyd George wanted to introduce a new scheme to amend the old rating system so that the ground landlord would carry a share in the burden. To meet the new demands he planned to rely exclusively upon direct taxation, carrying further the principle that the rich should pay proportionately more.

The Easter break cured Lloyd George's throat problems and gave him renewed vigour to involve himself with the repercussions of the Curragh incident, when it looked as though the army might mutiny if called upon to quell Ulster resistance to home rule. In May, Lloyd George and Asquith represented the government at the Buckingham Palace conference called by the king for dealing with Irish problems. Birrell, the Irish Secretary, was not there, but yet again the Chancellor of the Exchequer was deeply involved. Frances says in her autobiography:

> There were constant talks and correspondence between John Redmond, Joe Devlin, John Dillon, Sir Edward Carson and other distinguished Irishmen on both sides. LG was busy and happy, happy because he was busy.

Happy also because his relations with Frances were running relatively smoothly and he enjoyed her total devotion, knowing he could count on her to drop anything and go to him when he called. This was not always easy for her.

On Sunday June 29th Frances went to help him prepare a speech he was shortly to make in the City. Birthdays were considered very important occasions in the Stevenson household and June 29th was Mrs Stevenson's birthday. Louise had been very annoyed that Frances should give any other appointment priority on her day, most especially an appointment with Lloyd George, and Frances arrived feeling guilty and flustered. Her guilt annoyed Lloyd George so Frances was working by herself on the speech in her office when a red despatch box came in from the Foreign Office.

At tea-time she delivered the box to Lloyd George who took out the telegram announcing the assassination of the Austrian Archduke Franz Ferdinand and his wife at Sarajevo. He told Frances that this would mean war, but she did not realise he meant a serious confrontation that would affect them all. As she travelled home on the tube to Wallington she assumed merely that there was about to be yet another upheaval in the Balkans, with Austria perhaps making threatening noises in the background.

The prospect of English involvement in a major dispute did not occur to her, nor would it seriously have disconcerted her. She shared the illusion that the great British Empire would quickly be victorious and that the professional armed forces would take the brunt of any action as they always had in the past. Conventional, in her feelings at least, she was disgusted by female acts of aggression. She was fervently convinced that the armed forces would be shown to advantage in acts of war.

Just as books could inspire her with ideals of love and dedication, Frances was always moved by calls on her sense of patriotism. In this she was like her brother, and most of their contemporaries, regarding the conflict in the nature of a crusade and with absolutely no idea of the pain and suffering a modern war might entail.

The days leading up to a declaration were very worrying ones for

Frances, not because she feared war, far from it, but because she was very perturbed that Lloyd George might oppose British involvement, just as he had opposed the Boer campaign. For Frances this would have been a catastrophe. She was never in any doubt that the war was necessary, and felt sure that Lloyd George would be not only mistaken but ruined if he made another unpopular stand.

Paul's effort to get into the army quickly rather than take up his scholarship to St John's College in Oxford made her proud. She would have been ashamed of him if he had not. It was incomprehensible to her that Lloyd George might genuinely think a war disastrous: costly and tragic. Even when the full implications of the war became to her she was glad that Germany had invaded Belgium so that Lloyd George had felt impelled to support a stand against this aggression on a small nation. This was to belittle his convictions and imply a cynical pragmatism, when in fact Lloyd George had never been a pacifist. His opposition to the Boer war had arisen because he felt it was an unnecessary and expensive mess. When Germany tried to take Agadir in 1911, Lloyd George surprised some, who misunderstood him and his motives before, by saying that Britain was fully prepared to go to war if the Kaiser maintained his pretensions in Morocco.

He very much felt that Germany must not be allowed to upset the status quo and that it would gravely threaten Britain's security should she do so. By 1914 he had relaxed his defensiveness, feeling that Germany had learnt her lesson at Agadir, or war would have broken out during the Bulgarian War of 1913.

Almost three weeks after the assassination of Franz Ferdinand, Lloyd George said in a speech on 17th July:

> We feel confident that the common sense, the patience, the goodwill, the forbearance, which enabled us to solve greater and more urgent problems last year will enable us to pull through these problems at the present moment ... and avoid 'creeping catastrophe.'

However, Germany had learnt a different lesson from Agadir and the near conflict of 1913. They now thought that conflict between the European powers was very likely. As a result, they believed they should get ready for war, choosing the best possible moment and give themselves the advantage. Confrontation had been avoided in 1913, principally because Germany had felt unready, but the near conflict had further convinced them that they must be fully prepared. By 1914 Germany felt surer of her ground and ready to encourage rather than restrain Austria.

On the 24th July the Austrians presented the Serbs with a virtually unacceptable ultimatum, which, astonishingly, Serbs could not accept, but they were amazingly conciliatory however and very apologetic so there was not really a plausible excuse for aggression. Austria declared war just the same. Germany rejected the English proposal for a four power conference and felt encouraged to think that the British would not interfere as they were clearly working so hard to avoid war. Germany judged that, without Britain, Russia and France were beatable.

The Entente with France and Russia did not oblige Britain to support them in event of war. Germany realised that Britain was loath to do so and understood that many Britons felt closer to the German nations than they did to their old rivals the French. Clearly, however, a French and Russian defeat would leave an unacceptably powerful Germany, and the British cabinet saw it would be very foolish to think they could remain secure in the long term against a powerful and victorious Central Powers alliance.

While Lloyd George believed that Germany did not want war, he did not think it was a serious danger to British security. When it was seen to pose a direct threat he was, as he had shown himself in 1911, determined to resist with all possible determination. That he did not leap to this conclusion as easily as Frances or most of his compatriots was because he knew enough about the horrors attached to the human sacrifice, and the exorbitant expense of war, to regard it as very much a final resort. He would have preferred a negotiated settlement every time, and he did not want to believe that such was then impossible.

Contemporary records from the first few days of August show him as torn. Asquith in a letter to Venetia Stanley said: 'Lloyd George all for peace, is more sensible and statesmanlike, for keeping the position still open.' [2] Riddell described him in his diary as 'ruffled', presenting a case whereby a defeated Germany would leave Russia and France too dominant in Europe.[3] Ideally, he wished things could stay as they were.

The importance of Belgium became clear to him as the crisis developed, not so much through its status as a small neutral victim, but because if the Germans gained control of the Belgian coast they could threaten British shipping. Also, if Germany kept out of Belgium the French army would have a much shorter frontier to defend and France could probably manage to survive on her own.

The invasion of Belgium did not so much provide Lloyd George with an excuse for supporting a war as give him even more evidence that Britain's vital interests were threatened. The idea that Belgium was a weak and innocent victim consolidated mass support for the war, but the government was prompted more by fears that Britain's security was at risk. For all Lloyd George would have liked to go on pressing for social

[2] Venetia Stanley, letters
[3] *War Diary* Lord Riddell

improvements and reform, he was forced to the conclusion that reform would little benefit a country open to attack.

When the cabinet decided to send their ultimatum to Germany, he was in agreement and committed finally to achieving the best and fastest possible victory for Britain. He was not impressed by Frances's jingoistic sentiments that Germany should be crushed in a glorious campaign. He knew and understood, far better than she did, that the cost in life, progress and grief would be a high one. At this time he was better able to open his heart to his wife, who had supported him in his isolation during the Boer war. He wrote to her on 3rd August: 'I am even more horrified that I should ever appear to have a share in it but I must bear my share of the ghastly burden though it scorches my flesh to do so'.[4]

He was writing to his wife, however, because Margaret had, as usual, packed up and taken the family to Criccieth for the summer, leaving Lloyd George in a partially closed up 11 Downing Street. Frances was therefore with him at this crucial time, actually staying at Downing Street.

Her nature was such that while she did not share his distress, she could be soothing and sympathetic to him. She later admitted that she had thought his reservations stemmed chiefly from fear of what his supporters would feel. Her love for Lloyd George made her anxious that he should not be discredited either with his supporters or with the country. It was a relief that Belgium provided an obvious reason for war likely to reconcile both sources of opinion. She never seems to have realised his genuine dilemma and was merely reassured when he finally announced his support for war, that his career would continue.

It was true that he was needed. Clearly a country at war would have to face enormous economic strains. As Chancellor he knew this and, having decided that there was no choice, he took vigorous protective steps. For several days they scarcely saw one another while he immersed himself in meetings to find strategies to protect the pound. Never particularly interested in balancing her own finances or understanding maths, Frances continued to be excluded from sharing his innermost thoughts and progress with any real perception for the first few weeks of the war.

Within days of the outbreak of hostilities, the Central Powers made frightening advances and it was clear that an all-out effort would be necessary if they were to be defeated. On 19th September a mass meeting was held at the Queen's Hall with the intention of boosting Kitchener's recruiting campaign. Lloyd George decided to make a strong speech in support of the war, explaining the Allied cause and his support for it and Frances and all his staff were caught up in the preparations.

[4] LG Family Papers op cit

Even the shortest and most unimportant speeches were prepared by Lloyd George with enormous attention to detail. He underlined words in different colours according to the stress he wanted to give them and went over and over his initial draft trying it out with Frances and making her run about to check up on facts and figures. On the occasions when he was called upon to speak spontaneously he could manage very well but he preferred to be thoroughly prepared.

He was intensely nervous about this speech, telling his friend Lord Riddell that it made him feel 'he was about to be executed,'.[5] Frances was ideal in such a situation. She liked nothing better than to support and encourage. Having expended the enormous effort necessary to drive the speech home he came home deflated and exhausted to the praise and reassurance of Frances. She told him she had seen a rush of men to the recruiting room when he finished, so he could gain comfort from her praise even before he saw the press on the Sunday and Monday. They were united in effusive praise for the speech.

Lloyd George may also have been better able to strike a chord with the young in his audience because he and Frances had invited Frances's brother Paul to spend some time with them at Walton Heath. After three daughters and seven years the Stevensons had had a longed for son, called Paul after Louise's talented brother who had died at nineteen. The little boy had been a sickly youngster and had preferred to sit inside reading rather than playing vigorously with the cousins. On winning a scholarship, to Christ's Hospital he blossomed and began to win not only academic awards but also to succeed in sport ending up as Captain of Cricket. Paul had been about to go up to St John's College Oxford with an exhibition when war was declared, so he had withdrawn from university and tried to get into the army at any level, but the initial confusion and delay caused him to take advantage of his experience in the School's OTC and apply for a commission. Roland Leighton could have been speaking for Paul when he wrote to Vera Brittain, 'I feel that I am meant to take an active part in this war. It is to me a very fascinating thing – something if often horrible, yet very ennobling and very beautiful.'[6]

Although Lloyd George knew more of what the war would very likely entail he could not fail to have been moved by the youthful idealism of the two Stevensons. It made him aware of a great source of dedication and spirit of self sacrifice available to the country at this time and to which he referred in his speech.

[5] Riddell, op cit
[6] *Testament of Youth* – Vera Brittain

For most generations sacrifice comes in drab and wariness of spirit. It comes to you today and comes today to us all in the form of the glow and thrill of a great movement for liberty, that impels millions throughout Europe to the same noble end. It is a great war for the emancipation of Europe from the thraldom of a military caste... [7]

Paul at this time was academic, idealistic and handsome with dark blue eyes and a youthful respect for his own ideas. He argued vigorously with his sister about the position of women and fortunately was innocent enough not to question the privileged standing on which his sister stood with Lloyd George. As an admired prefect and prize winner at school, he had gained confidence and he spoke freely to the Chancellor of the Exchequer without quite the awe he might have developed later. Joining the army was a rough brush with reality.

19th September not only heralded Lloyd George's public commitment to the war, it also began the opening of the couple's closest years together, working exhausting hours and helping each other through difficult times. The war saw their relationship forged in strong metal and able to withstand all external pressures. The pitch at which they were working, as the strain of the war's demands became all consuming, developed their inter dependence. They provided each other with immediate relaxation and comfort. The obvious demands placed on Lloyd George by the work also gave him a good excuse to spend even less time with his family. Frances's role meant he could justify the time he spent with her.

When the family returned from Criccieth on the 21st September forcing Frances to return home, she wrote in her diary that the previous two weeks had been the happiest of her life. She had shared some precious times with LG (as she now referred to him in public) and had a chance to draw closer to her young brother.

Paul had also enjoyed himself and was shocked by the army where his opinions, as a second lieutenant, were of no interest to anyone and where he found his naïve idealism and intolerance aroused irritation and contempt in his older and more worldly colleagues. If he had been less of a prig he would, no doubt, have had a much easier time, but by the 23rd October Frances received 'a rather disquieting letter from Paul who is not happy at St. Albans. He says the other officers are rotters. I expect they are so called "men of the world" and he has known nothing of the world yet, poor little beggar.'

Part of Frances's charm lay in the fact that she would turn to others for advice or help in an appealing fashion and then take it appreciatively. Among Lloyd George's admirers was a certain James Murray, a Liberal

[7] Speech by Lloyd George 19 September 1914

MP, to whom she confided her worries about her brother. He offered to drive her to St Albans to see Paul and try to speak the young officer himself 'man to man' to see if he could give him some practical advice.

Frances was delighted. She felt that the interest shown in a young subaltern by a distinguished middle-aged MP would help his standing with the others. She also wanted, if possible, to rush to the rescue. On a par with giving presents, helping people, finding them jobs, introducing them to contacts and generally being useful gave Frances enormous satisfaction. Her new position provided the opportunity to indulge this passion. She had just found her old college friend, Grace Steenthal, a secretarial position with a Liberal business man. Now she hoped her contacts would help her baby brother, the darling of her family.

James Murray was tactful. He showed interest in the whole regiment and did not make it obvious that he had come to preach pragmatism to one young subbie. Frances felt that his common sense attitude did encourage Paul to feel less hostile to his colleagues. Whatever he felt about his brother officers, his main concern, when Butler and Frances visited him, was that he should not be left behind when the regiment got sent to the front. As he had not yet learnt to fit in easily and was blatantly treated as the baby of the mess, he was afraid he might be expected to go through further training. Frances sympathised with this fear and expressed no relief that this might protect him from danger for a little longer. Life had been too gentle for her to imagine danger realistically. When she did hear of Paul's death the following year she was completely devastated. 'I did not worry about him for it seemed to me that he, at least, would come safely back, that death at least would spare one so promising and so dear and necessary to us.'[8]

The reality of the horrors at the front did not yet impinge on Frances, absorbed as she was by her passion for Lloyd George and the demands of their work together. She did try to play her part in the 'war effort' and began to attend Red Cross classes, but she was further distracted by the increasing problems in her home life: Mama was being very difficult.

Like many of her generation, Louise Stevenson was finding it very hard to adjust to domestic changes brought about by the war. Her resilient disposition could have coped had she not been so disturbed by the developments in the lives of her children. Paul's eagerness to get to the front filled her with dismay and pessimism: not sharing Frances's confidence in her son's safe return. She after all, had known young and cruel death with that of her enormously gifted brother. It must have seemed to her that here potentially was just such another instance. Her only son, beautiful, talented and a source of great pride and joy was exposing himself to great

[8] Diary by F S op cit

risk. As Christmas 1914 approached and it became apparent that not only would Paul not get leave, but also that he did not mind, Mama became still more bad-tempered and upset.

Worrying about Paul distracted her somewhat from the continual harassment of Frances over LG until Frances confided to her, very shortly before Paul left for France in February 1915, that she thought she was pregnant.

From the end of December, Frances and LG had been able to live together at Walton Heath while the rest of his family continued their Christmas holiday in Criccieth. Frances later told her daughter that 'precautions are never one hundred per cent reliable.' This was said with some bitterness, because she had always wanted children. Having conceived it was doubly hard to take positive action to terminate the pregnancy. It happened twice: the second time she seems to have suffered less and coped more realistically. Living in her 'idyll' at Walton Heath however, she had lulled herself into a false belief that all things might be possible. She talked often with LG about her yearning to have his child and he was not able to tell her brutally that 'a love child' was simply far too great a risk. It may be that at this time her 'precautions' were blatantly inadequate because she did not really want them to work.

In October of 1914 her preoccupation was already evident. Riddell described a meeting in his diary, at which, he said discussion had been principally about oratory and style. All Frances could recollect of the same occasion, (in her own diary), was a discussion about the unmarried woman and her status, quoting views that supported the opinion 'that a woman had a perfect right to have a child from any man she pleases.' She joined 'The Women's Freedom League' and dreamed of a time when perhaps LG could free himself from the constraints of his career and promote schemes for reform. 'He could earn enough for his needs by writing for he is a man of simple tastes and prefers a simple life and simple fare to luxury.'[9]

She was deceiving herself. LG could never give up politics and in fact cared more for his wife and for his comforts than Frances quite appreciated at this time.

On February 23rd she wrote:

C and I have wanted for so long to have a child, and we thought this week that our wish was about to be realised. But when I told Mama of what was going to happen she was terribly upset and is still. She says she would rather see me dead than that such a thing should

[9] Ibid

happen. She has raised all sorts of issues to persuade me, but behind it all is the spectre of respectability which haunts her with horrible pictures of what can happen to 'disgraced' women. She does not think it possible for a woman to give a child to the man she loves, but who is unable to marry her, and still be happy and willing to face the criticism of the world. She does not understand that if anything happened to C my only chance of happiness would be for me to have someone to remind me of him, and to whom I can devote my life. She can only think of the wickedness of it, his wickedness she calls it, and will not understand that our only fault is that we love each other too well and that where love is, the greatest trials can be sustained. If she would only look at things clearly and judge the facts fairly! But she will not – there is one part of her which has never come out into the clear light – which may not do so, in case the futility of conventions should be revealed and the crippling bonds of middle routine be weakened. She does not understand that I would be proud to have his child and would be willing to suffer for it, nay I should glory in suffering, rather than die childless – I would suffer so that the child should not. I would spend my life so that he might be happy and I would brave the coldness of the world, for I know there are some friends who would stand by me, and I should not be entirely alone.

But it is not to be. I fear that if I insisted upon this, she would be so upset that people would see what had happened and I cannot be responsible for the ruin of C's career. And then too, my love for Mama makes me hesitate from hurting her too much. I hate myself for inflicting this upon her, and I fear that the wound is a deep one. C says that in love lies do not pass for such, just as in war killing is not called murder. But the long and the short of it is, that much as I love Mama and Dada, I love C better and will never leave him, and am impelled to put everything else subordinate to his love. But the idea of our love child will have to go for the time being. I fear too, that I shall not be able to stay at home after this, for Dada does not yet know what has happened and I do not know what his attitude will be. I dread hurting him, but one thing is certain, I cannot give C up.

I can't help hating myself for making Mama so miserable. The thought haunts me all day long and I would do anything to prevent it. But what can I do? Some years ago Harold Spender said to C, 'You are the most lonely man I know.' I think I have changed all that now and I cannot think that I have done wrong. I am not vicious or evil and my only fault in this matter and his, is love. 'Love justifies many audacities.' I think the justification for these audacities is the length of love's duration and I know C and I belong to each other for ever. I should be so happy were it not for the fact that I am causing unhappiness to two people whom I love and who have been so good and loving to me.[10]

She had finished her Red Cross lessons before Christmas and this time took up some Red Cross work to distract herself and improve her self-esteem. However, this did not last very long as the abortion took a heavy physical toll on her for a while.

Frances's idea that LG was delighted at the prospect of a 'love child' was an illusion. He did indeed love children and was always delighted to meet and play with any he encountered. Even in the height of the war Beaverbrook's daughter was to remember his infinite kindness and patience with her as a small girl, but at this point he felt it was impera-tive that no risk to his career should be taken. He stressed how lonely he was before Frances started to love him and encouraged her to think that her mother might be so distressed as to cause a public scandal. Frances was persuaded it was an impossible time for their 'love child', while being assured that there would be a child some time. She went ahead with the abortion.

Although LG loathed illness and normally steered clear of anyone who was ill, in this instance he nursed Frances tenderly back to health with a gentleness that was rarely to figure again in their life together. 'There was no little thing that he did not think of for my comfort, no tenderness that he did not lavish on me.'[11]

However, guilt and fear caused his agile mind to do some serious think-ing as he expressed his care. He did not like a situation whereby he had to worry about getting caught. Nor did he like the fact that he had to deprive Frances of her long-expressed longing for his child. It must have seemed to him likely that there would come a time when he would no longer be able to stop her, and quite plainly he wanted his love to have an easier time away from the nagging doubts constantly expressed by her mother. It must have seemed to him that life had been a lot simpler when he had a mistress with a complaisant husband and the idea came to him that it might be possible to set Frances up with a husband who would make no demands but would provide her with the security and status whereby they could continue their relationship and perhaps have children.

It would also be much better if it were possible to get Frances away from home. The atmosphere at Wallington was tense and depressing. Not only was Mrs Stevenson upset by the whole pregnancy episode, she was also reaching a new pitch in her fears about her son. Paul's regiment was due to leave from Southampton at the beginning of March. In his embarkation

[10] Diary in DLG papers, House of Lords
[11] Diary by F S op cit

leave he spent the time at home arguing non-stop with Frances about women's rights. With her yearning to have a child with or without a husband, Frances had become rather more extreme in her position.

When Paul finally did leave for France on March 25th, Frances tried to shake off her lethargy and illness so that she could comfort her parents. LG had sent her to Walton Heath to be nursed by Sarah, but she dragged herself home for the weekend, to find her mother proclaiming that she was certain Paul would never come back and that her children were a grave disappointment to her. Frances was sickened.

> Poor Mother! She cannot realise, and I fear she never will, that parents cannot control their children's lives for ever – that children exist for their own and the next generation, and not for that of their parents, which is past. However, it is hopeless to argue with her; but I fear she will never be happy unless she takes a wider view. What is more, if she is not careful, she will lose the sympathy and respect of her children.[12]

Frances felt her mother should be proud of Paul, rather than complaining. They were receiving cheerful letters from him at the front and Frances's main concern on behalf of her brother was that he should not be too terrified when he first came under fire.

Home was grating on her, and although she tried to immerse herself in work, she made one of her more critical comments at that time, muttering that it was all 'Liquor and Welsh disestablishment'. War news was depressing and Lloyd George was promoting an idea whereby the country should commit itself to giving up alcohol until the war was won. Frances succumbed to a cold made worse by depression, and allowed herself to be packed off for another holiday to recover, this time in Brighton.

It was a busy hotel but Frances found herself with too much time alone to think and feel lonely. She brought her diary up to date and read Meredith's *Egoist*. The novel supported irregular relations between men and women and interested her, while diminishing her hopes that in the future Lloyd George might make any sacrifices for her as it accepted that selfishness, in a man who is working for a cause, should be understood and allowed. Childless and manless, the world seemed very gloomy until her fourteen-year-old sister arrived for the weekend and needed entertaining.

Muriel, the youngest sister, now half her age, was nervous and prone to depression on a more serious level than anything Frances ever experienced, but she was also highly intelligent and very witty. Even more than in the developing relationship with her brother, Frances found in

[12] LG papers, House of Lords

her youngest sister a member of the family with whom she could share thoughts and better still a sense of humour. Muriel wanted to be a writer; she was all for having an exciting career and very admiring of her sister's apparent success. Her respect and lively company did much to restore her older sister's joie de vivre and Frances finally returned to Walton Heath to share once again L G's progress and schemes. 'He wrote me his scheme for Drink was progressing, but that it would be a hard fight, and I am anxious to hear all about it from his own lips.'[13]

Frances settled back down to hard work relieved by moments when the couple could escape together for picnics, walks, a shared salmon, enjoyed in moments between cabinet discussions over the failure in the Dardenelles, or LG's hopes for a Drinks Bill and putting through his budget.

In May Frances spent a weekend with an old college friend in the countryside near Newbury and, despite the sunshine and her friend's appealing little boy, she did not suffer from a reawakening of her depression in jealousy for someone happy as a wife and mother. In fact she told herself that the little boy looked likely to be 'a dreadful handful later on.'

Another friend asked her to be godmother to her baby and she reflected in her diary as to whether she was unfit to take responsibility for her moral welfare. 'But I do not, oh I do not think that I am wicked and unfit to help in the upbringing of a child. Surely my experiences have made me more fit for this: for knowledge is safety.'[14]

Fortunately, for the time being, there were no further scares that she might be called upon to find out. She submerged herself in work as times became more critical. The government faced a crisis in public confidence – almost a complete collapse when it was revealed how inadequate were the supplies of ammunition reaching the front. It was finally decided that the emergency of war necessitated drawing upon all the talent available in parliament, and a coalition was formed on May 18th.

Frances's role as a discreet but understanding confidante was much in demand, though it had to be understood her loyalty was to Lloyd George. Some members of the War Office were disgusted with LG's stated intention to interfere actively with munitions production and the likelihood that he might replace Kitchener as Secretary of State for War. LG was initially very intrigued by the idea – thinking it might give him more control over the running of the war – but Kitchener still retained his support in the country, and hostility to Lloyd George within the department would obviously impede his efforts there.

Frances was able to tell LG that Humbert Wolfe, the Secretary to the

[13] ibid
[14] ibid

Committee for War, had informed her of Sir Percy Girouard's and Sir Alfred Booth's intention to control the output of munitions and keep this firmly within the bounds of War Office control. LG had asked for a tour of production to judge progress for himself. Wolffe had told Frances that it was planned to show LG only certain parts and keep him in the dark.

It was clear to Frances, as to many members of the government, that things could not continue as they were. To her mind, of course, LG seemed to offer the solution, but she was nervous that a change in position might weaken his influence. The hostility in the War Office and the responsibility the task would entail kept her awake at night, although the prospect also excited her. When he informed her that it would not be a sensible move she was relieved, but she was aghast when instead he informed her that he intended to set up a Ministry for the production of Munitions with himself as the Minister.

Lloyd George was also a little hesitant about leaving the Treasury for a job that looked likely to offer small reward and little prestige – however necessary it was that it should be done. He initially suggested that he should organise munitions while remaining Chancellor, or perhaps leave the Exchequer in the hands of the Prime Minister for a limited period while he devoted himself to the job. For an ambitious man it was hard to say goodbye to the Treasury, which was a recognised step to the premiership. Moreover, Lloyd George was hardly enamoured of handing over the task of controlling pensions and tax to one of their new Conservative partners. Frances admitted that she was afraid munitions might turn out to be a quagmire which even her adored LG would slide into, showing himself unable to solve the problems and losing his political reputation at the same time. The challenge intrigued LG and it was clearly vital that something be done. On the understanding that he could return to his post as Chancellor when the situation was resolved he left the Treasury to become Minister for Munitions.

On the 25th May the new department was created with a skeleton staff, little furniture and an enormous amount to do. The first day involved Frances and her fellow secretary, J.T. Davies, in a battle to keep the only two chairs in their office. Order was going to have to come out of chaos, but Frances missed the rest of the fight. The evening after their crazy first day, the team decided to eat out and go on to see a popular musical, *Rosy Rapture of the Beauty Chorus*. In the last act Frances noticed that J.T. Davies had arrived with some news for Lloyd George, but with so many developments going on, this did not surprise or worry her. After the play L G asked her to accompany him back to Downing Street and it was here that she discovered it had been news for her that J.T. Davies had brought. Her brother had died of wounds received earlier that week in France.

Her first reaction was total disbelief and confusion. She had not believed that her mother's fears were reasonable and she just could not accept that Paul had truly died, but she made her way back urgently to Wallington to try and support her parents.

Mama cried and wailed and said that she had known. Indeed, Muriel told Frances that Mama had refused to make a cake for Paul that week, and had known for days that news of his death was coming. Papa was shattered and bewildered. Unable to receive comfort or give much to his wife, he wandered around the house desolate and distraught. All the daughters assembled at home to be of what use they could, and Frances spent the next few weeks commuting from Wallington rather than Walton Heath.

It was fortunate that there was such a huge job involved in creating a new ministry. Work served as a panacea. There was so much to do and no rules by which to do it. Frances had to concentrate on finding means to organise an office and found she was working a fourteen or fifteen hour day, and then having to travel by public transport out to Wallington. She began to find no purpose in continuing to live at home. Initially, Mama had clung to her oldest children but now Frances felt that, on top of the demands made by the job, she had no energy left for comfort and support. She started to look for a flat in the centre of London where she could enjoy more immediate rest and privacy with Lloyd George.

She had managed to find her first flat and had already moved out when her brother's batman came to visit Mrs Stevenson and give her details of Paul's final journey. Apparently he had been in considerable pain when taken to a small hospital in Annezin where he died the next day. Mrs Stevenson managed to control herself in front of the batman, but she completely broke down when the parcel containing Paul's blood-stained clothes and his other possessions was returned. She wept over the telephone to Frances, 'need they have done this to me?' and, according to Muriel, she made it plain that any of the girls would have been a welcome sacrifice in exchange. Frances was fortunate in being totally absorbed in work that often kept her in the office until midnight, but she did say that her mother never really recovered from the loss of her beloved son.

Frances was particularly in demand at this time because of her linguistic abilities. LG was building up a strong relationship with the French Minister of Munitions, Albert Thomas, despite the fact that neither was fluent in the other's language. Frances was the intermediary.

LG was busy during the summer speaking to the munitions workers, persuading them to give of their best, setting up new factories with improved conditions and negotiating for women to be allowed to play a part in jobs previously restricted to union members. He looked into new inventions and worked to extend arms co-operation between the allies. He was very busy with his own work, but he also continued to worry about strategy at the front and fear that the government were not pushing effectively enough. Despite the vast amount of work and thinking he needed to do, it was also during this summer that his notion of a safe cover for Frances came a little closer to fruition.

He found a man who seemed prepared to become a husband in name only to Frances. Billy Owen was a liaison officer for the Ministry of Munitions to the War Office. He declared himself a devoted admirer of Lloyd George, prepared to assist the 'Chief' in any way he could. It seems he must have liked Frances also and declared himself ready to marry her and have a wife in name only. From his summer break in Criccieth, LG wrote to Frances that Owen was consumed by a desire 'to get on' and would marry her unconditionally. 'There is peril and pollution in the other course. I love my pure little darling.'[15]

Frances also found the idea of security and a cover for any possible family fairly attractive. It would solve some difficulties. Her mother would cease to plague her and admirers would realise that she was unavailable and cease to court her (a mixed blessing). Her position as a married woman would be established and while the war continued, she would be able to justify the fact that, although married, she also worked. She would also have a cover if she were to conceive another child by Lloyd George

Marriage to Owen, however, would form another serious barrier to her innermost hope that one day marriage to Lloyd George might be possible. Would Owen continue to accept the situation? She was bound to silence by love; was his loyalty sufficient to bind him indefinitely? Could she protect herself from the possibility that Owen might one day demand his marital rights?

Owen was not a man she could tremendously respect. If she were to contemplate marriage seriously, it was far more likely to be with someone she actually admired. His obsequiousness was irritating and she did not want to be married to Lloyd George's abject servant. However, she allowed LG to think she was considering the idea. Owen was, after all, very good-looking and flattering in his devoted attention to herself as well as LG. She did not reject the idea out of hand and went down to Walton Heath with LG and Owen for a weekend.

In part, it was pleasant to drift along with the idea, as marriage to anyone would please so many people; her family, her friends and, it appeared, LG. Of course, while she drifted she could avoid any nasty confrontations and definite decisions. She became secretly engaged to Billy Owen, but the mere fact of accepting something as formal as an

[15] FLG papers

engagement frightened her and she broke it off. No one seemed to take this as final however.

Lloyd George seems to have been torn. He liked to have his Frances constantly available and, although he believed that Owen would respect their relations, she would need to live in very close proximity to a young, good-looking man. LG found it hard to accept that others could be more faithful than he found it possible to be himself. Frances was technically free and very attractive. Nor was she above giving him a little bit of a scare occasionally and allowing him to know she had admirers in whom she was interested. His jealousy and possessiveness were extreme and even a husband provided by himself might be seen to pose a threat.

> D was making himself miserable over the idea of my belonging to someone else even in name. Several times he has cried and sobbed as a child when speaking of it, begging me all the time to take no notice of him. But I could not bear to give him pain and I know he is relieved now that I have broken it off. I must be free to be with him always, and marriage I know would forge new bonds. Owen is very upset but wishes to be friends still. He is very weak and a very little satisfies him.[16]

That of course meant they were still in the same difficult and dangerous situation and LG, having checked that Frances would not sacrifice his faintest need for Owen, went back to thinking she should perhaps marry him. On the 23rd October she wrote:

> D is now on the marriage tack again! He says there are many advantages to be gained by marriage provided that Owen understands clearly what our relations are and promises to respect them. Am dining with Owen tonight to discuss the matter.[17]

LG was in the middle of one of his intermittent periods of fearing exposure. At the same time he started insisting that Frances travel down to Walton Heath by train instead of going down with him in the car, 'in case people fix on it for a scandal' Frances wrote. She was rather discouraged by this inconvenience and felt that it added to the humiliation and discomfort of her position, for all LG professed to think that 'We are doing the World in spite of its spitefulness.' Frances had the harder part in this 'doing' and so yet again she paid lip service to the idea of marriage to Billy Owen.

The scheme was allowed to drift, but in fact Frances was much more

(16) LG papers op cit

excited about her plans to set herself up independently in a flat with her old friend Mary Phillips. They had found a flat in Chester Square which was sufficiently close to Westminster to provide a comfortable and easily available refuge. LG brought her some presents from France to help her furnish it, a Napoleon clock and two Napoleon candlesticks, and she spent far more than she could afford in comfortable furnishings and enhancing the rooms to their best effect. Despite having been brought up by an artist's daughter with a strong interest in the arts, Louise Stevenson had furnished the villa in Wallington just as her neighbours furnished theirs. The children were brought into an environment of dark wood, marquetry tables, grotesque ornaments and thick chenille curtains. The effect was very dreary but socially acceptable. As she reached middle age and put up with her children's disparaging comments Louise did admit that she would like to make changes, but changes for changes' sake cost money and that was never abundant. The furnishings were socially correct and anyway familiar. The children were constantly warned not to knock the ornaments over: hideous they may have been but they had also been expensive.

It hardly sounds the sort of environment from which daughters with a passion for furnishing and decorating beautiful homes would emerge. However, in this instance genes had more effect than social conditioning and Frances reacted strongly against the ugliness of her roots and took an intense, almost physical delight in beauty. She did not inherit her grandfather's ability to paint, but she created beautiful and soothing homes, lovely gardens and had the knack for picking the one beautiful item from a stall full of bric-a-brac.

Just after moving in at the end of November 1915, she added in a brief aside in her diary that she did not think she could possibly marry.

> I have come to the conclusion that D needs all my energies and devotion, and I think that marriage might bring an element of unhappiness and worry into his life, even on the most favourable terms (to him). Owen and I are therefore not engaged and I have not seen him for some time.[18]

Life in Chester Square was a joy. She was tasting freedom for the first time and leading life according to her own tastes and convenience. The role of wife to a Liaison Officer for whom she did not have much respect could scarcely compete with the heady excitement of independence in her own home.

[17] ibid
[18] ibid

She poured whatever energy was left over from the demands of her work in the Ministry of Munitions and attending to LG, into making her flat beautiful and comfortable, while enjoying life in the centre of London. She established a delightful routine. Sharing expenses with Mary meant that they could afford to employ a live-in-cook, and a maid of all work. On Saturday afternoons a hairdresser came to the flat and did their hair. Free evenings were few. On the occasions when Frances did manage to leave the office at a reasonable hour, she would return to find friends popping in, or more likely she would have ensured her departure from the office in order to indulge her enthusiasm for the theatre. Every new play or show was seen and actively discussed as a refreshing change from the constant preoccupation with war.

Owen did not disappear from the scene completely, however. He is mentioned in Frances's diary several times at the beginning of 1916, humbly accompanying the couple on outings or even attending the occasional meal, filling the role of unobtrusive third according to Frances and 'looking after D very nicely.'

Owen would have had to be a great deal more attractive to her than he was to figure as an alternative to life in her new home, but he was an amiable man and did provide admirable cover as Frances's sometime fiancé.

Chapter Three

Secretary to the Prime Minister

In among Frances's papers is a 'Political Operation Order' for December 6th 1916.

1. The Lloyd Georges will relieve the Asquiths at 10 Downing Street to-morrow 7th inst., under arrangements enumerated below.

2. An advance party consisting of Mrs Lloyd George and Megan will arrive at the junction of Whitehall and Downing Street at 10 a.m. where they will be met by Mrs Asquith and Violet.
   No arms will be carried by either party.

3. The Lloyd George advance party will proceed to view the premises at 10 Downing Street.
   Every facility for this inspection will be afforded by the Asquiths who will hand over all dixies, toast racks, ablution benches etc. and take receipts therefore.

4. Clean billet certificates in duplicate signed by Mrs Lloyd George will be forwarded by Mrs Asquith to reach House of Commons by 4 p.m. 7th inst.

5. No stores of any description will be removed by the outgoing party from 10 Downing Street. Special attention must be paid to the inventory of 'unconsidered trifles' which must be left intact and complete.
   Mrs Lloyd George will 'wait and see' that this is done.

6. The female element of the outgoing party will clear Downing Street by 3 p.m. No escort is necessary.

7. Lloyd George will arrive at 10 Downing Street at 4 p.m.
   The Speaker will detail an escort of 3 politicians and 6 men to report at War Office at 3 p.m.

8. Upon arrival of Lloyd George, Asquith will immediately hand over all scraps of paper, anti-Northcliffe Defence Schemes, friends' relatives' exemption certificates and the National Imprest Account.

9. Completion of relief will be wired in code to House of Commons and the Daily Mail.

10. Upon relief, Asquith will proceed by route march to 'Procrastination Cottage' Berks. The route will be lined at 10 paces intervals by young exempted and indispensable eligibles from Government Departments in Whitehall. Upon arrival at destination, Asquith will change his mind.
11. Bonar Law and Carson will hold themselves in readiness for action at two hours' notice.
12. The Unionists, Liberals, Labour party, Nationalists, Ulsterites, and Mrs Pankhurst will remain in their present billets until further orders.
13. The leave granted to Lord Haldane is extended indefinitely.
14. The privilege of writing such expressions as 'Business Government at last', 'I told you so' or reproducing posters from two years ago is withdrawn from Horatio Bottomley.
15. Members of the outgoing Government will assemble at the National Liberal Club, Athenaeum or other places within the meaning of the act, where they may continue their debates which will not longer be reported.

ACKNOWLEDGE   John Bull. Captain
                                         for the British Public

Issued at 7 p.m. G/12/16
Copies to:
No. 1 Herbert Henry
     2 David
     3 Daily Mail
     4 House of Commons
     5 J L Garvin
     6 File [1]

It seems that internal upheavals within a party, such as this, are more bitter than the mere replacement by the opposition. Certainly the Asquiths and their supporters were very bitter indeed and felt that LG had disloyally worked for power against the man who had supported and upheld him through various crises of the past. They never accepted the idea that perhaps LG was better able to cope with the demands of war. Asquith rejected out of hand the suggestion that the country might continue to benefit from his vast intelligence and experience by his remaining within the government, but a government led by Lloyd George.

The situation LG inherited could scarcely have provided him with a greater challenge and inevitably he did suffer from qualms, but he had many

[1] FLG papers

ideas for making the government a more efficient war machine. Almost immediately he imposed his scheme for a small War Cabinet composed of highly intelligent men who had no other responsibility. It met for the first time on Saturday 9th December, thirty-six hours after he had become Prime Minister, and for the first time also he introduced the idea that a Cabinet Secretary should sit in on meetings and take notes. Maurice Hankey had been very highly regarded when working for Asquith and, as a civil servant, he continued to give his allegiance to the acting Prime Minister. Thus LG acquired one of his most invaluable assistants.

The overall situation was described by Hankey in a memorandum to Lloyd George, and following its points it can be seen that the situation was grave indeed. Hankey began with the crisis at sea. Although Britain still had a superb navy, shipping was being crippled and imports being strangled by the hazard of German Submarines.

1.   The maintenance of sea-power is the first consideration, and the restoration of our complete maritime supremacy against submarines should be a first charge on all our resources.

2.   We must be absolutely secure for Home Defence, but the present margin of military force is unnecessarily large...

3.   The Western Front must continue to absorb the larger part of our forces as it is essential not only to make it absolutely secure but to be capable of taking a very powerful offensive there to counter or anticipate another Verdun. In fact, I think an offensive is absolutely unavoidable, although I have still the gravest doubt whether we can smash the German Army by means of it.

4.   Subject to the Russian Conference, I would drop the project of overwhelming Bulgaria, and adopt a defensive role at Salonika...

5.   Subject to its practicability and to the consent of the Italians, I should carry out the scheme of transferring guns to Italy with a view to a great attack on the Carso, the objective being Pola.

6.   I should prepare for an intensification of the operations from Egypt by transferring Divisions from Salonika and possibly one from Mesopotamia.

7.   I should stimulate to the utmost production of every kind in this country, with a view to a gradual diminution of our dependence on overseas resources... In order to do this I would not hesitate to adopt Industrial Compulsion in whatever form Labour will consent (to), nor to the introduction of foreign labour for our munitions factories, ports, mines and agriculture.

8.   I should adopt an entirely conciliatory policy towards Ireland.
     In any public pronouncement I should adopt the attitude that victory is only to be achieved by a tremendous national effort,

but that if this effort is made there is little doubt that a satisfactory and lasting peace can be delivered.'[2]

Hankey had delivered this memorandum to LG before his first Cabinet Meeting and it summarizes the principle concerns facing the Government. In addition, LG was determined arrange his own organisation so that he could keep his finger on the pulse of things and effect his ideas as quickly and efficiently as possible. Even at the first meeting, he mentioned his idea to extend his Secretariat. Realising that a Prime Minister's power had been confined by the lack of the resources of a department, LG decided to create a Prime Minister's department with men of exceptional ability. In the short term they were based in huts in the gardens of 10 and 11 Downing Street and evolved into what became known as the Garden Suburb.

With all these plans and developments taking place, Frances was having to work late into the night, grabbing food when she could and managing to see LG only in his official capacity. The talent and ideas flying around, as well as the demands made upon her, made her feel tired and tense. Just at this moment she did not feel up to providing LG with his soft carpet to sink into and they quarrelled. However, LG's family spent the entire Christmas season in Criccieth and Frances was able to spend the whole period with him, which gave them a chance to recover their harmony.

Despite all the new staff, Frances was still a very senior secretary and she was provided with a beautiful, spacious office right next door to the original Cabinet Office; no garden hut for her. She was thus very centrally placed for acting as a sounding board for views, or keeping track of who was needing what. It was an enormous challenge to keep some sort of organisation and record of what was going on. As Hankey wrote on the 12th January, 'The horribly unbusinesslike methods of Lloyd George's render organisation almost impossible.'[3]

Nonetheless, organisation did come about, although LG's comfort in 10 Downing Street was not progressing at the same rate and he continued to retire often to Walton Heath. The way he reported it to Frances stirred her ready sympathy and anger on his behalf. He claimed that Margaret did not bother about his requirements at all. When they moved in on the 7th December, Margaret did not organise a room in which he could work, so he had to come back down to the offices. Little considerations such as keeping his window open at night were neglected and he complained that the house was looking hideous. Margaret insisted on

[2] *Hankey: Man of Secrets* – Stephen Roskill p353 (quoting from Hankey's diary)
[3] ibid

hanging ugly family portraits done by 'some cheap artist', despite LG's taking them down more than once.

Probably there is some exaggeration in the reports LG made about his wife to his mistress, but it was true that Margaret was not overly worried about his comfort. As ever, she was uncompromising. Her children came first and she seems to have thought that since LG was a grown man, he should be able to cope. Frances could see for herself that 10 Downing Street was not pleasantly decorated, and it might not have been outside the bounds of possibility for the Lloyd George family to keep him company in London over Christmas, when they must have been aware that pressure of work was unlikely to allow him a long break in Wales. No doubt LG encouraged the family evacuation: it did after all leave him free to be with Frances, but it does not seem to reflect a very great degree of support and concern for him on the part of by the family.

The relationship between them was as strong as ever at the beginning of 1917: 'We had a supremely happy week before he left, and saw the New Year in together.'

When LG decided to travel to France and Rome and try for a main offensive on the Italian front, Frances was sleepless with anxiety. Illogical fears were stirred when the portrait of Bacon in the Cabinet room fell down while he was away and smashed the big clock on the mantelpiece in its fall. 'This of course was a bad omen and depressed me very much'.

She had reason, to think that LG could well be a target, especially now he was Prime Minister, but she was also mightily superstitious. Finding four-leafed clovers she was delighted and handed them all to LG 'as he needs luck at present more than anyone!' In 1916 she had been seriously concerned by a psychic message to beware the 28th and 29th January. 'I never can quite bring myself to disbelieve in these psychic people.' Although nothing did happen, she still manage to explain the warning because the boat LG travelled in on the 28th was sunk on the 29th.

The Prime Minister may have laughed at these intuitions and superstitions, but he respected her assessment of people and called her, 'wise little judge'. Her position in the big office by the cabinet meant that she was comprehensively abreast of developments, and found herself acting as an intermediary on behalf of people who felt she would state their case. She was truly at the heart of state affairs, and yearnings for family and security were relegated to the back of her mind. When Owen was heard to be returning by boat from New York, she wrote on 26th February: 'It will be strange meeting him after all this time.'

The next day she wrote that she had heard that his boat, the *Laconia*, had been torpedoed and shortly afterwards had received a wire from Owen saying that he was safe.

It is extraordinary how little impression the fact that Owen might be drowned made upon me. What I was worried about was that I should have to appear to be so dreadfully upset to everyone when in reality I did not care at all – not more than if it had been any other acquaintance. However, the engagement will be broken off while he is at home and there will be no more need for pretending.[4]

This time she was emphatic. Any idea of marriage was dropped and she made this plain to everyone. On the 7th March she received a letter from her mother:

I have known all along that you did not care sufficiently for Owen to marry him – the pity is that you ever engaged yourself to him.

However, I am quite of the opinion that it is quite right not to go on with it if you feel as you say – I must admit that I had looked forward to your being married to a good man who really cared for you, and that I am sure Owen does – however, least said soonest mended.

I suppose you have well thought the matter over, and that there is no chance of you altering your mind.

I have known that your heart was not in this engagement for some long time, but as you did not say anything to me I did not like to force your confidence, but you must know my darling, how much your happiness is to both Dada and myself.

Will you be coming home before Saty?, I should like to see you. Muriel is very upset.[5]

It must have been easy to let the family go on believing that she would embrace respectability and marry a man they all liked, but from her own papers, it is clear that she had not seriously considered this marriage for some time, if at all. Her sister Ninette, her third sister, wrote from Carshalton,

I am awfully sorry to hear that you have broken off your engagement. Why have you? ...

Somehow I feel that you do care for each other, and it's on account of some difficulty which might be got over if only you think it over. Have you quarrelled? Do tell me. I feel that you are very unhappy over it, and I can't bear to think that you are miserable...

[4] LG papers, House of Lords
[5] ibid

I do wish you would come and see me, or I could come and see you, so as you might tell me all about it.[6]

In fact Frances and Owen broke up in an entirely friendly fashion, with no hard feelings on either side, and there are a couple of cheerful letters from Owen to Frances in 1918, one accompanying a parcel of 'things which I think you find difficult to get at home' seemingly written on 12 April 1918. Presumably she maintained a suitable demeanour with her family, since cheerfulness would not have seemed appropriate, but really the whole business hardly bothered her.

She was far too busy and concerned supporting LG, as he was not only coping with the premiership, but his much loved Uncle Lloyd died on 1 March and Megan developed measles less than a week later. LG was always terrified of illness, and having lost one daughter, he started imagining the worst and talking of meningitis. Frances had enough to deal with calming LG without worrying about Owen.

On 1st March she wrote that LG had told her she was

his only devoted friend now ... D needs so much someone who will not hesitate to give him everything and if necessary to give up everything, and whose sole thought and occupation is for him. Without that it is hopeless to try and serve him.

Her tender ministrations led her to invent a concoction of egg, port wine, honey and cream which she persuaded him to drink each morning, 'which seemed to buck him up a lot.'

Even so, she did have bouts of depression when his need of her was not so evident. A month later she wrote that, after a week when LG was too busy to see her, he had taken her down to Walton Heath for lunch and 'two hours of bliss'. She had been feeling lonely and LG was 'very tender and kind'. 'I feel as though I ought not to mind when he is busy and cannot pay me very much attention, but I suppose I am only human and I get depressed. But he soon puts me right again.'[7]

War news did not absorb her so completely that her own emotions could be ignored. Nor could she deny every feeling for LG's all-consuming needs. If she had had no requirements of her own she would have been very happy, not lonely and depressed, as America had finally committed itself and declared war against Germany on 1st April. War prospects looked more hopeful, but naturally enough her own life did preoccupy Frances intermittently.

[6] LG papers, House of Lords
[7] ibid

Two weeks later she was invited down to Colonel Stern's beautiful house at Goring on Sea. Stern was away in France, but Mrs Stevenson told Frances she had heard talk of marriage between them. Frances took her mother's suggestion seriously and worried that perhaps Stern harboured such thoughts. Deciding that it was unlikely, as he seemed to know what relations were between herself and LG and invited them down together, she concluded that he probably just liked her. Her doubts about her own status and the opinion in which she was generally regarded nagged at her.

He is most kind and considerate. But it is always a question of how deeply these qualities penetrate − whether they are merely on the surface and displayed from a point of view of diplomacy, or whether they are genuinely spontaneous and natural. I have never found Col. Stern lacking for one moment in them so unless he is extraordinarily clever, I am inclined to assume they are natural − and indeed I prefer to do so, for it is bad for me to be continually looking for a hidden motive in every kind action, though public life rather tends towards fostering this attitude.[8]

In her papers at this time are invitations to balls, and to large country houses for weekends, clear indications that she was beginning to social-ize in a world in which she did not feel entirely at ease. On her own, yet unavailable, there must have been times when she longed to lay claim to a position at LG's side rather than waiting discreetly in town while LG visited Lord Derby or the King, keeping her distance at social occasions and generally behaving as an employee rather than a wife. In her diary she shows some bitterness towards his 'real family'.

On November 11th 1916 she had described Margaret as 'a lump of flesh, possessing, like the jellyfish, the power of irritating'. On the 1st February 1917 she commented that Margaret 'does not study him (LG) in the least' and just over a week later in reaction to a newspaper article written by T P O'Connor she wrote,

T P must know D well enough to realise the conditions of his home life. Of course D is fond of his children, but as he himself said to me when I made the same remark in defence of someone else: 'Every animal is fond of its young.' As a matter of fact, he and Olwen are continually at loggerheads and yet he is always pleased when the papers make a fuss of her, simply because she is his child. Of course D is very clever in the way he pretends at being the happy family man... He

[8] F S Diary op cit

makes me very angry sometimes, but he tells me that it is necessary...
I think he rather overdoes it, and it hurts me when I read articles like
T. P.'s where they hold him up to be a model family man. It amounts
to hypocrisy.[9]

She was still getting on well with her old pupil, Megan, now a very
lively young woman. On April 29th 1917 Frances described how she had
been placed next to her at the Mansion House lunch.

> She is an amusing little person, but is getting rather artificial. D thinks
> she is growing selfish, but that is not her fault, for she has not been
> taught to be unselfish. I think she is wonderfully unspoilt, considering
> the way she has been brought up. Many children would have been
> unbearable. She informed me that her mother reminded her of a char-
> acter out of Dickens: 'But this is only for your ear!' she added.

Frances took pleasure in recording it, however, in her diary.
Here was an area in which her normally sound judgement of people
was heavily affected by her own emotions. Plainly LG could not confide
his true feelings about his family to his mistress. With regard to others LG
would frequently come into her room, sit himself on her desk swinging
a leg and discuss people in the Ministry. It was not that he allowed
her opinions to affect his own use for a man, but he liked to hear her
views.
She described Lord Northcliffe as 'an extraordinarily commonplace
man, with a very good brain for business. He is rather dull to talk to, very
vain, but kindhearted I should say. Nothing original,' and then cynically
added, 'Those are the men that get on.' On the same day in her diary, she
described Harold Spender as

> a frightful bore, and D himself though he likes him, says he is one of
> the most tactless persons he has ever come across. His latest example
> of tactlessness, though perhaps he is not to blame for it has been to ask
> me if I would get Mrs Lloyd George to dictate to me anecdotes about
> D.!!! I hope he will suggest the same thing to Mrs Ll G.

No doubt it would have astonished these people to realise that the
gentle and responsive young woman was actually making such harsh
assessments. LG enjoyed her barbed comments and humour, perhaps all
the more because they seemed so out of keeping with her gentle exte-
rior and because she could make them very funny. She was much more

[9] ibid

entertaining about people in her papers when not liking them than when rhapsodizing in sentimental fashion. It was not that she was exactly deceitful, appearing pleasant while actually trying to hurt, but she liked to make herself agreeable to everyone and her harsh opinions would only come out in company where she felt sure of herself and could relax enough to say what she thought.

In her autobiography she wrote about the people who surrounded her in normal every-day circumstances and whom, in consequence, she did not think to mention or describe in her diary. For the most part, her descriptions here are revealing but much more complimentary. She says for instance that she liked Lord Northcliffe, 'but found him just a little sinister.'

Towards people in genuine hardship she did demonstrate a very lively sympathy. She managed to organize that the Church Army should use some funds sent to LG by the Maharajah of Gwalior, in order to investigate and relieve suffering as a result of the war. Although now Prime Minister, and faced with immense problems individual suffering could still awake a ready response from LG and Frances was ideally positioned to alert his attention and take advantage of this.

The crisis which had seemed imminent from the many U-Boat attacks was to a great extent relieved by a system of convoys. Food was again arriving in Britain, but during the summer of 1917 there was a bloody and unsuccessful British offensive in Flanders and by the autumn it was clear that the Italians were foundering. On the 24th October they were heavily defeated at Caporetto and, in order to prevent them falling out of the war, LG set off to a conference at Rapallo. Frances accompanied him.

This gave Frances the chance to visit Paris again (a very different Paris from the city she had known and loved before the war) and the chance to see her French relations. She described in her diary a city full of uniforms and women in black, and how sad and thin her cousin Suzanne had become.

Leaving Paris, her spirits improved and she later described how the Rapallo Conference was 'one of the most interesting and exciting incidents in my life. I had never been to Italy before, and the journey itself was a revelation'.

In her diary she described the scenery of the Alps and the Savoie:

As we went on the scenery became more and more wonderful. The sky was deep blue, the mountains were capped with snow, and all up the sides were autumn tints of the trees – from bright yellow to golden brown, and the deep green of the firs. Lower down the slopes were the vineyards, also with their autumn tints.

In Rapallo she described how, 'For the first time in my life I have seen olives and oranges growing in the open. I am thrilled with all the surroundings, but it is a place where one wants to be lazy.'

She had opportunities to go for walks and shop for lace. Here was a foretaste of the delights of travel with LG. The Italian government was assured that troops would be sent from both the British and French armies and LG was at last able to initiate his idea for a long overdue reorganisation of the command system, whereby any decision on strategy would be taken by an inter-Allied Military Council at Versailles. In the event the Supreme War Council could at first only advise and discuss, but it was a move in the right direction for a cohesive war effort out of the sole control of the generals.

They returned refreshed, leaving Italy able to withstand the onslaught from Austria, and returned to a cold, damp and depressing London where reports from the Western Front continued to appal and dismay. Cambrai, the Somme, the Bolsheviks making a separate peace for Russia with Germany; the news remained unremittingly grim. It was to get worse yet.

Not until March 21st, when German troops broke through the Western Front, did LG's idea for a Supreme War Council gain effective power. Haig showed himself to be a remarkable politician, and whereas he had resisted any idea that British forces led by himself should be commanded by the French, in the crisis of the German advance, a meeting was called at Doullens and he volunteered to place the British army under his command under the Supreme Command of Foch. He further suggested that Foch should be placed in command of the Allied Army as a whole. French pride was delighted, but Haig had shown amazing shrewdness, for in the battle situation as it existed, reserves would all flow to support the British line and bolster up Haig's command.

A map in the Cabinet Room had a British line marked on it in red and every day Frances saw it moving back and back with increasing dismay. The pressure seemed to lift LG to new vigour and apparent confidence, but Frances was horrified to realise that the Germans were very close to marching over Bethune where her brother was buried. In her distress she distractedly made her way to Wallington to be with her family. To her immense relief, that was as far as the Germans managed to advance, but attacks on the government caused fresh alarm.

It is now clear that the German army did not have the strength in reserve to follow through on their advances. They were moving across land devastated by four years of war, without roads or buildings to help them. As well as this, the German men came across provisions hastily left by the retreating allies. They had been virtually starving and these marvellous supplies distracted them from the main aim.

On April 1st, the advance ground to a halt. Another conference was held at Beauvais on April 3rd, attended this time by LG and the American

Generals, to arrange Foch's command over the Americans. Haig wrote in his diary:

> The PM looked as if he had been thoroughly frightened, and he seemed still in a funk... LG is a fatiguing companion in a motor. He talks and argues so! And he appears to me to be a thorough imposter.[10]

It was true that LG had been thoroughly alarmed, and with reason. If, after four years of grinding warfare the Germans could gather enough intelligence and use the lessons from what had gone before to make such advances, they were clearly a very formidable foe, and he had no evidence to see that the English generals had taken similar instruction. However, his secretary Hankey, who was by no means disposed to flatter LG, did not notice any failure of nerve on LG's part and a regular army colonel is reported later to have stated that, while LG kept up a confident front, Haig appeared white and shaken. It was a further indication of the wide gap and lack of confidence shown between the government and the army command.

On May 7th the British General, Sir Frederick Maurice, published a letter in the *Times* and the *Morning Post* declaring that the government had deliberately misled the British people and were impeding the best efforts of the army by failing to provide them with as many men as they claimed. It was a very serious attack on the honour of LG's administration, claiming that the government had lied when they announced there were more men at the front in January 1918 than in January 1917.

LG and many other government members had probably been rather loth to commit too many men to the supreme control of Haig and his fellows, convinced as they were that the generals had little regard for individuals and were more concerned with advancing a few feet than with the cost in human life. No doubt, in the winter of 1917–1918 the government were of the opinion that it had been a long war and enough lives had been lost already, so they probably did want just to sit tight until the Americans arrived.

However, did LG deliberately mislead the British public and allow the Western front to be materially weakened, thus allowing the Germans to take advantage of such a mentality? Maurice knew he was probably wrecking his future in the army when he publicly accused the government of lying about the numbers of men at the front, but he plainly felt it was desperately important that the British public should not be deceived and that the army should get all the help it could. Asquith allowed his supporters

---

[10] Sir D Haig to Lady Haig quoted in R Blake (ed) 1952 *The Private Papers of Douglas Haig 1914–19*, Eyre and Spottiswoode

to persuade him to demand an enquiry in the House. If it was shown that the government had deliberately been keeping the army short of men, then the disasters of the German advance since March 21st might be laid at their door, so it was imperative that LG refute this attack. He carefully prepared a speech in front of Milner and Chamberlain.

LG was at his most brilliant. He demolished Asquith and made Maurice look ridiculous. In fact, the situation seems to have been that the government were by no means deliberately lying. The figures they had received had been supplied by Maurice's own department while Maurice was still Director of Military Operations, and they did show that more men had left for the front in 1918 than in the previous year. The fact that many had gone to the Italian front rather than to the Western front had not come to light. This particular detail seems to have gone astray and, strangely enough, Maurice and his supporters did not refer to it, even to justify their position. LG and his government were triumphant and Asquith and his supporters totally discredited as trying to blacken the government in time of war.

Clearly there would be no possible rapprochement between the Asquithian liberals and the supporters of LG after this.

Frances later described how she came across the document showing the missing particulars with J T Davies some days after LG's triumph in parliament. J T Davies apparently put it in the fire remarking, 'Only you and I, Frances, know of the existence of this paper'.[11] Its revelation would have made the situation a little less clear cut, though the general thrust of the situation remained the same. The attack on the government was badly timed and did smack of undermining and even treachery. Moreover, the government had not deliberately lied. They had made statements based on figures supplied by the war office. The fact that these figures had then been amended appears not to have come to light. However, this oversight and the debate it engendered immeasurably strengthened LG's government for the remainder of the war by wholly discrediting its attackers. Frances never regretted their joint act of concealment, feeling it was an essential step at the time.

By summer, the outlook for LG was far more optimistic. American troops were arriving, his government was strong and on 30th June his friend Lord Riddell rented a beautiful Elizabethan house called Danny near Hassocks in Sussex, so that he could go for a change of air and scene whenever the opportunity offered. Frances spent a great deal of the summer there, often surrounded by LG's government and officials working from this base. She had developed an inflammation of the kidneys and Riddell organised that two nurses should be on duty to care

[11] Autobiography FLG op cit p130

for her. As she lay in bed she could occasionally catch the distant hum of male voices in conference together on the terrace below her room, but she seems to have been too lethargic and unwell to have been caught up in much of the excitement of the improving war situation.

LG was frequently away but managed to spend several weekends down there and would send her passionate little notes interspersed with cartoons to cheer her up.

How are you today cariad bach anwyl anwyl?[12]

    I am in love today with two such darlings. One the little sofa girl with the blue dressing gown and the other a little love in pink with braided hair falling one each side of the sweetest face you ever saw nestling on a pillow. Fond tender love to both, D.'

He was with his family for a fortnight in Criccieth in the last part of August, but quite often during the six weeks that Frances was there, he was able to pop in. Although illness always repelled him, he was attentive to her, coming in to report on the good war news and thinking out loud about settlements and post-war arrangements. He had a growing awareness of the election soon to be inevitable and, had many plans for a post war Britain that he was anxious to secure victory.

LG suffered a bad bout of flu in September while speaking in Manchester, but he was so exhilarated by the way the war was going that he managed to shake it off relatively quickly and return to Danny for recuperative walks over the Downs with Frances and a picnic on Beachy Head. Convalescing together, they enjoyed the sea air and accounts of Allenby's victories in Palestine, and the Allied Armies' approach on the Salonika front. These victories clearly indicated the beginning of the end.

Developments on the front were happening thick and fast and another Allied conference was obviously due. On the 5th October LG set off for Paris leaving Frances 'Instructions how to behave on my departure for and during my absence on the Continent.' He told her to take it easy, but, although she still felt rather weak and lowered by a cold on top of her long illness, Frances made her way back to the office and to work. No doubt she felt she had been away for far too long as it was, and with the approach of victory and peace she understandably wanted to be back at the centre of events.

When talk was not about negotiations and peace settlements, it was clear that many members of the government were thinking about their future after an election. Letters and approaches were even being made

[12] *Darling Pussy* op cit

from Asquith, who wanted to be involved in any peace conference. Unfortunately, LG felt he could not offer him a place at the expense of one of his loyal supporters, and Asquith remained out and in opposition. Churchill offended LG considerably by asking if he could take his own line at the election. LG felt he had taken a risk bringing Churchill into the government at all and now demanded total loyalty. Frances was never able to form any kind of rapport with Churchill and later was to feel antagonistic to his glory, as though it somehow diminished LG's achievements, but the main problem probably arose from the fact that neither Winston Churchill or his wife could be bothered to be polite to LG's secretary and later when they took over Frances' London flat, they were extraordinarily abrupt. In her rather dubious position, Frances inevitably took possible slights to heart and was hurt by an appearance of contempt.

Still, events were too exciting for her to be much troubled by Churchill and anyone in society who had no time for her. She was invited to the Lord Mayor's inauguration dinner on the 9th November and it was at this moment she was able to feel thrilled at the conclusion of the war. Although the Armistice had not been signed LG was able to announce that the Kaiser had fled and the Germans had asked for terms. When the bells actually rang out for peace Frances, like many bereaved by the war, was less than totally ecstatic. She watched, from a window in her office, the gathering on Horse Guards Parade. She found herself suffering a sort of anticlimax and reaction to all the long strain, as did LG who quietly dined with two or three colleagues. They did not celebrate together, but went almost immediately into the hectic business of organising the 'Coupon election'.

Chapter Four

The Peace

On 14th December, just five weeks after the armistice, LG was returned with a massive majority. The epidemic of victory fever put him in an appallingly precarious position: a Prime Minister without a party. His coupon support, given to all those deemed reliable supporters of a coalition, went across the board and incorporated a majority of the old Conservative party, who in the long run were unlikely to feel any loyalty to their Liberal leader. While borne on a wave of national victory euphoria he could achieve almost anything, but when the problems of the peace became more and more apparent it would prove hard to proceed without a firm political base.

Even the greatest optimist might have quailed at the problems facing him at Versailles. A totally emasculated Germany would leave an ominous power vacuum at the centre of Europe and no one quite knew just how alarming the new threat of communism in Russia might become. Many people believed that the old world of wealth and privilege would soon be swept away. Even as he began negotiations in Paris, Lloyd George was aware of serious industrial unrest at home. Meanwhile, on a more basic level, there was the impossibility of satisfying all the victor's demands, even if Austro-German interests were entirely ignored. To cap it all, the American present had decided that this was the moment to usher in an ideal world. His 'fourteen points' discounted French demands for vengeance in view of the suffering their country had received from Prussian hands twice in less than fifty years. Lloyd George, ever a great optimist, had enormous confidence in his own powers of persuasion and envisaged the establishment of some sort of lasting balance. That at last there was a peace to negotiate was sufficient triumph to ensure that party problems did not discourage him.

Frances arrived in her favourite city full of zest for the challenge ahead and was installed in the Hotel Majestic with the rest of the British delegation. She had been made a Commander of the Order of the British Empire in the New Year's Honours list and was pleased and proud that she had some kind of recognition for her role. She later wrote the first of her two published books describing the characters at Versailles: and the excitement and triumph of being at the heart of these earth moving events.[1]

In her book she described the atmosphere at the Hotel Majestic. It was more or less completely taken over by the British to the extent that the French staff were packed off. There were cheery little waitresses from Manchester and Wigan tending to their needs. Solid British food replaced French fare at the restaurant and a British telephone exchange was installed, linking lines directly from Paris to London. British cars waited in a row outside the hotel with British Tommies as chauffeurs, and a branch of Lloyds Bank opened in the foyer. So a 'piece of Whitehall was planted bodily' at the heart of Paris.

Lloyd George was living in a flat in Rue Nitot and visited by his family, but she was able to work closely with him in an office there. Her excellent French was again proving itself invaluable, as well as her calm soothing presence in the midst of so much tension and gaiety. Intimacy in the evening was initially something of a problem as the young Megan had persuaded her father to allow her to come to Paris. Realising that she would have far more fun in the Hotel Majestic than at the quiet family flat, she invited herself to share Frances's room. She was still totally unaware that her former teacher was considerably more than her father's secretary.

Social life was hectic. Statesmen arrived to breakfast at the hotel, invitations were fixed for lunch and every Saturday there was dancing. In moments between work, expeditions were made to the Palace of Saint Germain, or to the Louvre where Frances admitted herself too frightened to embark on the rather rickety affair that constituted an early escalator. On Sundays, when they could get away, Lloyd George was particularly keen that they should all visit battle sites and memorials such as the beautiful cathedral at Reims which had been badly damaged in the war. Megan began to find her excitement at this sort of routine waning and was persuaded to attend a Parisian finishing school allowing Frances a return to some privacy.

At this time Megan liked and respected Frances, referring to her as Miss Stevenson in her diary and clearly wanting to spend time with her. It was probably due to the fact that she had liked and trusted Frances (and that she did not want to blame her father for his unfaithfulness to her mother) that she became so very bitter when the truth was gradually brought home to her.

Unlike Megan, Frances did not tire of life in Paris among the dignitaries arranging the peace. For one thing she had serious work to do which provided her with satisfaction; for another she was in close harmony with the man she loved; but perhaps most of all there was her

[1] *Makers of the New World* written by Frances Stevenson but published anonymously by Cassell in 1922

fascination with the developing negotiations themselves. She was entranced with being at the centre of this maelstrom and for the rest of her life would tell stories of the famous characters she had observed at work in Paris.

One story she was fond of repeating was of the Polish Prime Minister: Paderewski. Not only was this man a great Polish patriot and leader, he was also one of the foremost pianists of his day, but he put aside music in order to work for the benefit of the country. He was often present at the flat Nitot but could never be persuaded to play for the entertainment of the others because as he explained, 'If I don't play for one day, I notice. If I don't play for two days my critics notice and if I don't play for three even my public notice, so I don't play.'[2]

Frances, who bore no such burden of expectation, returned to her old role as music maker, accompanying the varying visitors in every kind of song.

Lloyd George loved entertaining and parties of every description. The cook who came with the flat found herself hard-pressed to cater for lunches and dinners when people numbered from six to sixteen. She was also expected to provide food for breakfast parties; a thing she had not encountered before. She visited a local market every day at six o'clock in the morning: after British rationing the fruits of her expertise were devoured enthusiastically.

It was not only political leaders who came to the flat. An ageing and rather grotesque Sarah Bernhardt came to call: Nancy Astor brought Ruth Draper, Gertrude Bell and Augustus John were introduced: even royalty made a visit: the Belgian king, Albert. Frances was fascinated by August John and disappointed when LG placed a veto on her attending any of the painter's parties. John's reputation with women worried LG.

Frances found that her office in the Rue Nitot was a stopping point for many members of delegations who wanted messages passed on to LG in the hope that something might be achieved. Keynes came in to complain to her that the financial clauses were far too harsh and Frances was somewhat amused when, on the very same afternoon, the Governor of the Bank of England, Lord Cunliffe, came in to say he was disgusted because the English were letting the Germans off far too lightly. T E Lawrence made a couple of visits persuading her that his terms for the Arabs were necessary and she felt that his charm and personality would have convinced anyone, except the intransigent French. Frances knew already of the Sykes-Picot Agreement which ensured that his dreams could not be realised.

Many of the men she met there were to make a lasting impression on

[2] Conversation with Frances Lloyd George

her and featured in her book *Makers of the New World* which came about when the Editor of the *Sunday Times* asked her to write a series of articles about the great men she had got to know in Paris. These came out anonymously in the summer of 1921 and were put together into a book which was released in the September. This did not constitute too much work in addition to the long hours still demanded of the Prime Minister's Private Secretary. The articles were inspired by her reaction to Maynard Keynes' book criticising the whole Peace Conference. Her first chapter is pure eulogy of the Prime Minister's genius and achievement. The book becomes more readable when she is critical, or when she repeats the stories she picked up at the conference.

The politician that had most in common with Lloyd George and with whom he might have been able to sort out some more equable terms was the ex-Premier of France, Aristide Briand. Frances described him as 'a wily politician... , making up for his indolence by a certain amount of craft.' One day for instance, the French minister Fréycinet made a long and well-reasoned statement at a meeting of the Cabinet upon a subject under discussion but possessing no gifts of oratory the statement made no impression. Others spoke, and at the end of the discussion Briand got up. He made an elaborate and profound speech, which attracted much attention. Freycinet remarked: 'What an intelligent fellow he is! How did he come to make such a brilliant speech on this subject?' 'He knew nothing about it when he came here,' was the reply of a colleague,' but he heard all that an hour ago from you'. She concluded that Briand was a little like Lloyd George, 'a blend of Lloyd George's mental equipment and the temperament of Mr Asquith. He is indolent by nature and seems to tire easily of a great task.' No wonder she wrote this anonymously. Asquith was still leader of the Liberal party.

Unfortunately for the peace terms, the French people had become impatient with Briand in 1918 and elected the formidable and ferocious old man, Clemenceau, to be their new Premier. Clemenceau was seventy-nine and it was said by many of him that 'His clock stopped in 1871' when the Germans having invaded, imposed their peace terms on the French government and burnt St Cloud. These memories made a him totally determined to ensure that Germany should pay to the limit and possibly beyond, so that she would be incapable of inflicting such suffering on France again.

On March 14th Clemenceau was battling to establish a separate republic under French control on the left bank of the Rhine, with bridgeheads on the right bank. Frances described how LG managed to persuade him to adopt a slightly more reasonable attitude through appealing to his pragmatism.

'You speak as though that would afford you security. Can you name a single river in this war that stopped an advance?' Clemenceau admitted the reason in this argument – a far more effective means of convincing him than Wilson's impractical idealism.

President Wilson infuriated the other leaders. Clemenceau was heard to exclaim, 'Fourteen points! Why the good God himself could only think of ten.' On the 15th March Frances reported that it looked as if there might be a row:

> The meeting of the Peace Conference had to be adjourned this afternoon because Wilson said he had not read the papers, and therefore could not discuss them. This is the sort of thing that will make D very angry. Moreover, Wilson insists on re-opening questions that have already been settled.

'Was there ever an idol who so forced attention to his feet of clay?' She described how the President might claim democratic principles, but he expected 'at least royal treatment' with a guarded mansion outside which pedestrians were not permitted to walk. The square had a shady garden that had been a favourite rendezvous for the nurses of the neighbourhood with their charges. It became a common occurrence to see a scuffle outside the Presidential palace with ruffled gendarmes defending themselves from nursemaids armed with perambulators, angry that their right of way had been taken away from them.

In her eyes the President had no personal magnetism and she felt that he bored his conference colleagues with vaguely relevant anecdotes. When Keynes published his book about the Peace Conference and claimed that Clemenceau slept through Wilson's speeches, Clemenceau retorted that, 'It would have been better for President Wilson and the Peace Treaty too, if he had slept instead of talking'.

Frances went on to say,

> As is always the case when a man just misses greatness he was unable to delegate the work to others, but attempted to do it entirely by himself. He consulted no one. Not even Lansing was admitted to his counsels... He might have been the President's little dog but for the fact that he was never patted – and always left at home!

On March 21st Frances reported that everyone was chafing at the delays in decisions from the Peace Conference, but as LG had himself remarked that 'Wilson can think of nothing but his League of Nations and that poor old Clemenceau is not the man he was.' LG decided to try and push some achievements through, because industrial disturbances at home were making it more imperative that he should get back to

London. He took Smuts, Henry Wilson, Philip Kerr and Hankey down to Fontainbleau 'to work out definite proposals for the kind of treaty of peace to which alone we were prepared to append our signature,' as Hankey reported. News was coming through of a Communist uprising in Hungary under Bela Kun and this heightened the feeling that one of the overriding concerns of the peace was to limit the extension of the Russian revolutionary movement.

Frances always thought it was romantic that Smuts should be such an important confidant during the final stages of the war and peace. She described in her book how a British General had last seen Smuts at the end of the South African war fleeing as England's foe. The next time he saw him, Smuts was a member of the British War Cabinet, having access to information that even the rest of the Cabinet did not know. Frances felt that he still had the eyes of a man who is for ever on the watch and, however friendly the conversation, at the back of it all there was a gateway with the words 'No thoroughfare'. However, he was a man who understood about war, privation and negotiation. LG found him invaluable and he remained a good friend to both Frances and LG.

Henry Wilson was probably the one military leader that LG trusted and could get on with. Frances showed the common civilian prejudice about military men when she described him, saying 'He does not strike you as being the type from which soldiers are usually drawn – he is too elusive, too artistic.' She said he was a genius who had predicted the German offensive that had come in March 1918, but had been written off then by his superior officers as a 'jester'.

Fortunately for the Allies, Wilson and Foch got on extremely well. Frances felt that because Wilson was an Irishman, 'he understands Frenchmen in a way that the ordinary Englishman never can. He loves their gaiety, their recklessness.' She repeated his story that 'a Frenchman, if he sees a cow in front of him on the road along which he is driving, says 'Voila un obstacle,' and immediately puts on the accelerator.'

When she wrote about Foch, the Supreme Military Commander, her main example of his single minded determination obviously inspired her admiration.

> During the war he lost his son, and when they told him the news someone approached him with words of consolation. He swept them aside with a magnificent gesture. 'No!' he commanded. 'Speak to me of it after the war'.

Frances plainly thought this admirable. It is to be wondered if his wife did.

If one is to assume that some of Frances's opinions were heavily influenced by her closeness to LG it is not surprising that the other military leaders had less success with him. She described Sir William Robertson as 'the typical British soldier – solid, immovable, thick-necked and broad shouldered.' She went on to say that he was an attractive character,

> a homely good-natured, simple person, fond of a good joke and able to crack one himself. As a Quartermaster-General he was admirable:... But he was never more than a butler on a great scale. Strategist he certainly was not. He designed one or two battles. They were sanguinary failures.

She also felt that he distrusted all foreigners and felt that 'In many respects allies were more dangerous than enemies. They had more opportunities for doing you in.' In consequence he did not get on very well in a big military alliance and found himself replaced by Wilson.

In addition to the two military advisers LG took down to Fontainbleau there were two civil servants with extraordinary understanding and intelligence: Philip Kerr and Maurice Hankey. These men were called secretaries, but they were not secretaries in the sense that Frances was, organising the files, writing the letters, providing an ordered environment enabling the work to progress efficiently. These men were something more and Frances acknowledged this, appreciating that they had an understanding and imagination that could contribute more than she could.

The Americans were making themselves more and more unpopular, attempting to increase their army and double their navy while preaching the gospel of the League of Nations. Frances felt it was a great pity that Wilson's speech had been left out of the report, because he had apparently claimed that the League of Nations would do better than Christianity. Lloyd George returned from Fontainebleau determined to sweep the Americans and French before him and anxious that the Peace should 'not leave bitterness for years to come, and probably lead to another war.' He was very much opposed to the idea of lopping off a slice of Germany continuing three million Germans and putting them under the Poles, which he believed would provoke another war. He found himself subject to vitriol in the press, particularly the Northcliffe papers, the *Times* and the *Daily Mail*. Although he enjoyed a fight, he found himself resorting to quiet dinners with Frances or scooping her off for a picnic in the St Germain woods to recover.

While these negotiations and upheavals were going on, Frances was able to pose for a portrait by Orpen, visit the opera and enjoy the dances at the Majestic. Taken out several times by Esmond Harmsworth, Lord Rothermere's son, she found herself enjoying long intimate discussions about the weight of responsibility he had acquired since both his older brothers had been killed in the war. He would have to take on his father's business and she felt that he had a far nicer nature than his father, though perhaps a little 'cold and calculating', but 'extraordinarily handsome' and she liked him![3] Lloyd George made jealous comments about their friendship, but Harmsworth was a less serious threat than Colonel Sir Albert Stern.

When Stern arrived in May, he told her that he had come to Paris to have a good time which, she said in her diary, meant that he had come to give others a good time.

'He is a most generous and thoughtful person and the best host I have ever met.' Over the next few days she saw him and dined with him practically every day, and a week later LG confronted her with his fears. He admitted that she thought Stern would marry her if she gave him any encouragement. Was she prepared to leave LG. She confessed that she was seriously tempted:

> I don't love him, but we are good friends and I know he would be very kind to me. It would mean a title and wealth, whereas now I may find myself old and friendless and having to earn my own living. If anything should happen to D. People will not be so anxious to marry me in ten years' time.[4]

She could not give up LG, but clearly after eight years as his mistress and no very definite future security in sight there were times when the precariousness of her position did frighten her. The more enthralling her life the weaker the temptation: it was to strengthen later. Stern's timing was wrong.

Apart from flirtations, dances and delightful picnics with LG, Frances's free time did contain some serious moments. Her visit to her brother's grave in April revived her grief, and plainly she was still bitter about the Germans. On 7th May 1919 the Germans were finally presented with a Peace settlement. The head of the German delegation, Brockdorff-Rantzau, seemed very arrogant and insolent and did not stand to make his speech. The allied delegates were infuriated and Frances said she was glad the Germans had behaved like this because it meant LG would remain stern to the end. 'If they had been submissive and cowed he might have been sorry for them' and she did not want that.[5]

On May 25th she was terribly shocked to see a young motor cyclist

[3] Diary by FLG op cit
[4] Ibid
[5] Ibid

killed in front of her eyes in an accident with a car.[6] The abruptness with which life could be brought short was re-emphasised, and while plunging herself with renewed vigour into enjoying it to the full, she also began to worry about her loved ones. Just because she loved them didn't necessarily make them secure. It also made her a very nervous driver. For a while she tried to enjoy the independence of driving herself around, but she had to have a companion and that companion would have to get out and inform anyone stationed behind France on a hill that she always went backwards before she went forwards, and they would be well advised to reverse away from her car. In the end, when she got no better, she decided to give it up as a bad job and rely on being chauffeured for the rest of her life, by her sister or friends, or when the could afford it, a hired driver.

On the 28th June Frances went to Versailles for the signature of the Peace. She knew it was a tremendously significant moment and her sense of drama was rather disappointed by the way the event was organised. The delegates had to push their way up the Hall of Mirrors and almost half the room was taken up with representatives of the Press. 'The Press is destroying all romance, all solemnity, all majesty.'[7]

Not in fact all. On the 29th June they returned home and LG's public reception thrilled her. Crowds lined the streets and the King and Prince of Wales drove down to the station to welcome him. When a laurel wreath was thrown into the royal carriage it fell on the King's lap and he handed it to LG. In a quiet moment later, LG gave it to Frances who treasured it and kept it carefully until she finally handed it on to the Lloyd George Memorial Museum where it is now on display.

Frances suffered badly with a sense of anti-climax. In France they had been free to meet and had been provided with every comfort

When at Downing Street ..., or Walton Heath it is another matter. There is never enough to go round and what there is, is very inferior. I have never seen anyone with such a capacity for making a place uncomfortable as Mrs Lloyd George.[8]

After all the fun of Paris, life settled down to more routine work and less freedom to be together. Margaret was much in evidence, living in London or down at the new house in Cobham. Frances repeatedly remarked in her diary on how she neglected her husband and caused his life to be uncomfortable, but she ignored Margaret's other considerations; her children and the constituency where her heart and loyalty lay.

[6] Conversation with M Stevenson
[7] FLG Diary Op cit
[8] Ibid

Margaret took the family back to Criccieth for the summer holiday and LG went to Deauville for a month to further negotiations with the French, in a house Riddell had taken at Hennequeville on the Normandy coast. Frances was a member of the party. Margaret can scarcely have failed to know. It makes it all the more commendable that she involved herself so thoroughly on her husband's behalf in his constituency. She did the local campaigning and dealt with local problems while her husband attended to great affairs of state. It sometimes is most forcibly apparent that Lloyd George was astonishingly lucky in the two women who shared his life. One was a devoted mother to their children and a strong support in his constituency, the other was a dedicated comforter and tender ministrant to his own requirements and a careful, efficient and discreet mediator and organiser.

Frances's gentle powers for creating a harmonious environment were stretched to the full at Hennequeville. Apart from Riddell, who was the host, Hankey, Sir Hamar Greenwood and his wife, the Waldorf Astors and F E Guest (the Chief Whip) made up the party. It was hoped that discussions at Hennequeville might end British intervention in Russia and come up with a plan to deal with Arab aspirations in former Turkish provinces. The Irish question and the increasing industrial unrest were also discussed, but socially the group gathered together was rather strained as the Greenwoods and the Astors did not get on. Frances had liked Nancy Astor a lot in Paris and had been grateful for the support she had offered at Paul's graveside, but Nancy was a fervent Christian Scientist and very judgemental. She was beginning to realise that Frances was not solely Lloyd George's secretary and was immensely critical, so naturally enough Frances also began to feel very uncomfortable with her.

Over the next ten days, Bonar Law, Eric Geddes (not one of Frances's favourite people) Horne and Lord Allenby joined the House party. Allenby had come to try and resolve British vacillations over the future status of Egypt and conflicting Arab/Zionist ambitions. Discussions covered all the issues, and LG was talking of a scheme for a new party which would give him a real political base. He raised the idea of a 'National Democratic Party,' but there was no enthusiasm for this intended mix of right and left and he allowed the idea to drop.

At the end of their stay, Lloyd George and Hankey motored to Paris to persuade the Americans to agree to their plans and it seemed that they had been successful, but shortly afterwards the Senate rejected the Versailles Treaty and the United States ceased to make a very significant contribution to the peace.

On the 29th November 1919 Frances wrote that Nancy Astor had been elected as the first woman M.P. She also wrote that she had concluded that Nancy was treacherous but remarked, 'she will get her reward in the

House of Commons! I do not think any wise woman would choose to sit in the House!'[9]

For someone as politically attuned and supposedly keen on rights for women this seems an extraordinary comment, but Frances was not an earth-shaker. She liked to fit in and although her life had tumbled her down a rather rebellious path, such was not her natural inclination. She did, however, have a historians's, or perhaps a journalist's perception for significant events and their place in history. She was thrilled to see the first lady M P take her place on December 1st 1919 and she was moved by the dignity of the occasion. It was the evening that summer in Normandy when Nancy and Ernest Evans performed an Apache dance that remained most vividly in Frances's memory. The dance had ended with Nancy flinging herself, after a series of cartwheels, into the lap of Lord Riddell.

With the intense demands of the war now over, there was less reason to work late every night and LG had no excuse not to spend a bit more time with his family. In consequence, Frances enjoyed a more hectic social life than before and started to mingle with the gay and the great in distinguished society. On December 18th she met the Prince of Wales for the first time and was charmed. Philip Sassoon the millionaire, started to invite her to frequent weekends at his luxurious country home, Lympne, and to many dinner parties at his Park Lane house in London. At first she put his friendly attentions down to ambition. He did want to work with Lloyd George. But they developed a genuine friendship and even when Lloyd George was out of power Philip continued to invite her to weekends and dinners. Some of his more luxurious tastes made a deep impression upon her and, during the many times she stayed at Lympne, she gained some of the ideas which ultimately made her own home so beautiful.

For all the kindness and fun she was enjoying, the focus for her passion was still Lloyd George and she felt desolate when he left to spend Christmas with his family. She wrote that they had been spending so much time together, without the constant burden of war, and she had become too used to it. She found it harder and harder to be self-effacing and allow for the prior claims of his family. She wrote in her diary, 'I get such a terrible feeling of loneliness when he goes, and almost feel frightened at his being so far away.'

Christmas was spent with her family in Wallington and a return to her role as daughter. The holiday was soon over, however, and she was back to the whirlwind of life with Lloyd George.

On the 8th January they were in Paris and were shocked by Clemenceau's defeat. Old enemies were being vicious to him in his fall

[9] ibid

from power and the humiliation made both Lloyd George and Frances a touch reflective.

February was a social whirl, getting to know the Prince of Wales and his mistress at the time, Mrs Dudley Ward. Although she had been awestruck, and felt that she was 'trembling all over' when she had first been introduced, she gradually succumbed to his boyish charm and found that he and his brothers were mortal and that she could converse with them like anyone else.

In some ways she was becoming used to the high life and was coming very much to like it. On 23rd February Lloyd George heard that the American millionaire, Carnegie, had left him £2,000 a year for his services in the war and he decided that Frances should benefit too. He told her he would arrange for her to have a bigger and more comfortable home. 'I am glad he wants me to have a bigger flat, though I love the one I have got, but it is getting too full of treasures (mostly his gifts).'[10]

On the 24th February she saw a film that had been made about Lloyd George's life and described it as,

> a perfectly appalling thing ... the man who was supposed to be D was simply a caricature. I begged D not to let it be shown. Mrs LG was angry with D because she said I had put D against it because I objected to the domestic scenes in it.

It was not so much that, though they may have influenced Frances, but without television or even sound there was no way that Lloyd George's magnetism could be revealed to a wider audience and Frances's fears that a 'caricature' would not do him justice may have had some truth. Certainly the film was not released then. In this instance her judgement coincided with his own. Her superstitions did not affect him so much and when she worried because she had seen 'the new moon through glass' he was inclined to tease her out of it. Still, he liked her to worry so much about him, and more and more he tried to have her with him whenever he could.

In April there was an Inter-Allied conference at San Remo. Frances went too and shared a cabin with Megan with whom she also shared a bout of serious sea-sickness. It was the last time Megan would want to share anything with Frances. With her father's obvious inclination for spending so much time with Frances, it gradually became clear to Megan over the summer of 1920 that Frances was rather more to her father than just a friend. Once realised, her bitterness and sense of betrayal knew no

[10] ibid

bounds. She would have done anything to hurt Frances, even risk her father's career.

It was at San Remo that Frances met and became friendly with Berthelot, the French Prime Minister's assistant, and found herself drawn into a flirtation. She never felt it was serious, but discovered that they were being watched and wondered about. While finding him fascinating she also described how his vitality seemed diminished when they spent time with Lloyd George; clear indication of who had the upper hand.

In the summer the Lees bequeathed their country home, Chequers, to be a country residence for the British Prime Minister, so that he would have somewhere relatively close to London in which to escape and enjoy rural delights. It also provided a beautiful house in which to entertain foreign dignitaries, with its long gallery and mementoes of Cromwell. Frances was enchanted. 'The peacefulness of the place is indescribably. There is healing in the atmosphere.'

She was allowed to organise the hospitality and put her own imprint on the entertaining and this infuriated Megan who felt that her mother was being ousted.

During 1920 Lloyd George barely visited Criccieth, claiming that he had to work. He was certainly hard-pressed with the dangerous Irish situation and with worries about Turkish nationalism and the Miners' strike. The Unionists in the Coalition were badgering Lloyd George about the economy. In consequence, he failed to support his reforming Minister of Health, Addison, who was trying to get houses built, thereby draining government resources as costs in the construction industry grew.

He spent that Christmas with Frances, refusing to go to Criccieth and spend any time with his family, and Hankey recorded in his diary that he was shocked by LG. Not only had he failed to support Addison in his democratic and reforming work, but he had been rude in the Cabinet and bullied Curzon, the Foreign Minister. In his diary Hankey concluded that, 'LG is suffering from a touch of swelled head,' though he finished his entry by saying that it 'is understandable as he is the biggest man among them.'

The Coalition was definitely not running harmoniously, but LG told Hankey that he was happy at the prospect of a period out of office. He would take a place in Kent with some fruit trees and write a book about the war, leaving his successors to make a mess before returning refreshed to attack them.

He may have been tired of life at the centre, but Frances was still loving it. At the end of the year a long article was written about her by the American journalist, Helen Ormsbee, describing how beautiful and unruffled she seemed in her office next to the Cabinet, at the heart of the British Empire. When asked what she felt was the most important quality for a secretary in her sort of position, she said that she thought it was discretion. She would record events for posterity and she certainly felt that history should be preserved but she would not by so much as a flicker betray to the public her particular position. Never would it have occurred to her to threaten Lloyd George with any bad publicity. She believed he was a great leader and any personal failings should be concealed in the interests of what he could contribute to the nation, just as she also felt that if he demanded her life he had a right to it. She never wavered in his conviction and could never understand how his children could be less unreserved in their support of everything he did.

She had no illusions that he was all gentleness and tenderness. He returned from yet more meetings in Paris in a thoroughly bad mood, saying that the rooms in the Crillon were overheated. On the 30th January he invited Tom Jones and Frances to join him for dinner and they were discussing the German indemnity which Jones pointed out was less than the capital of Lord Leverhulme's companies. This brought the conversation on to talk of Leverhulme cutting out his head from Augustus John's portrait. LG said he could sympathise, he did not like the portrait John had done of him. Frances said that John was a genius who had seen the savage side of the Prime Minister. Jones agreed with her and said it was good to show 'the square jaw I had sometimes seen in cabinet and which I was sure Briand had seen last week.' Frances was delighted to hear Jones saying this and said forcefully that 'there are more than enough of the Sunday School portraits of the Prime Minister about and that it is important that posterity see his other face.'[11] None of this was said with any bitterness. Frances loved him, savagery and all, and the evening ended happily enough with Frances playing Welsh music to them on the piano.

On the 17th March Bonar Law resigned on the grounds of ill health. Lloyd George was very sad – they had worked well together. Kerr commented perceptively, 'LG is so tied up in his various pledges to Germany, to France, to the Arabs and to his Irish policy that he ought to clear out for a year or two;' and that he was in the position Asquith had been in in 1916, 'hanging on without any particular policy or support and it would only end ... by being kicked out ignominiously.'[12] But the grind of every day office was too all dominating for Lloyd George to look clearly at the situation. He was distracted by immediate issues such as getting the miners back to work and he still felt he was the only person who could fulfill his various pledges.

Kerr decided to distance himself a little and on May 7th he quit his position as one of Lloyd George's secretaries to become Editor of the *Daily Chronicle* and lead a quieter life. He had been a calming influence

[11] *Whitehall Diary* – T Jones
[12] Roskill op cit

and generally liked. Frances felt very sad that he would no longer be working so closely with them. It did not occur to her that a period out of power might have been a good thing for Lloyd George and, in the same diary entry that she talks about Kerr leaving, says that Lloyd George must try to write his war memoirs in the autumn recess.

On June 2nd Frances wrote that she 'lost all my Derby bets yesterday. "From him that hath not shall be taken away even that which he has".' That sounds a little extreme, but Frances was always extravagant. However rich she became, she always spent her money twice and no doubt she had counted on the Derby bets to alleviate some pressing debts. Still, she was earning some welcome extra funds from her *Sunday Times* articles and on June 20th she wrote that she had heard they were to appear in book form. She felt very proud of herself.

On July 6th the Chancellor of the Exchequer, Horne, reported to LG that people had been talking about him and Frances. Apparently, Megan had been spreading rumours critical of Frances, hoping to put a spoke in the relationship. Lloyd George told Horne he would rather go out of public life than do without Frances, but Frances made plans to be more discreet and travelled down to Chequers by train rather than in Lloyd George's car – she did not want to be the cause of him retiring from public life.

His health was beginning to show the effects of all the strain he had been under. Frances had to call for a dentist to come to see Lloyd George at home because he did not have time to go to him. On another occasion, they walked up the hill from Chequers and just sat and lazed in the sun, because Lloyd George had no energy left for his usual walking. He was beginning to talk more and more of a period out of office. He spoke to her of a need to find a home fairly close to London, but in the country, so that he could keep tabs on events, but enjoy the country pursuits he loved so much, practise some of his farming ideas, write the books he had planned and enjoy long walks. He wanted a place also where he and Frances could be together, away from the family. Frances was sent out house-hunting in Kent and Surrey, with the idea of finding somewhere with a view and land for growing fruit.

Lord Dawson, the renowned doctor to the king and other notables, saw LG and told him that he was not fit enough for a strenuous foreign holiday taking Frances motoring through the Tyrol and the Italian lakes, but that he should have a complete break somewhere remote.

A holiday must last a month at least to be any use to you. The first week you will be quite certain that things cannot go on without you; the second week you will be a little less certain. The third week you will have come to the conclusion that they can; and the fourth week you will not care a damn whether they do or not. That is when you can feel quite sure that your holiday has done you good.[13]

Unfortunately, Dawson took his responsibilities so seriously that he found the remote spot, a house near the sea in Scotland opposite the Island of Skye. It was very beautiful, but inconvenient in the extreme if you did not intend to take Dawson's advice to heart and needed to stay in touch. There was no telephone. There was only one car and the house was thirty miles from the nearest station. The summer was dry and sunny elsewhere, but it rained every day at Gairloch and everyone got wet through playing golf or trying to take walks. Margaret was in residence in the house, but Lloyd George persuaded Frances to join some others in the local hotel where she went down with a bad cold and, in consequence, a bad case also of depression.

Lloyd George could not bring himself to ignore world events and take a real holiday, especially with the talks on Ireland beginning to make progress, so he demanded that members of the Cabinet come to see him in his remote and wet holiday location, whatever their own plans had been for the summer recess. Their annoyance was exacerbated when he developed a serious abscess of the tooth and could see no one and do nothing for several days. Jokey little notes were delivered to Frances at the hotel with cartoons Lloyd George drew of himself blown up on one side by his abscess, but Frances felt desperate to get away and go home. Lord Dawson had been called over from his holiday in Scotland to look at the abscess, and when he found Frances in a bout of tears he was very encouraging and told her that Lloyd George still needed and depended on her. It had been hard to feel sure of that when she was isolated from him in her hotel and heard intermittently from him through scrappy, if fond notes.

> My sweet,
> I heard the doctor's report and it gave me joy. I have been increas-ingly enquiring about you and I do miss you so much.
> Police very vigilant today so cannot write, but my love is beyond all police supervision.
> Ever and ever your own sweetheart and lover and husband DAI.[14]

He began to realise that they were not going to spend time together in Scotland so he sent her off to do some more house-hunting. She left as soon as she was well enough in order to look at an estate that had become available in Churt near Hindhead in Surrey.

---

[13] FLG *Autobiography* op cit
[14] Edited Letters op cit

She visited it on a glorious September day and fell in love with it so completely that she wrote telling him that it was the appointed place. He wired back asking one question. Did it face south? She confidently assured him that it did, feeling so sure that it must do that she did not actually check. On her assurance he gave the order to go ahead and buy the sixty acres.

As soon as he came back from Scotland he came down to see it on a raw and misty autumn day with the view almost obscured. Frances indicated where the view lay and he brought out his watch which he used for a compass and said that it lay north.

Frances was distraught and very close to tears, wondering frantically if she could raise enough money somehow to buy the estate herself, but he suddenly decided to relent and, laughing at her, said that they would call it 'Bron-y-de' which means 'breast of the south'.

Plans for a beautiful home here were a delightful distraction from the arduous talks with the Irish which continued throughout the autumn. Frances was transfixed by the struggle. Her diary for November is completely absorbed in Lloyd George's negotiations and how he finally seemed to be getting the Sinn Feiners to the point of signing an agreement. She sat in her study next to the Cabinet room, waiting for the last stages to be agreed upon until nearly 3 am on December 6th 1921, and she shared Lloyd George's passionate sense of achievement when he at last brought out a treaty and told her to keep it in a safe place. She felt, as did many others at the time, that Lloyd George had managed to solve the insoluble.

Many others did not. The papers were almost universally angry with Lloyd George and attacked him for his autocratic ways and problems in the domestic economy. Although many of the Press Barons had benefitted from Lloyd George's distribution of honours, they were also attacking the level which the sale of honours had reached. Lloyd George could argue that ever since 1850, every party had sold honours when in power. He felt that at least it was better than what went on in the United States, where policy pledges could be bought with party donations. So he could justify it to himself but the scale on which he allowed the sales to take place did begin to cheapen their value. Certain dubious characters, who would normally have stood no chance even of buying an honour, managed to obtain peerages at this time. As a money-raising exercise the sale of honours was very successful and helped create Lloyd George's enormous political fund, but that in itself made people afraid he was getting too powerful for a truly democratic society.

Lloyd George did not seem to allow himself to get unduly discouraged by the opprobrium in the press. With a staggering degree of optimism he seemed to feel that he could still solve the problems of Europe, and early in January he went to Cannes intending to offer the French a security pact on certain conditions. He worked well with the French Prime

Minister, Briand, and the conference seemed to be going so well that Lloyd George took Briand off for a jovial game of golf. The press used that apparent light-heartedness as an opportunity to pour vitriol on Briand, and caused him to resign. Poincaré took over and the chance for any amelioration of the Treaty of Versailles receded. At this point even Lloyd George saw that the outlook was bleak and did talk frequently of resignation, but he could not bring himself to do it. He had achieved so much and he trusted himself to achieve more if only he could count on support. The Unionists under Austen Chamberlain assured him that they wanted the Coalition to continue and so he went on planning for a final bid to restore the European conference at Genoa.

Frances was sympathetic to his talk of resignation and said that she thought a period of rest and recuperation would do him good. She envisaged it as being very temporary and enabling them both to be a little out of the spotlight. She was still enjoying the involvement and getting used to influencing affairs. In the summer of 1922 Birkenhead tried to get Horne to accept a peerage and go into the House of Lords as he thought Churchill would be a better Chancellor. He approached Horne saying that Lloyd George had asked if he would like a peerage. Horne was very upset, assuming that Lloyd George was trying to get rid of him. Frances persuaded him to confide in her and she was than able to get Lloyd George to talk to him directly and assure him that this was not the case. Her tactful and intelligent mediation meant that Horne stayed in position and loyally maintained his support for Lloyd George later in the year when things got critical.

In March, tired from all the attacks in the papers, Lloyd George escaped for a rest in Criccieth. From there he wrote to Frances telling her how the rest was restoring him – despite his yearning to be with her – and warned her that whatever decisions he came to, he would have to expect tough times when he returned, so he needed a complete rest. After three weeks LG came back to persuade the Cabinet that he should make terms with Russia and if they did not support him he would resign. His terms were moderately couched, so he clearly wanted them to be accepted and to continue with his self-appointed task of securing peace in Europe, but as J T Davies wrote to Frances,

> he means to stick to Coalition with the Tories... leading a great progressive party of Liberals and modern Labour requires new stunts, new programmes, new policies, new campaigns and I doubt whether the PM is fit enough for that now even with six months rest.[15]

---

[15] J T Davies to FLS 21 March 1922 quoted in Beaverbrook *Decline and Fall of Lloyd George*, Collins

Frances did not go to Genoa. She was busy overseeing the building of Bron-y-de and was feeling quite run down herself, apart from the fact that Margaret and Megan had gone with Lloyd George. Megan was by this stage so bitterly angry over his relationship with Frances that LG admitted to Frances that she was 'quite capable of taking advantage of that to say she insists upon returning home because you are here. That would create a first class scandal as the place is a hotbed of gossip.'

Failure seemed to stare Lloyd George in the face. Russia revealed that they had come to an agreement with Germany. France was even less likely to be accommodating therefore, and yet Lloyd George persisted; but he wrote to Frances:

> If this Conference were to fail I should like to take Pussy to an obscure island in the South Seas where there are no cables, letters or newspapers and then come back in five years – with the kittens – and see what had happened.[16]

If this conference were to fail! The conference was failing. The United States had refused to have anything to do with it. Poincaré headed a bitter French government and Russia had worked out its own future with Germany. These dreams of retiring to the South Seas were really a cruelly tantalising lure. Lloyd George could as much cut himself off so completely as stop his blood from circulating, but the promise of kittens was rather heartless. Frances was now thirty-three and her yearnings for children had not diminished, although while they were both so busy she could ignore them.

For the time being she had a big home of their own in Surrey to organise and furnish. Bron-y-de was Frances's home just as Brynawelon in Criccieth was Margaret's. Obviously whenever Margaret visited she had a superior claim to be there as the wife, but a visitor is what Margaret was there. Frances had to disappear quickly, but the servants, the décor and the every-day running of the place were all down to Frances.

As she organised their future domestic arrangements Frances informed Lloyd George that she had appointed maids, one of whom had qualified in her eyes by ten years' experience of looking after a fidgety old woman of seventy. Frances knew that Lloyd George would demand comfort and she was determined to provide it, more efficiently than Margaret had ever managed. The other maid was apparently a 'derelict old widow who looks ninety'. Her other consideration was probably that Lloyd George would not be surrounded by anyone too attractive as he had been known to upset young maids with unwelcome sexual attention.

[16] *My Darling Pussy* ed A J P Taylor, Weidenfeld & Nicholson

Frances does not seem to have found that behaviour serious or threatening. Their relationship was so strong at this period that she possibly regarded his attention to a pretty face as a sign of exuberance, not to be attended to. She knew that her only serious rival was Margaret and it is about her that she is really unkind in her diary. She knew that Margaret and David shared things she could not — a family, a history, similar roots, and an old understanding. She would comfort herself that Margaret did not look after David, which was true, and that he was bored by her, which was not true. David was a lucky man. He wanted and needed aspects of them both and he managed to persuade both of them to continue to give their support despite the presence of the other.

After nearly seven weeks away in Genoa, Lloyd George returned to another great reception at the station, just as he had when he returned from Versailles, but this time with even less reason. He had certainly not achieved the European security he had hoped for and he found the fabric of his government unravelling. Worse was to follow. First, in June, Henry Wilson was murdered by the IRA so that his Irish achievement was cast into doubt. Then in July, the full scale of the sale of honours was exposed and constituted a serious scandal. The civil service were sick of the so-called 'garden suburb', the Foreign Office were fed up with a Prime Minister who dealt with foreign affairs himself without consultation and, worst of all, there was a crisis approaching between Turkey and Greece.

Lloyd George badly misread the feeling of the country and the level of support and trust for himself when he suggested that a military stand should be made to stop the Turkish approach. His Greek sympathies were not universally shared, but far stronger than this was a passionate abhorrence for the risk of war. Brinkmanship played some part in Lloyd George's approach, but the threat had to be convincing to stop the Turks in their tracks, and unfortunately, it was so convincing as to convince the British also that the Prime Minister was prepared to risk war again. Frances was as appalled as any other member of the public. She considered sending LG a note to warn him against sending a threatening message. 'But then again, I thought, he will never agree to such a telegram being sent... The next thing I knew was that the telegram had gone.'[17]

Most infuriating for the Unionists was the fact that Lloyd George was acting so recklessly without referring to the Foreign Office. He excused himself by saying that Curzon was so often unavailable and residing in the country, but Curzon had been working for peace, and although the Turks did withdraw, there was a widespread condemnation of the 'amateurs in Downing Street whose interfering in diplomacy could lead to war.'

[17] Autobiography FLG op cit

On the 19th October the famous Carlton Club meeting and the Unionists decided to disassociate themselves from Lloyd George. He was left with no choice but to resign. On the 23rd October Jones described him giving a hilarious imitation of himself making a deputation to the future Prime Minister. 'Everyone laughed, except Frances'. Later on Tom Jones recorded that he 'withdrew from L G's office into Miss Stevenson's room and found her burning masses of papers in the fireplace and looking sadder than I have ever seen her.'[18]

She had reason. Their life together was about to enter new and uncharted territory. As his most ardent supporter and admirer, she hated to see Lloyd George turned out and humiliated. He may have put a brave face on it, but he wished he could have bone at a time of his own choosing and she later wrote: 'The most humiliating and shattering thing about adversity is that it gives one's enemies an opportunity for triumph.'[19]

She did feel shattered and she was offered a senior position in the Civil Service. She would not even consider it, feeling as she did that Lloyd George had been betrayed and let down on all sides. She wanted to support him and all her maternal feelings ached with pain at his defeat in the election that November. In public he maintained a boisterous public face, but privately to her he confided that he felt old, so she encouraged him to seek out the sun and they set off for a holiday in Algeciras, getting strength up to face the direction their lives must now take.

[18] T Jones op cit
[19] *Autobiography* FLG op cit

Chapter Five

Adjustments

Lloyd George suffered a reaction to the electoral rejection that occurred in November 1922, and although he did not appear discouraged in public, he privately admitted to Frances that he wanted to get away to recover his energy and equilibrium.

They went together to Algeciras, somewhere Frances loved and used as the setting for the start to the affair, in a novel she began to draft on her way home. She put down notes to herself to expand about walks under a crescent moon in the dark, with her hand in his and the scent of orange blossom and lilies.[1]

Painfully, she had to disappear discreetly from the scene as Margaret and Megan came out to join LG. Without a fuss, she was expected to be gone leaving no trace, so to comfort herself she returned via Paris and a few days in the splendour and pampering warmth of the Hotel Crillon. Here she drafted notes for the intended novel about a young, single, intelligent and educated young woman called Ann, who falls in love with a married MP called Michael.

There are lots of gaps and not much development or description. Frances was in her favourite city, with many old friends to visit and relatives to see, so she did not have a great deal of time alone to work on this book. At home in London there would be even less time for finishing it. She was returning to very heavy new demands as LG's only secretary, in place of the entire team he was used to in 10 Downing Street. However, she must have had a few moments in Paris in which to write, as there are several passages that show rather clearly how a young, intelligent woman felt on being asked to make no demands from her married lover.

Frances always felt that she was justified in taking Dame Margaret's husband because Dame Margaret was such a neglectful wife. Margaret preferred to be in Wales with the children, or if she did come to London, she did not bother to ensure that David returned home to warmth and comfort after a heavy day. Frances began her novel by describing the House of Commons as watched by a young woman caught up in a debate

[1] FLG papers

in which a very charismatic speaker is making an important speech. She is so transfixed and thoughtful afterwards that she doesn't see him come into the visitor's gallery and approach her. He has come to find out what she thought and take her to tea – just as Lloyd George had done so often in the early days of their courtship.

The heroine asks the M.P about his wife: 'She is away,' he answered shortly, 'I asked her to come up for my speech, but she did not see her way to do so.' On the way out they bump into the M.P's adult daughter who is with a young man and clearly distracted. She too has missed the speech, but is very irritated to see that Ann has been there and is now with her father. The young woman is initialled M in this early draft, and very pointedly ignores Ann – the sort of behaviour Frances was now beginning to expect from Megan.

Frances was now thirty-four. She had just had to tear herself away from a romantic idyll with Lloyd George to face the uncertain future and perhaps she was feeling especially bitter. Certainly the idyll is very quickly glossed over in the notes and the novel moves quickly on to Ann's realisation that work always takes first place for her lover. After a very few days in Algeciras he is called back to take a position in the government.

The heroine, Ann, apparently has 'an unuttered hope that he may refuse.' In a row that follows Ann taunts the M.P. that he is selfish and will not give up anything vital for her. He replies that he is not his own master: 'he serves the state and that must be his first consideration.' She replies: 'Motherhood is a woman's right. You deny it me. The pain is not now, but in long years ahead.'

He says she is unreasonable, becomes impatient and goes. It is hard to imagine that this sort of incident happened too often, or both parties would have become impatient, but obviously there were times when Frances felt she was making all the sacrifices. During the war and the busy years afterwards she had been preoccupied by the huge amount to do, but now suddenly everything was in a state of flux and, as she spent time on her own in Paris, the yearnings she always felt for a child were engulfing her again. In a later scene the heroine says, 'I adore children. There is a mystery about them which attracts and overwhelms me. Perhaps that is because I haven't a child of my own. If I had, I might be more sophisticated in this respect.'

Then Frances continued:

A child of her own! How sadly the words came from her lips. An infinite longing – an unsatisfied tenderness. All the tragedy of a hungry heart. Because he loved her, he ought to be able to fulfill her womanhood. But he knew her mind. He hinted at the possibility.

'No! No! A thousand times no! Bear a child in secrecy and like a hunted thing. Leave it to others after I had brought it into the world, or else resort to some subterfuge in order to have it with me. It would be a fine thing to bear children to you my lover, even without marriage, but a hideous shame to cover the fulfilment of our love with lies and fear.'

'That would mean ruin to me, Ann.'

'I know, so it must not happen. Don't think I'm complaining Mike darling. I'm perfectly happy with you as I am. Think, if I had a child I would want to spend at least half my time with him, and how jealous you would be.'

He folded her tenderly to him. 'I want you all to myself' he murmured. 'There must be no one else.'

Doubly selfish! He felt it in his heart, but how alter it? Fate decreed it, and if something told him that he was trying to get the best of both worlds – well it wasn't his fault. And she was happy with him, there was no denying that.

She gave a shrill little laugh, that ended in a sob. She passed her hand quickly from her forehead over her soft curls. always a sign of torment with her –

'Oh Michael – what a desperately unfair thing life is for a woman – even now.'

So Frances clearly minded sometimes, very badly indeed. She had always wanted and expected to have children. Grandmaman had predicted that Frances would marry a country clergyman and have ten children. No doubt the clergyman would have ended up a bishop whether he wanted to or not, but this destiny would have fulfilled Frances whereas the life of a courtesan did not.[2] While she was busy and and the centre of an exciting affair she could push it to the back of her thoughts most of the time but it must have shown even to LG sometimes, as he wrote in a letter just then saying how much he was missing her, 'even a Pussy bach at her worst.'

Clearly she was not the soft and tender ministrator the whole time. She did make demands and ructions. Occasionally she wanted to rebel, but in her letter to LG from Paris she is her usual devoted and efficient self, reporting on the attitude of the French to their invasion of the Ruhr and their anger with Bonar Law.

The notes from the novel act as a sort of commentary on what she felt about her situation. Frances describes Ann as being interested in politics because of her love of a politician – much as she said in other notes that she felt herself to be someone who needed to be inspired to

[2] Conversation with J Longford

devotion and then there was nothing she would not give to help the object of that devotion. A character she names N.A. and who certainly possesses many of Nancy Astor's attributes, remarks to the politician hero that Ann is

> not really interested in politics you know. I saw her going through the *Times* the other day and the articles she marked for keeping were one on 'Wood Lilies' and another on 'Italian painting'.
>
> And how genuinely, I wonder are you interested in politics? You use them solely for self advancement. Ann is at least interested in them for the sake of another person.

On the back of the sheet of paper where she describes this engagement, Frances wrote:

Times complimentary leader
Prognostices Liberal reunion
Free trade platform
Daily News very complimentary
emphasises success final meeting
Asquith's speech
Mail attacks Government
Features Chief.

Like her heroine she was very fond of flowers, and lilies were very much a favourite. Italian painting was also naturally of interest since she had grown up with an Italian artist grandfather. At thirty-four she was sufficiently aware of her own character to recognise that her interest in politics stemmed from her love of Lloyd George, but as he wrote to her, 'The Paris letter was so invaluable as a report that I mean to keep it.'

Politics may not have been her own passion originally, but she was sufficiently devoted to Lloyd George and all his concerns to have adopted his passions as her own and when politics affected her life as much as it inevitably did, it naturally came to be very important to her too.

Understandably in such an early draft, the novel shows a tendency to indulge her wishful thinking. For instance, the hero here is very rude back to the 'N.A.' character. In her diary she describes how Nancy Astor had attacked her in March 1922, but she does not enlarge on what she said. In the notes for the novel 'N.A.' tells Ann how important Michael's wife is to him and how much they have shared and then, on another occasion, snubs her. Ann describes the internal conflict facing her as 'this woman with her great position, her power, her wealth, her poisonous tongue, could do her great harm.'

More significantly Frances makes the plot develop by allowing Ann to become pregnant – despite that speech assuring her lover that he is enough. Instead of coming to an arrangement, she goes away to have her baby in solitude, leaving a letter in which she twice assures the hero,

'I will not let you down.'

However, in the world according to Frances, the hero is devastated when he discovers she has gone. His marriage collapses and he does no good work. Obviously leaving the finer details for another occasion, Frances turned to the back of the note book and wrote:

'But Michael what about your future, your career?'
Folding her closer, tenderly
'There can be no future, no career without you.'
The end.

A romantic dream, but there was not the remotest chance that LG would give up his future and career for her. He had told her from the beginning that he felt he owed it to the country to sustain his position and if this meant he could never risk the disgrace of divorce, then unfortunately that was the price they both had to pay. To be honest, she would also have lost her career and her position at the centre of events and, understandably, she had never been prepared to take the risk of losing her own job and her love. Unlike her heroine she was not a successful novelist with a life apart from the hero. Frances had made her role as his confidante, support and ally. To have withdrawn her support and to bully him into realising what life was like without her, would have been against everything she normally tried to do. Nevertheless her romantic dreams are understandable given that she was now thirty-four and facing a new beginning with Lloyd George outside office.

She did hope that the fresh start would bring her some changes too. It must have figured in her mind that he spent a considerable time still with his family, although appearances were not quite so important for a private man. He was earning a substantial amount from journalism and was in demand as a political commentator. Why not make his voice felt through his writing?

Frances's close circle of friends by now included her lawyer's wife, Elsie Morris, who had been divorced, and Felicia Brook who was a single mother. A letter she felt important enough to keep came to her that summer from someone signing themselves 'Yours Etienne' and in that he wrote 'I must get my divorce affair done with in one way or another.' Obviously she had written and helped him.

So I have scarcely the time to thank you for your letter written so late in the night. I must say when I am reading you all my deepest interest is as much taken as when you are speaking to me most gently or most cleverly. You express yourself so clearly and so thoroughly at the same time. One would say you know only solid luminous words.

Frances, Frances what shall we do? What shall we be able to do? I assure you the question is very momentous on my part. Much more than you can believe.[3]

There were always men showing her considerable interest and alternative futures. This one was a distinguished French economist who wrote a pamphlet criticising J M Keynes' famous book *The Economic Consequences of the Peace*. He was deeply in love with Frances and she liked him a lot and treasured the memory, but she did not fall in love with him.

Her yearning for children did not go away. If anything it was becoming more pressing with the passing of time and she now knew of unmarried mothers and divorced people who were accepted in society, although not wholly respectable.

When they all arrived back in England, Frances found that Lloyd George still expected all the work he had demanded in Downing Street days to be produced in the office he had taken in Abingdon Street. She had typists available to help her, but found herself swamped by the minutiae of notes, records, letters and reports, not to mention taking dictation for his articles and books, looking up references and dealing with visitors and requests. In her autobiography she wrote, 'One of LG's weaknesses was that he was quite incapable of comprehending how much work one person could do in a given time, however willing, nor could he grasp how long any given job would take.'[4]

In August LG went to Criccieth and Frances went to stay with friends at Beattock in Dumfrieshire. They parted on bad terms – but whereas in her novel, Frances made her heroine risk pregnancy and face the probable end of the affair, she herself could not bring herself to do anything so drastic.

I want to tell you again and again how much I love you and how desperately sorry I am for any pain I have caused you. I can only say that I was very tired too – more tired than I realised, as I am just beginning to find out. But when you return my darling, you will find a completely renewed and rejuvenated young woman awaiting you who

[3] FLG papers
[4] Conversation with J Longford

will spare no effort to make life sweet and happy and who wants to be such a help to you.[5]

In her novel she wrote, 'Supreme sacrifice – not death – giving up a loved one', and the heroine decides to do this because she is pregnant and thinks that 'motherhood and the child' must come first and that there is 'surely some other career but politics'. But in the novel the hero 'realises what she is to him. Moves heaven and earth to find her. Fails. Becomes listless and loses interest in his work.'

The heroine flees to Florence to have her baby and there meets an old flame. He realises her predicament and tries to persuade her to marry him. She nobly refuses because she still loves the hero, but this suitor is aware of the situation when he returns to London and seeing the hero observes 'the tragedy in his face, and hears in the club that M has left his wife and is doing no good work.' He tells the hero where to find the heroine in consequence and hence the 'happy ending'. But Frances was a realist, for all her romantic yearnings; her French blood perhaps. She simply could not take the risk that Lloyd George would collapse without her – nor, to be honest, did she want to cause him great pain.

He for his part had become aware that he was working her too hard and, with the approach of an American tour, he needed a male secretary to join his staff. Hankey had introduced LG to one A J Sylvester, a champion typist and shorthand expert and an exceptionally hard working man who had been a dedicated factotum to Hankey in the Cabinet Secretariat. With the promise that he would receive a pension equal to the civil service one he would have to forego if he left, plus a pay rise, LG inveigled Sylvester into joining his personal staff.

Sylvester was a rather unctuous and very obliging man, but with an enormous vanity. He demanded that in addition to the pay rise he must be known as 'Principal Private Secretary.' Frances was rather hurt when this particular term was agreed to. She felt she had the experience and years in office to entitle her to at least equal rank, and she felt quite frankly that there was no need to differentiate at all, but Sylvester made it clear that, since he could not compete with Frances in all respects, he would demand certain privileges. As Frances could see that he would be a very useful addition to the staff and also knew that she towered in importance over Sylvester on the personal front she metaphorically shrugged her shoulders and allowed Sylvester his grandiose title. There was a less easy relationship between them, however, than that which had existed between Frances and J T Davies.

She returned to the office from Scotland revived enough to enjoy thor-

[5] *Darling Pussy* op cit

oughly a chance encounter with Beaverbrook on the train during which they discussed the political situation. Beaverbrook said he had wanted Bonar Law to be Prime Minister, but now it had fallen to Baldwin he wished LG were back in power.

In fact the government were struggling badly and Baldwin was not coping. While LG had a glorious tour of America and Frances went to Florence and San Gimignano for an autumn holiday with a girlfriend, the Conservatives decided to go to the country in an election over Free Trade.

Lloyd George returned refreshed and encouraged from America and was lulled into false confidence by huge crowds who came to hear him speak as he campaigned all over the country. However, there was still no reconciliation with the main Liberal party and the country did not trust them or want them in government. Labour was providing a new option for those discontented with the ruling party and the results were that Conservatives won 258 seats, Labour 191 and Liberals 159. As this was clearly not a vote of confidence in the Conservatives, Baldwin stood down and allowed the next second largest party to attempt to make a government, if they could, with the support of the Liberals. Ramsay Macdonald became the first Labour Prime Minister and Frances felt anguish for LG as a mother feels about pain being caused to her son.

1924 was a fairly domestic year with both Frances and LG spending a lot of time at Bron-y-de, concerned with farming matters and working full tilt on the monthly articles LG had been commissioned to write. Many of these were concerned with foreign affairs and he did not feel it was essential to be in London or near the Commons while he worked on them.

In fact LG was battling to be reaccepted as a true Liberal with a platform – but the internal bitterness within the party was making it very difficult for him. Any initial expectation that Labour might introduce some legislation to transform the economy was quickly shown to be unfounded. The Labour leaders were too busy trying to prove themselves as a viable alternative government that could operate the systems already in place. As a result they passed up any chance to use Liberal support to institute new measures. Macdonald and Henderson showed almost irrational fear of Lloyd George, and the last thing they wanted was this old and experienced Government member stealing their thunder, so they would not consider any of his schemes for a minute.

LG began to realise that the country was not threatened by extremism but by excessive moderation and if both the Conservatives and Labour were inhabiting the centre ground, what place was there for the Liberals? He scorned Baldwin, Macdonald, and even Asquith for appearing more interested in preserving their parties than in solving the problems of the country, and he decided that he must show himself as the man with ideas. He used some of his political fund to begin the first of his great reports calling on experts to work on solving the problems in coal and the land.

He refused to hand any of the money to support the Liberals until they became more responsive to his ideas. While they showed such hostility towards him, he felt he was better staying somewhat aloof and working on schemes that would provide a platform for change.

At the Liberal Summer School, which had become established now as a chance for like minds to get together and discuss policy, Lloyd George tried to persuade the Liberals that they had two choices. They could continue to be a small group dedicated to keeping their doctrine pure, or they could opt to act like a party preparing for government with a challenging programme.

In addition to his work on the problems in the coal industry, LG was devoting more and more attention to his long-held concern with the land. During the war, particularly in 1917 when U-boats virtually held the island of Britain to ransom, he had come to see how vital food production on this island was. He had an innate fascination with agriculture anyway, with watching things grow and increase. The heathlands around Bron-y-de in Churt were already being transformed by him into luxuriant, fruit-producing orchards. He took enormous pleasure in walking around the estate and watching the improvements, and then enjoying home-grown produce. Frances had never been a great one for exercise, but she was expected to walk miles with him and, as with politics, his interest became her interest. Unfortunately she was later to try farming herself and, without his resources or strength of character, this turned out to be a financial disaster, but she certainly enjoyed seeing the orchards of Churt grow and prosper.

On 26th August Lloyd George gathered a number of agricultural experts together to stay with them down at Bron-y-de and discuss the future for land in Britain forming a 'Land Committee'. However, the relations with the Liberal party were getting worse. In September LG agreed to donate £100,000 to Liberal party funds on the condition that Mond would lead an investigation into the running of the party's organisation. Three Asquithians were appointed to the committee whose conclusions were that nothing needed to be done. LG wrote, 'You seem to have excluded every independent person who knows anything about our task in the country with the exception of Stott'. Mond's reaction to this was to replace Stott with E D Simon, so LG contributed £50,000 to the party funds. The Liberals were so divided and short of funds that they were in no position to prosecute a vigorous campaign when yet another election was held in the autumn of 1924, and as a result they were overwhelmed. Only forty-two members were returned and even Asquith lost his seat.

LG had not predicted this débâcle, but he had not bothered to canvass the country or make many speeches outside his own constituency. He felt that real issues were not important at this election as there was a hysterical anti-communist reaction in the country. He felt it was better to hang fast on to the money and wait for some climate of opinion where real achievements might be made.

At the end of 1924, Frances bought a new leather diary for 1925. She had not kept up with a diary at all in 1923 or 1924 but after the election she began to think that Asquith would not be able to remain leader of the Liberals and that surely LG would be given the opportunity and events would start to matter again. With her usual concern to record 'history' she wrote a long entry on December 24th 1924 under the section for 'Memoranda'. LG had just left her in London to go and spend Christmas in Wales.

He intends ... to speak plainly to 21 Abingdon St. on his return, specially to Godfrey Collins for the shabby way they are treating him. Asquith said before he left that it was indisputable that anyone else but L G should be the leader but he failed to say this publicly or to make it clear to his own people. But LG wrote to G C and told him what A had said, but G C did not think fit to mention it at the Party Meeting therefore LG says that the only result of their meanness is that he has been elected leader in spite of the machinations and without the least help on A's part or on the part of anyone else.

No 21 are counting on getting A back into the house but they don't realise that Fisher is not going to resign his seat until October even if he is elected for New College. D ascertained this in a talk with the Fishers on Sunday. This helps D considerably.

I lunched today with Cara Copeland and Orpen. The former is a niece of Asquith's and tells me that A told her before he left for Egypt that it was untrue that he was going to fight a bye-election. She says however that he gets no peace from the rest of his family. I think if A were left to himself he would hand over to LG.

In fact, Asquith accepted a peerage and went into the House of Lords from where it was obviously more complicated to lead Commons members. For all that, he held on to the leadership for a while.

LG was taken ill on February 21st when speaking at Walsall and it was a few days before he could be moved from Birmingham to Churt where Frances nursed him. She wrote in this new diary on the 17th March, for the first time since Christmas, 'Came up today for the first time since D's illness. He is by no means well yet – has been considerably pulled down.' Frances must have kept the diary in her London flat, as every time she writes in it she refers to the fact that they have come up to town and they are not doing this as often as they might. In fact they came up again on the 24th March and, although they had business in London again the next day, LG preferred to travel down to Churt for the night and come back up again the following morning. LG had been intending to go and speak in Manchester at the weekend but Frances describes him as 'dead tired' and records that he decided not to go.

> Am very glad as was worrying about it. Churt is the happiest place of all now. D. I think would for two pins give up politics – at any rate party politics for a time. The discussions at H Q make him sick, and the behaviour of the Radical group in the House is also nauseous.
>
> We return to Churt tonight ... D is superintending emptying the fish ponds.

Domesticity, the farm and life in Churt were giving increasing pleasure to them both – but he continued to argue with the Liberals to try to get a party base.

On March 24th Frances wrote that,

> D delivered magnificent speech this afternoon ... Liberals, as usual, silent and undemonstrative. They are intolerable ...
>
> This morning D went to No 21 for a meeting. He was much shocked at the expression as he says of absolute hatred on Wedgwood Benn's face on finding him looking so fit. D retaliated by reproving the party for falling on Baldwin's neck because of his 'peace' speech in the House last week. As D says, it was Baldwin who did most to injure national unity. D told someone after the meeting: 'W Benn reached up on tip toe to embrace Baldwin – like Nero, performing his nuptials in public.' Then he found Benn was just behind listening!

As ever, when Lloyd George felt himself under attack he attacked back viciously. Even old friends would be felled and turned out if they seemed to LG to be betraying him or hurting him. He was not very good at keeping long-term friendships. Frances herself came up against his vicious verbal attacks and would feel she could take no more, but Frances mattered so much to LG that he would pursue her and woo her back, using all the old charm that had melted her in the first place. With the Asquithian group, LG preferred to do without them than to charm them back into support. It was a pity he could be so impatient and belligerent here, when on other occasions he would take so much trouble to win people to his point of view.

Frances reported on the 24th March,

D attended meeting at the National Liberal Club, on appointment of Chief Organiser. He had previously expressed himself very vigorously to Godfrey Collins and to Asquith against appointment of Vivien Phillips. Asquith spoke first and made a vague speech, keeping his eye on D all the time. D made a most wily speech, begging them to take time to appoint no one now, and then gave a vivid description of the sort of person they ought to appoint – everything that V Phillips was not! They set up a committee to consider the appointment.

They also attended Curzon's funeral while they were up in London. Curzon was another character who had suffered sorely from LG's impatience and rather blatant rudeness, and yet LG felt no personal animosity towards him. His funeral found LG reflective:

He said that looking on the pall with its embroidered coronets, and thinking of the class to which he (D) belonged and which Curzon did not understand, and thinking of the underworld which even he (D) had no adequate knowledge of D felt as though it were the passing of the old order. (Nevertheless he quoted someone later in the day as saying that swells stood a better chance of winning seats even as Labour candidates!) D says that in the Abbey Miss Asquith got her own back for having been given a back seat, by walking out immediately after the corpse!

Frances would have liked that detail. She went on to mention that 'Winston is very friendly. D thinks it may be something to do with an alleged oil deal that W was supposed to be in – and which might, if it got out, be unpleasant. D is dining with him next week.'

Although he and Churchill had worked together and found a lot in common, he interpreted his friendliness as being from calculating motives. Does this say more about Lloyd George or Churchill?

In April LG took a cruise to Madeira with Margaret and his second daughter, Olwen. He felt he needed to recuperate after his February illness and wrote to Frances, 'I worked too hard the last three weeks before I had fully recovered. This voyage was a necessity.'

Frances was usually good at agreeing that his physical needs were paramount – frequent attentions were expressed in her diary about how he needed rest and pampering and how she worried about him, but it must have been rather galling for her that it was Margaret 'the neglectful wife' who had gone on the restorative cruise with him.

In the novel, she had written that the heroine was so in love with the hero that she had become 'his slave, his plaything, his chattel' and she had written, 'Always the woman who pays.' These words suggest that there were times when she was not wholly reconciled to being entirely at Lloyd George's beck and call, without the security and status of marriage to shelter her during their storms.

LG obviously knew that she was a little peeved at this holiday away from her, so he wrote stressing that she had all the security she could wish for.

A new birth came in October 1922. A new tenderness and new clear and firm purpose came to us both. Before that to use a legal term applicable to the law of domicile – there was a certain animus revertendi. More marked in your case than mine naturally. Since then we have settled our domicile. Your love is henceforth my country and mine is yours. So we have a right to expect loyalty and patriotism to our new domicile. We did not quite feel it was due before. I love you more tenderly than ever in a different way altogether. I cannot think of life apart from you now. I could give up everything for you without a qualm – even with some relief.[6]

A change was entering their relationship. The glorious shared love and absorption in a demanding and difficult job had slipped away and so LG was reassuring her that what had come in its place was better, that they were more committed to each other. He could safely promise her that he would give up every thing for her without a qualm, because he must have known she would not expect him to follow this through. He could not have been wholly sure that she would not go elsewhere for her security, however, and whereas he had always known that his 'Pussy bach' was attractive to other men and that she had had opportunities to marry, his serious signs of jealousy start to become very evident in 1925 when every other letter contains a reference to her flirting and temptation.

When Frances spent time in London she found that her large, beautiful flat in Morpeth Mansions did seem rather empty and, since she was spending so much time down in Churt, it started to seem like a very good idea to share it. In 1925 her youngest and most intelligent sister, Muriel, was twenty-three and had been found work as secretary to the Editor of the *Sunday Times*. Muriel had always been a pessimistic and nervous child. Whereas Frances had her Scottish father's blond looks and optimism, Muriel had inherited the Italian genes and was very dark, very slim and very intense. Never the easiest of people to live with she and Frances did share a sense of humour. She was totally sympathetic to the dilemma of her extra-marital position and being twelve years younger than Frances was then fairly amenable. Frances's beautiful home was very much to her

[6] ibid

Frances Stevenson at Downing Street, 1916

David Lloyd George, M. Albert Thomas and Mr Edwin Montagu (Under Secretary for Munitions) at the Munitions Conference in Paris, 1916

L.G. LOSES GIFTED ADVISER

COLONEL TWEED

" Penetrating political instinct "

COLONEL T. F. TWEED, who died yesterday after a long illness, was Mr. Lloyd George's political adviser and one of the ablest men in English politics.

It has always surprised me that so gifted and realistic a student of politics never sought entrance to Parliament.

In his young days, I believe, he was a militant Socialist. He saw many sides of life and had even worked as a dock labourer.

In the last war he was a battalion commander at 26. After the war his abilities as an organiser were used to great advantage in North Country Liberalism, and he belonged to the small group of Liberal politicians and economists who at Grasmere in 1921 started the Liberal Summer School.

This was perhaps the most vital post-war movement originated by the Liberal Party. Its success was largely due to his energy and organising genius

From 1927 until 1931 Colonel Tweed was chief organiser of the Liberal Party He resigned on the formation of the National Government, since when he remained in close political association with Mr Lloyd George. He was widely travelled. keenly observant. a shrewd judge of men and affairs

Colonel Tweed was a brilliantly witty conversationalist whose air of cynicism hardly served to conceal his genuine kindness of heart. He had a host of friends who will deeply regret his passing. He was 50 years of age.

A J C

The death of Colonel T.F. Tweed, reported in the Manchester News Chronicle, 1st May 1940

ABOVE: Jennifer & Taid, 1932
ABOVE RIGHT: Jennifer & Miss Neale, her first Nanny, 1931
RIGHT: Jennifer, 1934

Out on the farm 'helping.' 'Taid to feed the chickens, 1932

Explaining the 'New Deal' to Jennifer, 1935

Lloyd George and his dogs, 1935

Frances in her Court dress, 1936

*Dame Margaret in the 1930's (A picture which Lloyd George kept at
Bron-y-de in the 1930's)*

Food from the Farm, 1938

Off to school in 1941

Frances and Lloyd George in the year of their marriage, 1943

Still working for him as his wife in 1943

Frances and Jennifer at Ty Newydd, 1945

Jennifer, 1955

Jennifer & Michael, 1956

Frances in her eighties in the garden at Avalon

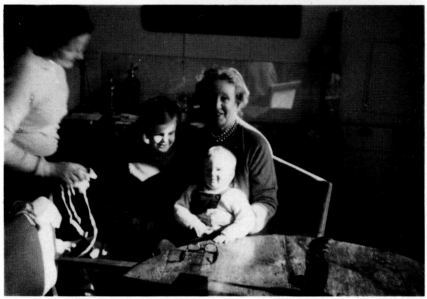

Jennifer, Ruth & Philip with Frances at Avalon, 1962

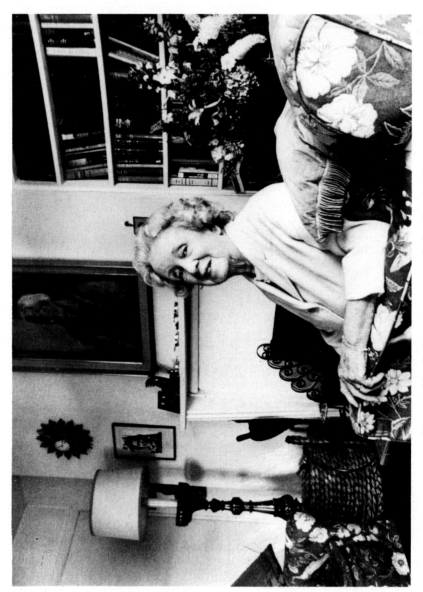

Frances Lloyd George, two years before her death

liking as was the freedom she enjoyed there while Frances was down at Churt.

They were getting on so well that Frances asked Muriel to come with her to Llandrindod in the summer. LG had recommended it as a centre where Frances might also enjoy a recuperative holiday – surrounded by aged invalids on a rest cure themselves and therefore unlikely to invade his territory. Muriel began to share her sister's life at the time when LG was no longer at his charming and attentive best, but more jealous and demanding, older and more spoilt. She slowly came to the conclusion that he was not worthy of her darling older sister and watched cynically his jealous demands on Frances, wondering how she put up with them.

Worse still, there were now more frequent instances of Lloyd George making a pass at a pretty young thing so his obsessive jealousy of Frances was probably the result of the lascivious indulgence that had come back into his own behaviour. If he behaved like that how could he reasonably expect her not to?

'Keep clear of the tropics in your excursions and if you do then you cannot cross the line. A good motto for both of us my sweet...' he wrote on 18th August 1925.

Yet he could still make her heart 'sing' with delight when sending her wonderful love letters.

I feel as though I were walking on air. You are a darling to write to me such a loving letter and you make me feel more than ever that my man is the most wonderful lover in the world and that no one could give me such tenderness and affection and love as you do.

Although he was now sixty-two, she was still powerfully affected by his physical demands. 'I want your lips today, cariad. I have been thinking of their sweetness and their thrillingness, and of course that leads me to think of other things!...'

She went on to say that although he could feel safe because most of the other guests at Llandrindod Wells are over sixty and ancient in outlook too, she knew better than to regard his material age as of any significance. 'There is an old man in North Wales ... who is a most danger-ous character and not one to take liberties with! So do be careful sweetheart mine, and come back to me without a spot on your escutcheon.'

There was a fair chance he might be the one to 'spot his escutcheon' and Frances by now knew it, yet both she and Margaret remained loyal and discreet, even loving. Both knew of his overactive libido and somehow reconciled themselves to it as part of the man they cared about, and so forgave him – so long as he did not actively hurt or humiliate them. Margaret did find Frances's presence a humiliation but she very seldom had to endure it and the relationship between the husband and wife seems to have been that of good friends who would not let each other down, so long as they made the basic bow to the formalities. Presumably Margaret found life more peaceful and a lot less demanding when her husband was elsewhere.

Frances was prepared, usually, to meet the demands. Sometimes he infuriated or upset her, but he could always charm her round his little finger when he set about it. He could make her laugh or cry, he could inspire her and he could thrill her with a feeling of romance that no one else ever could. Fleeting sexual peccadillos hurt at the beginning, but were another aspect of him that she forced into the file of painful attributes she had to accept in order to enjoy the glory that she continued to feel with him whenever he made the effort.

She was aware that she was very attractive to many men. Several had made it plain that they wanted her either as their wife or their mistress and she had never shown any interest. In Llandrindod she was amused to discover that a young family, a naval Captain and his two sons were all rather in love with her – but with the boys '16 & 20 ... I'm quite impartial'. She liked to keep LG alert and aware that she did not have to rely on him – others were interested too.

Now thirty-six, Frances was conscious of the fashion for pencil-shaped women that held sway in the mid twenties. Naturally she wanted to keep up with 'the look'. In her twenties she had been quite slim, though shapely in the way enjoyed by Edwardians, but just as the fashion started to be for virtually flat-chested boy-shaped young women, she began to fill out and become quite matronly in stature. LG assured her that he liked a fuller figure himself, but as with most women she wanted to please her own taste in her looks and she made a serious effort to slim on this holiday.

In their first days together she had dressed erratically and obviously not too expensively. Her youthful prettiness had shone through. When they began to go to conferences she was advised to go to Worth and get some beautiful clothes made for her. Now she made great efforts to dress well and elegantly. In her novel she described a fitting where the seamstresses buzzed about the heroine and went to enormous trouble to make her clothes perfect, as they found her responsiveness charming. It not only suited her nature to be pleasant and friendly but she found it also paid dividends too.

Returning from their separate holidays recharged and, in Frances' case, sleeker and glossier, they began to work hard on land reform. On 17th September LG launched the policy at a rally in Killerton. In October and November he and his agricultural advisers brought out the 'Green Book' and the 'Brown Book' on rural and urban land reform. The Liberals were furious that LG should be publicising policy so vigorously without consultation or general agreement, but they decided to accept the policy with modification and the question of finance was then reawakened.

LG was very dubious about handing over what amounted to his most significant weapon. Frances was definite; he should not do it.

> They have misused what money they had and cannot raise any more, so what on earth is the use of your giving them more, which will only go the same futile way? You may be quite sure that if there is any special bit of organising to be done, or any propaganda you will have to do it yourself, and pay for it too. You are far too trustful of them even now, even of Vivien Phillips who is a nice fool and nothing more. The Old Man counts for nothing and if he is decent about things it doesn't carry any weight. If you are not careful that section of the party is going to be like an old man of the sea about your neck. That is what I am afraid of.[7]

LG allowed himself to be persuaded! In October he launched the 'Land and Nation League' which received £240,000 from the LG fund over the next few years. The Asquithians were very angry as they felt the main party should have the money, and they were dubious about the policies represented in this particular campaign. They were looking for an opportunity to attack LG and perhaps get this giant thorn out of their flesh.

Over Christmas of 1925 Frances accompanied LG and a large party to Italy where LG met Mussolini and signally failed to be impressed. This was their last holiday abroad together for several years and marks the beginning of one of the most perilous periods for their relationship.

1926 was a year for serious confrontations. The first was between LG and the Asquithians. LG took a conciliatory stance over the General Strike. This struck the Asquithians as sinister and probably opportunistic, when they reflected that only the previous year LG had been urging Baldwin to make a stand, but in fact LG wanted the government to act less like a bully cowering weakly before the Unions when they were ill prepared in 1925 and then giving them nothing at all in 1926.

LG wanted attention to be paid to the problems that had caused the strike, not wholly concentrated on breaking it, but this was opposite to the official Liberal view. On the 12th May, a week after the strike ended, Asquith sent LG a letter virtually expelling him from the party. Frances was as aghast as he was.

In brief it was obvious that the Old Gang thought D's luck and popu-

[7] ibid

larity were down as a result of the strike and that it was time to get rid of him. Dirty work. The Asquith women are of course at the bottom of it. My chief concern last night was to get D into a calm state of mind. It was a blow for him — rather a cruel one, the like of which he had not quite experienced before. He has now before him a fight for his political life.

LG went off to see C P Scott who advised him to be temperate in his reply and produce a moderate and sad letter in response to Asquith's attack, thereby helping to put Asquith more firmly in the wrong when both letters were published on 26th May.

Frances said that when he returned to London he was 'outwardly very cheerful and determined, but inwardly trembling with excitement, keyed up to the highest pitch — higher than I can remember and deep down hurt almost like a child unjustly punished.'

Asquith and his close friends failed to realise that LG actually reflected typical rank and file Liberal feeling about the strike and that the majority of the party thought LG was too important to throw out. Asquith wrote an open letter on June 12th saying he would not 'continue to hold the leadership for a day unless I am satisfied that I retain in full measure the confidence of the party.' Very quickly it became apparent that he did not, when Liberal associations everywhere refused to condemn LG. Asquith was brought to the unwelcome conclusion that, since he did not enjoy a full measure of confidence, he should resign as leader. LG was invited to take his place, but not in total triumph, as it was done on a yearly contractual basis. Those at the heart of the party would always remain nervous of him and his independent ways.

The next crisis that occurred in 1926 was not on such a dramatic level but involved a lot of unpleasantness. LG was asked by the editor of his paper, the *Chronicle*, if Frances would like to be on the board. The Lloyd George family decided this was the final affront and that they must tackle him on his relations with Frances. She was led to believe that he received a letter 'written signed by his wife and all his children, demanding that I should be removed from the secretariat ... or else ...'[8]

LG told Frances that he would not allow such audacity and informed Frances that he had written to Dame Margaret, 'upbraiding her and the children for attacking him and offering her a divorce, which he said he would welcome.'

A J Sylvester later reported that he had no recollection of this exchange, but then it is fair to wonder how far he would have been involved in it. Lloyd George's eldest son, Dick recalled being offered a

[8] Autobiography FLG op cit

lucrative position on the board as Gwilym, Dick's younger brother, refused to sit on it with Frances. He described how he had turned it down also, rather amused that Lloyd George should be so anxious both to placate Frances and get a member of the family on to the board. What had actually upset Frances most was that she had not had any forewarning that Gwilym was going to make this stand against her. She was used to regarding Gwilym as a friend with whom she joked and chatted on the frequent occasions when he visited his father. She was shocked that he should take such a stand although she did realise that family counsels had put great pressure on him.

That Margaret did write to LG seems evident from his reference to such a letter and to a quarrel that had occurred with Gwilym since. More clearly Gwilym had made it very plain to LG that 'family counsels' had taken place and LG did write rather harshly that:

> It appears that my children are following the example of the children of Noah by exposing their father's nakedness to the world. It is not the reputation of Noah that has suffered. But his children have gone down the ages as first class skunks for turning on the old man...
>
> I must tell you how deeply pained I am to learn that you and Megan have turned against me. I have been for some time sick of public life. I work hard – very very hard – and get nothing but kicks. I have been contemplating clearing out and writing my book in retirement. I propose on Thursday to tell them to find another candidate. I am an old man. I mean henceforth to enjoy the leisure which is my due.[9]

Well, it is not exactly an explicit offer of divorce but it could well be presented to Frances as such, and it was clearly understood by the family to mean that he would retire from public life rather than allow them to tell him what to do. The family did not continue with the attack on Frances, but nor did L G continue to try and get Frances on to the board of the *Chronicle*. Instead, he sold the paper at a considerable profit and, since Frances and all the members of the family had shares in the paper, they all benefited from a small windfall.

Frances felt very hurt by the whole business. She had been stunned by Gwilym's attitude and it was also a very nasty surprise to discover just how hostile the family felt towards her. In truth, she was made to face the fact that the closest they had all come to discussing divorce had resulted in nothing. Her situation would continue unchanged for the foreseeable future, unless she herself changed it.

Like a small maggot in the beautiful, healthy-looking apple, a small

[9] *Darling Pussy* op cit

change was occurring at the heart of her relationship with Lloyd George. A long-term Liberal and friend from various Summer Schools, Colonel T F Tweed, joined Lloyd George's immediate staff, which meant that he was frequently around at Bron-y-de.

Tweed was another fascinating and exciting man; a very successful novelist and a hero from the First World War who had won the Military Cross, surviving to become the youngest Lieutenant Colonel in the British army at the time. The war had done permanent damage to his health and his marriage. He was very much struck by Frances – so much so that she became the inspiration for Pendle Malloy in his hugely successful book *Rinehard* later made into the film *Gabriel over the White House*.

Both Frances and her sister Muriel were enchanted by this witty, sad, slightly unwell war hero. They felt great sympathy for him, trapped as he was in a loveless marriage to a woman thirteen years older than himself. He told them that just before the war when he was twenty-three, he had been attracted to a highly intellectual and musical girl from a background quite unlike his own. She had told him she was twenty-six, but in fact had been thirty-six when they married. They had a girl and a boy quickly, and then he discovered the age difference and felt that he had been deliberately tricked. Living through the entire war in the trenches, he coped by becoming very cold in his emotions generally. He showed no interest in his children and he told Muriel that he stayed married because he felt he should 'fulfill an obligation'. So he continued to live with his wife and support the children, but he did not feel duty-bound to be faithful.[10]

At the same time as he came into proximity with Frances, she was reaching a crisis in her own feelings. Clearly divorce was impossible. Dame Margaret had been offered such an avenue and had declined to take it. LG was indulging his promiscuous tastes and assuming that she did too. Constant jealous taunts did make it seem that she might as well be unfaithful, since he assumed she had been anyway.

Always the romantic, she had not in fact ever slept with any of the ardent admirers she had encountered before. Her passion had been concentrated solely on Lloyd George, but in her later thirties a restlessness and general dissatisfaction with her life led her to allow herself to fall passionately in love with Tweed. If she had had children with LG, she might have resisted this temptation. Her yearning for a child was getting stronger and had it already been satisfied, she might have felt fulfilled and less resentful about her position. She would have been concerned for their stability and security. Had she actually been a wife, she might have felt more loyal to a legal husband, though childless as she then was, she might

[10] Conversation with M Stevenson

still have allowed herself to fall in love with a new and very attractive man. Deeply committed to LG's comfort and support in his political aims, she could not fail to notice that he took time off from their relationship to go on holiday with his own family. He also assumed she was unfaithful anyway and he noticed the attraction Frances felt for his new young agent. His letters to Frances in 1928 are pointedly suspicious.[11]

12 September 1928
Now keep out of mischief my sweet heart. You are (an) enticing little devil and you know it and you like to exert your power and to enjoy the rewards. Don't I beg of you. I promise to be good if I feel confident that you are.

and on 14th September 1928

Continue to write me my own girl – who is not and never has been naughty – my girl who thro' life has resisted temptation! Oh you little devil. I'll pay you out – in person and scrag it out of you.

On this occasion he was right to be suspicious. There are two letters wrapped carefully in an outer envelope to Frances from Tweed that August. He was on a cruise off the coast of Norway and wrote on August 9 1928:[12]

Darling,
A few moments of peace as we are sailing down the Skatterack towards Copenhagen gives me the long wanted, but hitherto seemingly impossible chance to get into spiritual communion with you – at least so far as the written word is concerned.
There is no real need for visible tokens of our love – you are with me at all times and sometimes I feel your presence so overwhelmingly that I expect to see you by my side when I open my eyes. There is one girl on board who looks very like you – and I hate her – not because she looks like you, but because she dares to be a constant reminder and yet is not you.
I am writing under some difficulty under an indifferent lamp on the back of a magazine and would get along a great deal faster if I did not leave off for long spells to gaze into vacancy – or at least into the inky blankness of the waste of waters across the deck, but I love just sitting and thinking of you. I suppose I ought to be thinking of magic case-

[11] *Darling Pussy* op cit
[12] FLG Papers

ments and gazing on perilous seas forlorn, but there ain't no magic casements and the seas are not a bit perilous and the only forlorn beings are you and I.

Still I don't need magic casements to picture little dream idylls in my heart and mind – funny little mixed up pictures all jumbled together but every bit of every one a caress and a balm to my loneliness and longing.

I wonder if you can recollect and place the odd pieces of the jigsaw – Cambridge and a starless night – wind and snow at Lynton – Red Chimney Pots and Cocktails – Riversmeet – the Grey And Red of the Howard – Victory and defeat at Barnstaple – a funny little tea shop near Beaux Arts – Churt and thrown kisses before a door closes – ivory flesh and love lit eyes – and over all harmony and an abiding peace and one man's – your man's great thankfulness for your love and the wonderful happiness you have brought him. Good night my beloved. You are very very near to me tonight.

Your sweet heart Chico.

Then on August 14th 1928,

Darling,

Just a short note. We are just approaching Stockholm and the dominating thought in my heart and mind is that this is the ultimate point on the cruise.

From now on every mile and every minute brings me nearer to holding you in my arms again – at least nearer to your physical self – because you have never been away from my side, when the sun goes down and in the morning I have stretched out my arms and almost felt the warmth and sweetness of your body within them.

In a curious sort of way I have almost enjoyed this forced severance because it has quickened my realisation of what your love means to me. I never realised quite so vividly my rich happiness and the joyous promise of the years which are yet to come, as much as I do at this moment when hundreds of miles of land and water separate us and yet we are together.

I am very much in love with you my sweetheart, my love, my wife and darling.

Your sweetheart, Chico.

In her published diary Frances describes LG's mood to 'retire from politics and write his book' with complete detachment. She says, 'he has had these moods before' and she comments for herself: 'Besides things are going so much better now, it would be a pity.'

The yearning for him to throw everything over for her had faded completely and she was back to wanting the very best for his career and to support him in that way. As LG wrote to her in early August: 'My little comforter and consoler and cheerer, my joy and delight and sustainer.'

Despite a romantic passion for Tweed, her maternal tenderness and devotion were still LG's to command whenever he needed them. Her support for his political aspirations, involvement in his achievements and interest in his interests all remained untouched by the new excitement of a love affair.

LG had his suspicions, and when they were confirmed by a tale-bearing maid in 1932 he coped magnanimously. The sexual and romantic side of his relationship with Frances was by now recognised as less important than her friendship and support. Her affair did not affect it, extraordinary as this may seem to those of us who find the different aspects of love hard to separate. LG was good at understanding how they could be separated and he had come to rely on Frances's devotion but it shows how neces-sary Frances was to him that he tolerated such a thing when he had previously shown such jealous possessiveness.

Frances had always been left when LG spent time with his family or in public places where the world might realise she was his mistress. There had always been occasions when, from filling every waking moment, LG would leave her suddenly on the side-lines with a massive vacuum, and in the autumn of 1927 this vacuum was irresistibly filled by Thomas Tweed.

His letters from the boat in the summer of 1928 show that an excit-ing and passionate affair had been going on for a while – certainly since 'wind and snow at Lynton' the previous winter. She remained in love with him until the thirties and there is evidence that she continued to seize time with him, but in January 1934 she made a promise to Lloyd George to cease any future exchanges with Tweed. When Tweed was very ill in May later that year, she was distraught, but kept her promise as was revealed in a diary entry on 19 October 1934.

> Saw the back of my beloved T. F. T. disappearing down the corridor and my heart bled with longing. It is dreadful to be in the same building and not to see or speak to him, but it is better for him that I should be firm.

She was still in love with him, but had broken off the affair at the end of 1933. That means that the affair was of six years duration and was of sufficient importance to them both for Frances to be mentioned in Tweed's will and for Frances to tell her daughter's fiancé that he had secretly been her husband; a fact which had been kept hidden from Lloyd George. Of course he was not. He had been a married man too, but

Frances wanted to give her daughter the benediction of legitimacy in case Jennifer's future husband cared about such things, and Tweed was her chosen instrument.[13]

Nor did she ever make it clear to Jennifer exactly who her father was. Both LG and Tweed believed themselves to be. The dates favour LG as he had flu over Christmas in 1928 and did not pay his winter visit to Criccieth. They were together until January 12th and Jennifer arrived on October 4th. It is also clear from the letters they exchanged after he had gone for his winter holiday that they had decided to try for a baby now, despite the risks, and Frances believed that she was pregnant when they parted. She told him that she felt unusually tired when she wrote to him on the 15th January, three days after their separation and LG wrote to her on the 22nd January saying, 'By the way I shall be expecting an interesting wire from you next Monday week. You know what I mean. If the usual thing happens wire 'transactions.' If not then 'no transactions'. I am hoping for the latter. Monday may be premature. If so wire on the critical date.'[14]

She replied to this that

I will wire you on Monday week , and I very much hope it will be 'no transactions'. I have a feeling that that may be so, but then I have had that feeling so often before. Only, although I feel so much better in myself, I still feel very lazy, and sometimes I think my eyes are a little tell-tale. However, we mustn't be premature. I have so often been disappointed!

On the 1st February she wrote:

There are no 'transactions' yet, cariad, but there are still two days to go and I am not letting myself be unduly excited in case of disappointment. But I do most passionately hope that the longed for thing may happen. It would just put the seal and crown upon our love and be a marvellous fulfilment.

On the 4th,

It really has happened this time, my love, and I am so thrilled about it, and hope that you will be too. I told you that I thought it might, as I had a curious lethargic feeling and on the other hand I thought that might be due to Torquay air. But now it seems that it wasn't only that.

[13] Conversation with J Longford
[14] *Darling Pussy* op cit

But I feel extraordinarily well (only a little lazy) and very rested and very fit in mind. I have been loving you so tremendously, my darling, so very completely and tenderly and what you say about my having looked after you while you were ill makes me so happy. I am so glad I had the opportunity (though it made my heart sore to see you ill) of showing you how really deeply and devotedly I care for you, and that you can depend upon me to love and cherish you 'till death do us part'. You are my husband, and my little child, and you will never cease to be. Do not doubt me, my darling; it upsets me when I think you are doing so, and under the present circumstances I want all your love and trust.

Tweed joined her in Torquay.[15]

However, it would have been an extraordinarily successful bluff if she had managed to convince Lloyd George that she was probably pregnant, then had become so and had had an early first baby to fit in with the dates that coincided with her time with Lloyd George. Jennifer knew who felt more like a father to her. Lloyd George was a loving and constant presence in her life. Tweed apparently talked of woman's maternal desires as the need they have 'for a kitten to play with'[16] and he did not bother with the children from his marriage or with the possible child of his affair. Jennifer thinks she may have met him once, as she remembers being introduced to a very nice writer who showed a lot of interest in her, but the only time he seems to have felt any paternal concern was when Frances was in labour. Family tradition has it that both men ran a temperature while Frances underwent her Caesarean operation.[17]

[15] Muriel Stevenson told Jennifer this and always preferred to think that Tweed had been Jennifer's father, but she had loved Tweed herself and had very mixed feelings about Lloyd George.

[16] Conversation with Muriel Stevenson.

[17] Conversation with Jennifer Longford.

Chapter Six

Motherhood

'We can conquer Unemployment' was brought out in March 1929, with Tweed working passionately to promote Lloyd George's cause. He came up with the idea that they should buy space in every important newspaper in the country and try to reach the British public directly with their ideas. Tweed initiated many modern methods of propaganda and canvassing and during the campaign for the by-election in 1928 in Middlesborough, Lloyd George's publicity machine had adopted the technique of checking what other parties were saying and finding out what affected people most.

Lloyd George's campaign certainly had the effect of publicizing the extent of unemployment, but he began it so early that by the time the election was announced, the party was running out of steam. Also, the growing Labour party seemed to many to be the natural vehicle for attempting to solve working men's problems, and it was remembered against him that Lloyd George had promised 'homes for heroes' after the war.

The General Election was therefore very disappointing to the Liberals. Despite offering new ideas and a genuine alternative to the other two parties, they only won fifty-nine seats. Technically they held the balance of power again, but in fact Baldwin and Macdonald preferred to work with each other rather than with Lloyd George.

Over the summer, everyone separated to recover and Frances went to France to see out the last and obvious phase of her pregnancy. She would be almost forty-one when the baby arrived and her doctor had advised her to return to London for delivery near to modern medical assistance there. It had been decided that she should have a Caesarian in order to protect her from the possibility of a stressful first labour at her age. So it was that she checked into a private nursing home for the operation on 4th October 1929 and gave birth to Jennifer Mary.

The operation did leave her quite exhausted but enormously exhilarated, because at last she had the yearned-for child of her own. Admittedly it was a daughter, but she had come to the conclusion that Lloyd George was better with girls and certainly his relations with his daughters was closer and happier than the one he had with his elder son. There may have been a doubt about the paternity, but there was never any doubt that Lloyd George would figure more largely in the baby's life than Tweed. Lloyd George was the established figure in her own life and he liked children.

He adored this one and was inspired by her birth to turn his hand to writing poetry again. Enclosed in an old wallet with telephone numbers and forecasts for the election in 1929, plus three quotations torn out of a daily diary, there are his jottings which, with crossings out and alternatives not altogether decided, runs thus:

> She sought for pleasure high and low
> She found it now and then
> The more she got the less she gained
> (By the embrace of men) (crossed out and replaced by) from festivals and men.
> One day a cherub came her way
> And lodged in her heart
> Its strings since then sing this sweet lay/out all day
> The twain shall never part.

Lloyd George definitely writes 'men' and not man so he knew she had not been exclusive to him and more appealingly he is touched that she is so happy at last to have a child and does not seem resentful that it is the child who is making Frances happy.

Also jotted down is the beginning of another one,

> Her fevered joys are now but dross
> These but a dead
> She counts them all but as a loss
> Her cherub is delight
> Cherub is all delight

This one is clearly even less developed then the first one, but the feelings expressed are clear and Tweed most definitely did not have any such feelings about the arrival of the baby. 'A kitten for Frances' since she wanted one.

As was still the habit among most of her social circle, Frances arranged for Jennifer to go to a wet nurse, for the time being. She was in constant attendance, however, and formed such a good relationship with Jennifer's first nurse that when the nurse later ran into financial difficulties, Frances bought and gave her the house she was living in.[1] Typical of her generos-

---

[1] Conversation with Muriel Stevenson

ity, this was by no means the only example of behaviour suggestive of riches. Compared with her own beginnings, she was rich, but unfortunately not nearly as much as she thought.

As soon as Frances had found a nurse she could trust, Jennifer was installed in the flat in Morpeth Mansions. An adoption order was arranged by her lawyer, John Morris, just in case there should be any difficult questions about the arrival of a small baby in the life of Miss Stevenson, and shortly after this Frances also arranged with John Morris to buy two houses and hold them in trust for Jennifer to provide her security. Her nanny, Miss Neale, signed this document as a witness and Muriel was made one of the trustees.

Although Muriel always claimed to dislike children and most definitely did not want any of her own, she managed to live with the new baby and formed a strong affection for her. Letters from Frances to Lloyd George became less ardently romantic and were filled with tracts about Jennifer's cleverness and beauty.

10 August 1930

'I have not got very much news for you – just a repetition of my last, namely that Jennifer is adorable, sweeter than ever, and much more intelligent even that I thought she was ...' Wrapped in an envelope and kept in among her important papers is a horoscope she had drawn up for Jennifer.

The child did not become her first priority. Lloyd George and his work continued to dominate her life and, in the same month, she wrote telling him that now she had found a good nurse she would be able to leave Jennifer without anxiety. She had promised him he would always come first and, to his great relief and satisfaction, he did. In this, she did not follow the example of his wife who had always put the concerns of her children above those of her husband.

She was initially a very unconfident parent. By coming to motherhood so late and leaving the nursing to someone else, she missed the chance to establish a secure feeling as prime carer for the baby she adored. At the end of August 1930, Lloyd George wrote to her to say that he was glad to hear that the new nurse was settling in well and that Jennifer had shown no signs of missing the first one. Frances had been worrying that Jennifer would pine and Lloyd George reassured her: 'I never believed in the 'peaking and pining' bogey. The little girl was obviously so devoted to her mother and so perfectly happy with her that I never thought she would miss anybody else.'[2]

Frances needed the reassurance as she was very diffident in her practical dealings with Jennifer. She was moving in circles that left a great deal

[2] *Darling Pussy* op cit

of daily childcare to nannies and naturally left any discipline to them. To make up for her absences she was the spoiling and fun 'Mummy' who told stories and brought presents. Since she still needed to be available for Lloyd George, she had to organise a home for Jennifer that would run without her.

Partly, no doubt, as a consequence, and also because she is naturally made that way, Jennifer quickly became used to an absent mother and developed into an independent and self-reliant child. This was sad for Frances, who tried hard to compensate for her absences and inadequacies, but lucky too, as a clingy child who cried whenever she left would have torn her in two.

As it was, she could see Jennifer was thriving without her and also that she thoroughly enjoyed the spoiling, so the pattern became established. Frances had to learn early that Jennifer would be delighted to see her and thrilled with presents and treats but, if she tried to swamp the child with physical demonstrations of affection, she would resist. From very early days, Jennifer was able to appreciate the fun that Mummy's arrival entailed, but she stubbornly refused to become a baby doll or the 'kitten' Tweed had suggested Frances wanted. She disliked being kissed her mother and Frances had to learn to moderate her embraces. It does seem to indicate that Jennifer was not wholly unaffected by her mother's many absences.[3]

While Frances was adjusting to motherhood, her career continued to be as demanding as ever. Unemployment was mounting and Macdonald was driven to overcome his dislike of Lloyd George and arranging meetings with him to discuss options. This was a clever move on Macdonald's part, because by keeping Lloyd George tied up in conversations and hoping to influence the governmen from within, he ensured that LG was not attacking them from without.

In the winter of 1931 Frances had a nasty attack of flu, so Lloyd George persuaded her to go and recover with her parents in Bognor and initially to leave Jennifer with her nanny in London. Throughout her childhood Jennifer remembers Lloyd George as a caring and constant figure, behaving as a grandfather might, and Lloyd George taught her to call him Taid, the Welsh for grandfather. She did not suspect that he might be her father, but she did know that he loved her and took an interest in her because he consistently showed that he did. While Frances was away, Lloyd George wrote to her about a visit to Jennifer,

I was there for half an hour the room crowded with Nurse's friends. I

---

[3] FLG papers and conversation with Jennifer Longford

forgot you had warned me that her sister was bringing two little charges to visit J. The latter was glad to see me. She took no special notice of the other kids, but went on with her usual tasks of nursing all the 'bas' in turn. She came to me sat on my knee opened my coat and asked for 'Ma'...

Jennifer was fifteen months old when he wrote this.

The letters between Frances and LG now moved from these more domestic interchanges on to politics, as ever. In February 1931 the talks with the government were dragging and LG wrote to Frances, 'I am full of trying to bring this cowardly government up to the mark – a hopeless task. Sisyphus is not in it with me. I am trying to roll a melting sloshing snowball up the hill.'

He did not give up however, and late in July 1931 he dictated this memorandum to Frances:

> Generally speaking, Labour would like an alliance. They would be willing to drop certain of their present Ministers ...
>
> Ramsay would be Prime Minister, Lloyd George would be Leader (of the House) at the Foreign Office or Treasury. Ramsay thinks he can adjourn early in August and resume late in the autumn and then continue till the next Budget. No fear of immediate Election ...

It was never likely that Macdonald would actually have risked inviting such a big cuckoo into his nest but Lloyd George evidently felt that his moment was coming – when one of those ironies of fate struck.

On the 26th July, Lloyd George fell ill while alone with Frances at his home in Addison Road. His wife and family had begun their summer holiday in Criccieth, but were told by the doctors that Lloyd George needed a serious operation on his prostate. They hastily returned and Frances was driven away to endure some of the most frustrating, infuriating and worrying days of her life. Lloyd George had been in acute pain and Frances felt that no one – certainly not Margaret – would be able to soothe him and make him comfortable as well as she could have done.

She was also frightened. It was a very serious operation and it was certainly quite possible that he might die. She had to rely on Sylvester to 'phone her with news when he safely could – away from Dame Margaret's eagle eye.

The operation took place on the 29th July and it was completely successful. To allay Frances's worries, Sylvester called round to see her on the 2nd August and told her that Lloyd George would like to see her. Obviously they had to be discreet, but an opportunity was to be created on the 4th August when Dame Margaret was persuaded by her son-in-law, the doctor Sir Thomas Carey Evans, that some fresh air and a drive to the park would do her good. Frances managed to see Lloyd George and he asked her to try and and come again.

Thomas Carey Evans was married to LG's second daughter, Olwen, so he could not be detached from the family feelings about Frances, but he probably felt that to be fretting about Frances was not doing Lloyd George any good. However, Frances foolishly left a beautiful bunch of flowers. The nurse on duty, not realising there was any need for discretion, told Margaret that the visitor who had brought them while she was out was Miss Stevenson. Margaret felt tricked and understandably angry, so Carey Evans said he would not risk getting drawn into any more family arguments and Frances would have to wait.

Frances was upset by this news and said it was for Lloyd George 'to put his foot down'. He was not, however, well enough for putting feet down and she had to accept the status quo and stay away.

While recovering, the financial crisis that had been looming finally flared up. Macdonald formed a National Government. Furious that everything was arranged while he was unable to affect anything, and particularly distressed that the new National Government seemed set to follow the same path that the Labour Government had chosen, Lloyd George decided to withdraw to Churt and claim that he was still too ill to be involved.

Margaret and Megan accompanied him down to Churt for a few days before leaving to resume their holiday in Criccieth. At last Frances could take over in her role as nurse and main carer. Lloyd George wrote her a poem of welcome.

> Cariad I have missed you so much
> Your sure understanding and your gentle touch
> It is largely due to instinctive art
> But I am sure that it comes straight from the heart
> I am looking forward to seeing you once more
> And your sweet face appear at the door
> It may send my temperature up a degree
> But you cannot expect joy without paying the fee.

The fee Dawson suggested he should pay was in sexual restraint for a while. He wrote to him on 18th September 1931,[4]

[4] FLG papers

My dear LG

Let me pick it up where we left off. My 'separation' had long been arranged for the long vacation so when I was confident you were not in danger I just slipped away. How wonderfully well you have done, though no doubt you realised that recovery is a tedious process and when the 'slump' days come, not without discouragement. To achieve the complete restoration you need to fulfil the dictates and desires of your active mind, you must keep yourself in a backwater for months, otherwise you will not regain your 100%.

When your days in the wilderness have been lived through – you will be ready to make use of the promised land – of complete health. And what a mercy for you to be out of the government – it will give you time: And the detachment, especially if a silent detachment, will give you freedom for what may seem the best part – a new chapter disentangled from previous commitments. Meanwhile you must witness Samuel's complete self-satisfaction with amusement. The pictures speak for themselves. To return to health – is not the return of business to its usual channel an outstanding event – more important than a maiden speech in the first admission to The Cabinet?

About sex – perhaps I can help you a bit – strictly the nearer you can keep to abstention for many months the better – but if the Pauline view about 'burning' obtrudes itself, come what may, the wise plan is to keep to well tried love. In this way you avoid the emotional stimulus which any new goddess must promote and to the patient's detriment. This view, I think, fulfils the dictates of statesmanship!

Anyhow the best of luck to you and I shall look forward to seeing you well on the road to being better than ever – 'Paradise regained!'

For myself I have found sea, sun and warmth to my great benefit and delight.

From, with affection

Dawson

Dawson clearly knew his patient well if he could advise him so frankly about sex. He must also have been aware that to remain detached from the political developments was going to be hard for Lloyd George, as indeed it turned out. September was not a month for mellow enjoyment of the farm's fruitfulness and his own recovery. There were alarming developments in international affairs that upset him. The 'Manchuria incident' gave Japan a feeble excuse for acting aggressively towards China. The League of Nations demanded Japanese evacuation to little effect and LG was very distressed by the success of overt aggression and militarism.

Worse still for LG was the announcement by the National Government that they would be holding a General Election on the 27th

October. It was far too soon for Lloyd George to prepare in time, even if he had been well, and he was dismayed to see the Liberals being sucked into a so-called 'National Government' but a government which did not in fact have any representation on the left. The bulk of the Labour party felt that Macdonald had betrayed them and withdrew to maintain an opposition, but the majority of the Liberal party preferred to cling to government and office. This caused the final severance of Lloyd George's relations with the Liberals, and although the party withdrew from the National Government in 1932, the link was never renewed and Lloyd George saw out his career as an Independent.

Still recovering from his operation, Lloyd George was not fit enough to fight a vigorous campaign around the country, but he made an impressive broadcast for the BBC and a film for the 'talkies' shown with the main film in the cinemas. In Caernarvon Boroughs, Margaret worked hard for his re-election and Sylvester wrote;[5] 'Dame Margaret has been working very hard both in the Boroughs and in Anglesey. Here she is loved, admired and is the uncrowned queen.'

It was a closer fight than Lloyd George had known for a long time. Over the rest of the country the National Government was returned with the biggest landslide in history.

Disheartened, for the time being, Lloyd George avoided the Commons, claiming the role of convalescent, and made plans for a long winter holiday in India and Ceylon. After their recent scare his family decided to accompany him on this long holiday, so Frances was not going to be required over Christmas and this gave her the opportunity to house-hunt.

Jennifer was now just two and very active. It was becoming plain that full-time residence in a London flat was far from ideal. Also Lloyd George was intending to spend less time in London and more time working on his farm and writing his memoirs in Churt. Frances decided to find a home in the country as well, for when she could not be in Bron-y-de, and so that her daughter would be nearby when she was there.

Frances spent the months that Lloyd George was away establishing a home for herself and principally for Jennifer and her nanny in Worplesdon, in a house called Heathercourt. Since Worplesdon is approximately twenty miles away from Churt and Lloyd George could be such a hard task master, this was to turn out to be rather unsatisfactory. There was little chance of popping in for a quick bed-time story, especially when she had to arrange for a driver to take her. In her autobiography she wrote that when he returned, 'We really got down to work on the memoirs. My time, of course, was all LG's, but he did not understand that Malcolm (Thomson) ever wanted to go home to his loving wife and child.'

[5] *Life with Lloyd George*: the diary of A J Sylvester ed. Colin Cross, Macmillan

This probably stands out in her memory because, of course, her time was not so easily 'all LG's', though in effect it remained so. She too had a loving child she would have liked to go home to, and the long hours Lloyd George worked did make things awkward. This is not mentioned in her autobiography, because the long years of ingrained discretion would not allow her to be completely honest about Jennifer, even in 1971 when the book was published. She wrote a chapter about Jennifer which she planned to incorporate at a later stage in the book and which began 'It was shortly before this time that I adopted my little girl'.[6]

Certainly, it was shortly before this time that she had taken out adoption papers to protect herself and Lloyd George from discovery, but Jennifer's birth certificate shows plainly that she is the daughter of Frances Stevenson, spinster, and there is no mention of a father. When she was nine Jennifer was told that she had been adopted and that her parents were missionaries killed in China, which gave her a useful story to use when questioned at school. When she discovered that these missionaries were figments of the imagination she was not distressed. They had never figured largely in her own sense of identity, but she did feel, as an adult, that if Frances was admitting publicly in her autobiography that she had been Lloyd George's mistress, then she ought to admit that she had had a child of her own. To incorporate suddenly a rather sentimental chapter mentioning the arrival of a child without any kind of build up, seemed to Jennifer to be bound to provoke prurient curiosity and an imbalance of attention, so she advised her mother to leave the chapter out or tell the truth. Frances kept the typescript but the autobiography stood complete without any further mention of a daughter, adopted or otherwise.

While Lloyd George recovered on a winter holiday in Ceylon and India, Frances organised her new home in Worplesdon from Bron-y-de. Jennifer was staying there with her, and Lloyd George suggested they should remain there for Christmas. It was a fascinating place for a child, with farm animals and plenty of space – a marvellous contrast to a flat in the heart of London.

Frances went from relating in a letter that 'Denny' loves the 'Baby Moo' to saying that the political situation was not moving much, 'excepting that increasing pressure is being put on Die-hard Tories to put duties on more things.'

They did not spend Christmas in Bron-y-de however, because it was arranged that they should be with the Stevensons in Bognor.

Although Frances's mother had said she would rather die than be presented with an illegitimate grandchild when confronted by such a

[6] Unpublished chapter left in her papers originally planned for her autobiography.

proposition in 1915, by 1931 she was apparently calm, even reconciled to the situation. Of her five children, only Ninette had so far married and had children of her own. Louise was therefore even quite glad to have Jennifer in her life and showed a constant interest in and love for her. She had become politically active on her own account since the war. Being outraged when the local council proposed to build new council houses without bathrooms and only an outside lavatory she had campaigned not only to persuade them to incorporate bathrooms in the plans, but also to join the council herself and influence such developments at first hand in the future. John, was of course, a gentle and delightful grandfather, but Louise was still stimulating and a little ferocious, and Jennifer felt a great respect and affection for her grandmother. Jennifer was never worried about pleasing 'Mummy' because 'Mummy' was always pleased whatever she did. If she did anything she knew was wrong, it was Granny's reaction that worried her.

Frances took her there for a good old Stevenson Christmas in the December of 1931 while she made final arrangements for sub-leasing her flat to Winston and Clementine Churchill.

The flat was very convenient for the Houses of Parliament and possessed a stunning view, so it was ideal for the Churchills, but they managed to offend the Stevenson sisters in their dealings. Muriel tells the story of how, having agreed to take the flat, they turned up one Saturday morning without any notice. Frances and Muriel had a hairdresser who came to the flat every Saturday to wash and set their hair. Muriel's hair was dripping wet and Frances's was in curlers when the Churchills arrived and asked to go around the flat to make notes on various sizes. Frances greeted them from her chair and left them to it, but Muriel, with her hair dripping down her back, felt she should show them what they wanted, and yet felt furious that they made no apology for interrupting them at such an inconvenient moment. When they had done everything they wanted the Churchills withdrew, still without making any acknowledgement of the disruption they had caused.

Frances never warmed to Churchill and frequently commented on how cold or self-engrossed he was. One of her favourite stories was of Lloyd George rebuking Churchill with the words 'Conversation, my dear Winston, is not a monologue.' In later years she understood that the two great war Prime Ministers were bound to be compared, but for her, the comparison was not of equals.

When Lloyd George returned from his months in Ceylon and India at the end of January 1932, he began to work seriously on his *War Memoirs*. This year was quite a stressful one for Frances. Lloyd George published *The Truth about Reparations and War Debts* and completed one hundred and twenty thousand words of his *War Memoirs*. He relied on her support and organisation greatly and often she was completely unable to get home, even to visit Jennifer.

Her removal to Worplesdon had another consequence she could not have foreseen. Her maid, Rowlands, had not wanted to work in Worplesdon and had taken employment with Olwen Carey Evans, Lloyd George's oldest living daughter. After some months an occasion arose where Frances was mentioned and Rowlands allowed Olwen to discover that Frances had been unfaithful to Lloyd George.

It is ironic, because by now the affair with Tweed was no longer physical at all. Frances once told Jennifer that she thought sex overrated and after Jennifer's birth there do not seem to have been any trysts. Frances continued to feel a romantic tenderness for Tweed that remained strong until he died, but she was able to promise not to meet him at all and to keep her promise, even when she knew he was dangerously ill, because by 1932 Tweed had turned from an unavailable and unwilling mistress to an ardent younger version. He had begun an intense affair with Frances's youngest sister, Muriel.

If he turned to Muriel because he thought she would be like her older sister he was very much mistaken. Muriel was passionate, intense, neurotic and demanding. There was not the slightest chance in the world that he would be able to enjoy affairs with them both and, however much he may have cared for Frances initially, he had to accept that if he wanted to continue with the exotic-looking and adoring Muriel, he would have to be exclusive to her. She was at least available whenever he was and able to devote herself to him.

By the end of 1932 Frances must certainly have put the affair behind her. There is not the remotest possibility that Muriel would have tolerated its continuance. Yet, Frances could not deny to Lloyd George that she had loved Tweed and still to some extent did. Sylvester recorded in his diary:

> 11 December 1932
> Yesterday evening LG phoned me personally saying, 'Come down to Churt early in the morning.' When I arrived Carey (Evans) met me at the door and said 'Look out'. I found LG in the library with Dame Margaret, Megan, Carey and Olwen. Presently he said 'Put a match to the fire in my bedroom and let us have a talk about Geddes.' After saying what information he wanted me to get from Geddes, he suddenly said: 'Now you owe your first duty to me, 'I said: 'There has never been any doubt about that on my part, ever.' He then said: 'Do you know about Frances and Tweed?' This was indeed a poser. I told him what I knew. He was terribly upset. I have never seen him so weighed down with grief in my life. Then I discovered that my information supported that brought to him by the family ...

14th December
The domestic situation has produced strained relationships and a peculiar atmosphere ... Tonight LG asked me to dine with Dame Margaret and Megan ... He was exceedingly tired, doubtless with all this anxiety on his mind ...

16th December
... Evelyn and I joined LG and Frances for dinner at Churt, during which he told us of the difficulty with which he was faced when Minister of Munitions.

It seems that, when confronted with evidence that Frances had been unfaithful, he could show great forbearance and even understanding. In the light of his total intolerance when faced with anything other than the most unswerving loyalty from his friends, family and even pets, this is extraordinary. The truth seems to be that he knew by this stage that he could not face life without Frances and, instead of casting her off, he returned to life with her as normal.

That is not to say that he did not continue to lead her a merry dance at times. There are references in Sylvester's diaries to huge rows taking place between them, and Jennifer remembers Frances arriving in tears, swearing that she would have nothing further to do with Lloyd George. This happened on more than one occasion, but it was never allowed to go on for more than a couple of days. Sometimes Frances apologised, but more often than not Lloyd George would come and charm her all over again, tell her how he relied on her and promise that all would be well in the future.

In 1933 Tweed published his very successful book *Rinehard*. It is about an American president, who after a car crash becomes a great reformer. In the book the President has a wonderful secretary of mixed heritage, like Frances. Independence, known as Pendie, has an Irish father; Frances's was Scottish. Pendie's mother was Polish-Russian; Frances's was French-Italian.

> ... the full red lips and the lurking pathos in her blue eyes made a vivid appeal to masculine susceptibilities ... but several of those who tried to philander were quickly made to realise that her small pointed jaw did not belie itself, and that the pathos of those china-blue eyes could quite quickly change to steely and unflinching contempt.

The fictional Pendie was also always ready to support her 'Chief' and sent him little notes about his speeches just as Frances always did. Tweed described her as,

... easy to look at, and her natural charm and dignity paved a way for her remarkable influence ... but it was not entirely charm and graciousness which compelled our respect. She had a first-class brain, a cool analytical mind and entire fearlessness in criticism.

Tweed wrote that he thought Rinehard was probably in love with Pendie,

But again for a man whose life was hardly monastic, his fondness for her was based on something deeper and more permanent than sexual attraction. It was more sentimental than that of a father for his daughter; more wholesome than that of a man for his mistress; and free of those latent antagonisms and differences of outlook which make life fretful and occasionally irksome for the happiest of married couples.

Frances was Lloyd George's mistress, so the analogy is not entirely appropriate, but this seems to sum up what Lloyd George felt for her more accurately than any other comment on the relationship between them. Who better to observe and understand what it was that he felt, than his rival for her attentions? Tweed's judgement of Frances's feelings for Lloyd George may have been clouded by his own desire to come first with her, but the description of Pendie's feelings for Rinehard also strikes a chord.

... her affections were more maternal than passionate. She realised all his weaknesses. She scorned his flamboyant style of oratory, and sometimes was openly contemptuous in her references to his many vanities. She had no illusions about him whatever. On the other hand, she had a real and intelligent appreciation of the many and varied gifts of his mind.

Rinehard is not Lloyd George, he is more probably based on Roosevelt. Later in the novel, however, Lloyd George is clearly described as the septuagenarian British Prime Minister, 'with his rosy apple cheeked face, flowing locks and abounding energy ...'
In contrasting him with the American President, Tweed said,

Only one physical trait had they in common, and that was in the blueness of their alert and penetrating eyes. Their temperaments were completely different – the British Prime Minister volatile, humorous and good tempered; Rinehard heavy, stern and humourless ...
   Their mutual attraction was strengthened, if not actually created, by the fact that they were men of great moral courage and originality of

outlook, who shared a contempt for the rigid mentality of the ortho-
dox whether politician or expert. Neither showed any hesitation in
sweeping aside established conventions or traditional usage if it
appeared that these were hampering progress.

Plainly, Tweed admired Lloyd George and he sums up the charm of the
man with whom he worked closely over many years. A fortnight before
he died (in 1940), Tweed wrote to Lloyd George congratulating him
heartily on the anniversary of his fifty years in parliament and his contribution in getting Chamberlain to resign. He concluded the letter,

And amongst those anonymous millions who have not forgotten twen-
tyfive years ago and whose regard and affection is undimmed by
neither time nor the fortunes of politics, please include one who in
humble duty signs himself, T.F.T.[7]

Tweed probably did not feel that he had been treacherous, at least not
deliberately, in having an affair with Frances. From the way he describes
the relationship between Pendie and Rinehard, it seems that he preferred
to regard Lloyd George's relationship with Frances as a close working one,
and his understanding of how things were between them does have strong
echoes of the truth although, of course, not the whole story.
    Lloyd George and Frances had far too much need of each other to fall
apart over a romance that either of them might have with another. The
romance, though cherished in Frances's memory, was not as important as
her life in service to Lloyd George. A small, torn out sheet of paper has
been carefully preserved by Frances describing her emotions when she
heard in 1934 that Tweed was very seriously ill.

May 18th
    After the brightness, the dark. My darling T.F.T. is very ill, ill unto
death. If he dies I do not think I shall be able to bear the scent of the
gorse and the lilac, when another spring comes round. All day long I
have been walking about, trying to staunch the wound at my heart and
to relieve my agony. I have never before had to bear pain like this, but
I knew it must come one day. People do die, and those who love them
live on. But what agony in between.
    My little Jennifer came to me, and puzzled at seeing traces of tears,
looked at me very searchingly, and said:- 'Grown-up ladies don't cry
do they, Mummy?'[8]

[7] FLG papers
[8] ibid

But she did not go to him. The diary was figuring prominently in Frances's life again in 1934 and Frances, now forty-six, seems to have put her mid-life crisis behind her. She would think nostalgically, even passionately of Tweed, but as her diary records, she did not break her promise and meet up with him at all, even after his illness. Her life apart from Lloyd George could revolve around Jennifer and her growing preoccupation with making a proper home for herself and her daughter. The diary shows that politics and life with Lloyd George were predominant again.

1934 began with Lloyd George away with his family in Portugal, working hard on his memoirs and enjoying the confrontation they stirred up when he attacked various members of his government or individuals in the armed forces for their part in the War. Frances wrote in her diary that Bernard Shaw had asked Lloyd George, 'Aren't you frightened of attacking people in the way you do?' She continued: 'Whatever the reason D. never hesitates to hit out, but I know that often he does not realise how hard he is hitting.' Indeed he seemed rather to enjoy old battles refought in newspaper columns now.

He was also fascinated and stimulated by developments in America and Germany, where policies he would have liked adopted in England were being put into practice. He too had wanted to provide work for the unemployed by building houses and roads and reclaiming land in great agricultural enterprises. A great part of 1934 was spent at Bron-y-de working hard on the memoirs and entertaining a great deal. As the year went on, he came to feel that if he could organise experts again to meet at his home and create a plan for English renewal, he would find again his place in British politics.

Lloyd George wrote 400,000 words of his memoirs in the first eight months of the year and Frances was expected to be on hand to produce files, letters and other references. The house in Worplesdon was clearly far too far away if she hoped to spend any time with her daughter. Initially she bought a barn just by the Bron-y-de estate and set about converting it into a home. Unfortunately she got quite carried away in her enthusiasm for the beautiful building, and Old Barn was transformed into a glorious but very grand home with a vaulted drawing room and minstrel gallery where superb parties were later held. It was going to cost a fortune to run and would need a lot of attention, so Frances leased 'Old Barn' and turned her attention to the building of a perfect home within easy walking distance of Bron-y-de.

Avalon takes its name from the 'Isles of the Blest' where Arthur's body was taken after his death – the Welsh 'afallon', is derived from 'afel' the Welsh for apple. In Tennyson's 'Idylls of the King it is spelt Avalon, and described as 'set in orchards fair' – which Frances often quoted. Tennyson's Avalon has the emphasis on the first syllable, where most people put it;

but for Frances, her family and Lloyd George, the emphasis was always on the second syllable, the Welsh pronunciation.

The house was designed by the architect Antony Chitty in accordance with Frances's ideas. Chitty protested occasionally, but was overruled. It was flat-roofed, one-storeyed, built in wood – to the horror of the local council, who refused to give it more than temporary planning permission. It was amazingly beautiful.

The main room was about forty feet long, divided by a small step and low, built-in bookshelves. The top third of the room had French windows opening to the north, giving onto a small paved terrace with steps leading down to a green walk with wide herbaceous borders on either side. At the end of the green walk there was a small rose garden with a low hedge behind, and beyond that a thirty-mile view over unspoilt countryside. Sitting and talking took place here, with the fire and the view. The walls were lined from floor to ceiling with bookshelves and there were very comfortable chairs and sofas. The other two thirds of the room faced south, with three pairs of glass doors running from end to end and from ceiling to floor, with thick velvet curtains of deep yellow. The floors were also of light oak, polished and covered with large, beautiful Persian rugs and home to a light walnut grand piano, a Bluthner. A round table in dark oak was near the door and could be served from a hatch leading into the kitchen. Immediately on the left as you entered the room was a big, low, seventeenth-century sideboard, with flowers and apples and a bowl of pot-pourri scenting the room always. There was an enormous mirror opposite the big door, which reflected the beautiful, south-facing courtyard outside, and the half wild, (but very carefully controlled) garden beyond that, with massive oak trees in the distance and azaleas and all sorts of other shrubs nearer to the house. And beyond everything, the orchards.

Jennifer was provided with a magnificent nursery, later known as the school room, with French windows on to a west facing terrace. Two other windows showed the distant view to the north, with a row of cherry trees in the foreground. Another window, with a cupboard on either side and bookshelves underneath, gave onto the front drive so Jennifer could watch the various arrivals and departures. There was also a large bedroom for Jennifer, a slightly smaller bedroom (with a less magnificent view) for the nanny.

Another of Avalon's glories was the front door, made of copper and needing a whole morning to polish. Visitors waiting on the doorstep saw themselves reflected in a door whose colour enhanced their own appearance, so they entered the house feeling happy.

The land with Old Barn, Avalon and the orchards in between already belonged to Frances. It was customary for her to buy, or for Lloyd George to buy and give her, land adjoining his own when it became available. He farmed all the land together until his death, but it was not necessary to upset his children (any more than they were upset already) by leaving Frances any part of the Bron-y-de estate.

Whenever they were free of guests, Lloyd George was happy that Jennifer should spend a lot of her day with them at Bron-y-de and he began the practice of walking with her around the farm before lunch. Jennifer with her 'Taid' was happy to be free of the nanny and looking at fruit trees, visiting the pigs and enjoying talking to him. She remembers feeling a bit bored by long, earnest and rather technical conversations Lloyd George had with the farm workers, but he made the walks a lot of fun. For example, if the current nanny said Jennifer was not to have any cherries when they were out as it would spoil her appetite for lunch, he would solemnly promise not to give her any – and then put cherries in his pocket and pretend to forget they were there. When Jennifer put her hand in his pocket he would look in the other direction and say it was most odd, it felt as though there were a little mouse in his pocket, he could not think how it had got there. On occasion he would set Jennifer and himself the task of finding on the farm every single thing to eat at lunch. The poor cook had to create it out of what they brought back. It was usually fruit and vegetables, of course, but one day they found a rabbit in a trap and bore it home in triumph. On that occasion Lloyd George hit it on the head with a walking stick, but Jennifer was taught early to kill chickens and rabbits herself. She was a country girl, brought up on a farm, after all, though there was one episode which distressed her. Very early one morning she was taken to see some fox cubs being dug out of an earth. The cubs were then imprisoned, but one was so desperate that it escaped over wire netting ten feet high and Jennifer was very pleased. After the 'cubbing' Jennifer used to lie in bed at Avalon and listen to a fox barking, imagining it was the mother desperately mourning her babies, and she grieved with her.

Lloyd George invented indoor entertainments too – sardine sandwiches that 'swam' through the air, and had to be caught; or an orange dropped into a glass of water to illustrate a recent novel, where the moon fell into the sea. When Frances fussed about the mess, he and Jennifer were delighted.

Jennifer had three nannies. She had nicknames for the first two - Noonoo for Miss Neale and Mooffy for Miss Moffat – but the third, Marjorie Hackett, who was much stricter and less loving, she called 'nanny' all the time. Jennifer has no recollection of any of them leaving, although she had some affection for all three. Miss Neale left when Jennifer was still too young for it to make much of an impact. Miss Moffat was the victim of the cherry joke, but her principal significance in

Jennifer's memory was the fact that her father looked after Bertram Mills' tigers when the Circus was in England but not actually performing, and Jennifer was taken on a visit to him to see the tigers. She also remembered that Miss Moffat was sea-sick on the trip they made to Portugal in the summer of 1934.

Lloyd George had enjoyed his stay there so much in the previous winter that Frances took the opportunity of his summer stay in Criccieth to go with Jennifer to Portugal. She stayed at the same hotel, the Estoril Palacio Hotel, and wrote to him on the 3rd of September,

My own darling little Man,
    Just a little line to let you know that everything is all right here – Jennifer quite recovered, and thoroughly enjoying life in every detail and every thrill. We shall be very reluctant to leave here, especially as we shan't be seeing you at the other end directly. It *is* a nice place, and the people are so kind and thoroughly honest. I haven't been very successful about villas, – not any particular one – but a good deal of general information which will be useful. I'll tell you all about it when I see you. Personally I think Cascais is the more attractive place, and beyond. I expect you know it, but I'll tell you everything when I see you.
    I received Miss Russell's letter and enclosure. I should think Layton will squirm when he receives your letter. But he deserved it! It is preposterous that he should have revealed everything to Samuel – an amazing thing for him to do. But I formed the opinion that he was only half-hearted about it all. You remember he was just the same when you were negotiating with Asquith – you never knew where he was.
    I may tell you that the handkerchiefs have been a great source of pleasure during the whole trip. They have been taken out and played with – but never used! When I suggested it, it was as though I were suggesting something quite sacrilegious!
    I see Ramsay Muir has been telling the Liberal Party again what to do and how to put everything right! They live in an entirely unreal world of their own, and will continue to do so until they are dead and ingloriously buried. And a good deal is done to spite you! Cutting off their nose to spite their faces!
    I am so sorry you have not been having very good weather in Wales. It is too bad, and you will have been envying us our sunshine.
    Yesterday we went for a drive to Cintra. I was doubtful about taking Jennifer, but she was thoroughly interested and thrilled with everything. It was a lovely drive, but I found the interiors of the palaces most depressing. Didn't you?
    It has seemed such a long time since we saw you, my darling and I

am longing for a glimpse of you again. I hope all goes well with you, and that you are enjoying your rest, and the change! – and that you are not working too hard. I expect I shall find a lot to do when I get back to Churt – otherwise I should have felt tempted to stay on here a bit longer – it is such a pleasant place –

Fondest and most devoted love to you, my darling from your own P & J.[9]

This wifely epistle is concerned with his health because Lloyd George had been quite unwell during the summer. He had thought he was becoming a diabetic, but Dawson had diagnosed 'glycosuria' and prescribed a special diet and some rest. Sir Walter Layton, to whom she refers with such disgust, was a Liberal MP who had been down to visit Lloyd George and had agreed with him that joining up with the National party had been a grave mistake. It seems he had now decided to make a grave mistake in his relations with Lloyd George by reporting everything that had been said back to Samuel.

They brought back memories of glorious white walls, bright red geraniums and a smell of drains. It was only towards the end of the holiday that they discovered that notices around the place referred to a typhoid epidemic in the town and advised inoculation. Jennifer recollects that she was nervous of the sea and that Frances had taken one hand, Mooffy the other and they had assured her that the waves would collapse and break long before they reached little Jennifer. The very next one did not do so and in fact went right over her head. Jennifer felt rather outraged, but it did seem to help her overcome her fear. Frances must have felt mortified at having her promise so immediately broken by the capricious behaviour of the sea.[10]

When Frances got back to Churt, she found Lloyd George immersing himself in plans for a so-called 'Council of Action'. She mentions that some of the technical experts seemed a little sceptical and rather scared at being mixed up in politics. She sounds not a little sceptical herself when she writes in her diary, 'However, when D sets his mind and his hand to anything, someone has got to shed blood. And even if the net result is negligible, there is bound to be a vast amount of publicity.'

At the end of a busy year making plans for an English 'New Deal' to be the equivalent of what was now working for Roosevelt in America, Lloyd George spent Christmas at Bron-y-de and took Jennifer to see *Cinderella*. The programme has on the cover in Lloyd George's writing,

[9] ibid
[10] Conversation with Jennifer Longford

'December 29th Jennifer's first pantomime.' Both Lloyd George and Frances were working hard on his speech announcing the 'British New Deal' at Bangor on the 17th January 1935. On the 10th January she wrote in her diary,

> His speech on the 17th is likely to be a momentous one. He has already drafted it, and Malcolm Thomson and I today went through it with a view to criticising it, which we have done rather drastically. I said to Malcolm: 'He will probably slay us for this', & Malcolm later typed out and passed me the following note:
>
> 'Attitude of meek but stubborn sincerity in which the criticisms of Miss Stevenson and Malcolm Thomson are advanced:
>
> THOUGH HE SLAYS ME, YET WILL I TRUST IN HIM:
> BUT I WILL MAINTAIN MINE OWN WAYS BEFORE HIM.'
> Job, xiii, 15
>
> As a matter of fact, I had already told D. that I should be slain for any criticism I should make, He said, 'Yes I will probably slay you. And afterwards I shall adopt all your suggestions.'

The meeting at Bangor seemed a success to both Frances and Lloyd George, and she was expecting a move from the government to ask Lloyd George to join them, though she perceived that Baldwin was unlikely to want this and was probably asking him to wait in the hope that the problem would go away. As the spring arrived, they became more and more certain that the government would have to invite him in despite themselves.

Spring had other excitements. At last Avalon was finished and on March 9th 1935 Jennifer, her nanny and the two Scottish servants, Margaret and Rose Cameron moved in there. The pattern became established that Jennifer would walk the mile from Avalon to Bron-y-de in the morning, stay to lunch, talk to Frances in the afternoon when Lloyd George had his usual nap and then walk home with the nanny, or with Frances, who would leave in order to be back at Bron-y-de for tea with Lloyd George.

As summer arrived, Lloyd George came to the conclusion that he was being strung along. Finally he could bear it no longer and he initiated the 'Council of Action' independently of the government on the 1st July. It was perceived by many as ensuring that Lloyd George could not now work with the government. He claimed not to mind, saying that he would smash them instead at the General Election, but as July turned into August it was apparent that support was falling away.

Also during the summer the Abyssinian crisis occurred, with Mussolini's annexation of Abyssinia. Again the League of Nations was wholly ineffectual and Lloyd George said that they had lost their standing during the Japanese incident, but that if he had been in power he would, at least, have sent arms to the Abyssinians. He regarded Mussolini as a bully. Increasingly, however, he looked at Germany with interest and sympathy as Hitler managed to establish some of the ideas Lloyd George proposed in his New Deal. Frances was aware of this when she decided she must take a holiday in Germany and set off for Freudenstadt with her sister, Muriel, on September 9th 1935.

She left Jennifer at the rented holiday home in Felpham with her new nanny, Marjorie Hackett. Louise wrote to Frances on the 13th September and added a note to say that she had just visited Jennifer, who was well and happy and at five, now able to add a brief note of her own in the letter.

In the unpublished chapter of the autobiography, Frances wrote that:

Jennifer was watched over by a strong-minded Nonconformist Nanny who took her regularly to Church (Methodist and Congregationalist only) and used by means of a hair-brush (this I only learned later) to instruct her in the ethics of speaking the truth, of being a good girl, and of being obedient. In the intervals of the spankings Jennifer's lovely golden curls were brushed straight. But Nannie tended her gently when she fell off a pony; and taught her to read and write and swim.

Jennifer recollected that, far from teaching her to tell the truth:

What she actually taught me, by beating me when she caught me out in a lie, was to lie more efficiently. She also taught me, inadvertently, to resent and oppose injustice, on any scale. For years I remembered her as having beaten me at least once a week whether or not I had done anything to deserve it, but I think it is more likely that she just found a great many things to beat me for – and some of them I had not even done. (For example, she beat me ferociously one morning for having left the lavatory lid up, when it should have been down – and I knew that I had not done this, therefore she must have done it herself.) At the same time, and equally without intent, I suppose she taught me how to tolerate the unjust person, while condemning their unjust deeds. Her beatings were painful, and so were her dosings with Syrup of Figs, a nauseous cure for constipation which she gave me whenever she thought I had been sulking.

It never occurred to Jennifer to tell Frances about this sort of treatment and everyone regarded Marjorie Hackett as a wonderful nanny, particularly because she was so conscientious in helping Jennifer with her reading, writing and arithmetic, and also in writing regular letters to Frances detailing Jennifer's activities, suitably censored it would seem.

Frances came home from her holiday in Germany not feeling very rested. She had spent the first two days travelling and the second two days in bed with a bad cold; nor did Muriel make a cheerful travelling companion. They both found Germany 'rather terrifying in her quiet and earnest preoccupation.'[11]

It was as well to have had some kind of break, however, because she returned shortly before they all swung into action for the election of November 1935. Jennifer remembers the campaign as, 'an exciting time for me, with everyone around me very active and hopeful – and masses of yellow pencils with "New Deal" on them.' The subsequent disappointment may have been the reason Frances wrote a long and clear article called 'A Parliamentary Impression', though perhaps she wrote it after the collapse of the Council of Action just before the Election. It reflects the growing cynicism she was beginning to feel for the world of politics and what they were able to achieve and was inspired in particular, by a moving maiden speech she heard delivered by James Griffiths to 'an apathetic House – which fell on deaf ears and unresponding hearts'.

> I lately heard that a certain Member of Parliament, capable and highly-esteemed by his Party, had decided not to seek re-election. I asked: Was his health bad; were his prospects such that he had no chance of retaining his seat; did his business preclude him from taking any further part in politics? The answer to all these questions was No: but the House of Commons was slowly breaking his heart.
>
> He was a man who all his life had taken an active part in municipal work. He had spent time and brains and energy in improving conditions in his native town, and had the satisfaction of seeing his efforts materialise. He had entered Parliament with the high hope of doing the same thing in a larger sphere; of serving the nation as hitherto he had served his own city. He was retiring from the House of Commons because he realised the utter futility of effecting any such thing and because he was aware of the impotence of a single member to have any influence upon the Parliamentary machine. To his mind therefore it was worse than useless to stay: it was merely heart-breaking to stand there seeing the thing that needed doing whilst being totally unable to advance it.

[11] Autobiography FLG op cit

So much has been written on the defects of the Parliamentary system that the subject might be considered hackneyed if it were not still one of real concern to a large number of people. No satisfactory solution to the problem has as yet been proffered or at any rate is likely of adoption, and debates in the House of Commons continue to drag on their weary way and to stifle any endeavour. Sir Oswald Mosley attracted a certain amount of support from many and varied quarters in his outline of plans which cut across parties, but that part of them to which least publicity has been given was the portion which demanded that the present parliamentary machinery should be superseded, that the Bauble of Parliamentary babble should be removed, and that as much business as possible should be done in as few words as possible.

Let anyone follow the actual workings of the machine as they appear to the onlooker from day to day, and he cannot but be filled with a sense of fury at the apparent impotence of the House of Commons to deal with matters of supreme urgency, or in other words to 'get a move on'. There used to be a common supposition that if wrongs were to be righted, grievances aired and measures carried, Parliament was the place to do it. I have listened spell-bound to a young Socialist Member from the Clyde giving in simple language a picture of the conditions under which his kith and kin lived, under which he himself had existed and with which he was familiar – a picture so moving and convincing that none but the hardest and most unbelieving hearer could fail to be sympathetic to his appeal for a remedy. The House was very thinly attended, but such members as were present were attentive and impressed. The speech finished, the speaker sat down, the House resumed its mood of indifference and boredom, and the eloquent speech and all that it represented passed into oblivion. One realised that it had not so much as ruffled the surface of the deep, deep sea of parliamentary inaction.

On another occasion a similarly moving appeal was made to the House by another young Socialist during a debate on unemployment. He himself had been one of the unemployed, and he spoke from his heart in begging Parliament to take the matter in hand. Speaker and speech were applauded; the machinery for dealing with unemployment was not quickened by a perceptible fraction and the unemployment figures continued to mount.

But it is on the occasions of full-dress debates, so to speak, that the futility and waste of time becomes most apparent. On such days time is allotted to the leaders of the three parties, so much time for their subordinates, and the remainder of the time may be used as the Speaker thinks fit and as the Whips decide amongst themselves. The speeches are made, the time is filled in, opinions and emotions are registered, the House is interested or bored according to the importance of the speaker: and one is painfully conscious at the end of the day that nothing has happened or is likely to happen as the result of so much talking.

The Unemployment Debates themselves have come to be regarded as important not so much because they give an opportunity of dealing with unemployment but because they may have to be regarded as Votes of Censure on the Government and so endanger its existence. Will the Government survive or not? That is the question. A full-dress performance is staged, skilled speakers belonging to all parties make their speeches, parry attacks, invent defences. The Government survives. As you were. Only the Unemployment figures are not quite as they were – just a little larger.

The Electoral Reform Bill is, we may suppose, a necessary measure. Let us grant that it is. Must day after day be passed in the delivery of speeches which everyone knows in advance will not influence or alter the ultimate voting by one single vote? The futility of Parliamentary procedure was illustrated by the account of the first day's Debate on this Bill in the papers the following morning. A long and picturesque account of the various speeches was followed by the announcement:- *Business done* Bill for the better protection of trout in Scotland – first reading.

Little as one may sympathise with Mr Maxton's political views, one cannot help thinking that he was making a sound criticism when he complained towards the end of two days spent in such speeches that Parliament had no right to consider the rearrangement of political machinery while people outside were crying for bread.

It is said that bad trade is the cause of our unemployment, and that we should concentrate on remedying that: it is not until measures are taken to improve the trade of the country that any change in unemployment can take place. But I have listened to debate after debate upon this all-important subject in a House not half-filled and wholly apathetic, with nothing accomplished at the end. And only the other day during a debate on public expenditure and economy (instigated by the Conservatives) the House was 'counted out' owing to insufficient interest and attendance.

One could quote endless similar examples. It is not the fault of any one party. It is the parliamentary system which, in allowing such an unconscionable waste of time, produces such apathy and despair of accomplishment. It is quite unable to adapt itself to meet the present discontents. Can it be repaired, this old machine, parts of which are outworn and other parts rusty with age and disuse? Or will it have to destroy itself and substitute a new machine? Something must surely happen soon, if Parliamentary representation is to mean anything to the nation in the future.[12]

Frances did not actually know very many people suffering from the trials of unemployment in the thirties, but she had the imagination and sympathy to care. She also felt that Lloyd George had answers and, because he had not played the parliamentary game, he was not getting a chance to introduce any of them. She was becoming very disillusioned and seldom spoke to Jennifer about politics other than to say that politics 'was a dirty business'.

But since politics were not her *raison d'etre*, she could still take great pleasure in making two homes beautiful, caring devotedly for Lloyd George and enormously enjoying the variety and excitement of life. At Christmas this year they were not working on any 'New Deal' or even feeling very hopeful, so they distracted themselves by going to Tangiers together in a party that included the Churchills. They were invited to lunch by the Glaoui, in his palace somewhere in the mountains, and they all had to sit on the floor, and eat a magnificent meal with their fingers. Churchill had said earlier that nothing would induce him to eat with his fingers, but one of Frances's favourite stories was of how, as soon as he had eaten the first mouthful, he said, with satisfaction, 'To hell with civilisation.' For Christmas they sent Jennifer a postcard from 'a couple of tangerines' followed shortly afterwards by an enormous box of the fruit.

Nobody thought to ask Jennifer if she minded being left at Christmas. She might even have said no, but the long term effect was to leave her with an ambivalent attitude towards Christmas. Lavish presents and treats organised by 'Nanny' did not entirely make up for a feeling that she was deserted. Nanny Hackett wrote long letters informing Frances of all these treats and reporting various adorable little sayings of Jennifer. Frances kept and treasured them all, but it was not the same as being there.

There are pages and pages of letters from Nanny Hackett, and obviously she was very efficient at making Jennifer write letters also, as there are almost as many pages from Jennifer in neatly drawn lines. Telegrams also are kept and details of how the dogs are or of political developments. The private code for telegrams was left each time Frances and Lloyd George went abroad, with invented words for political developments and Jennifer's progress. Certain words always featured: 'Jennifer well and happy' was 'Jappy', and 'Jennifer sends love and greetings was 'Joves', 'Please send news regarding' was 'fools' and 'Please wire here news of' always 'goats'.

A typical letter from Nanny Hackett written on November 23rd 1936:

[12] FLG papers

Dear Miss Stevenson,

Jennifer's cold is no worse but as it was so cold and foggy this morning she did not go to school. The appetite is still very good.

Yesterday afternoon was spent in playing snakes and ladders and ludo, and Jennifer won every game. I put her to bed 5.45 and she was asleep by 6.30.

Your cable came over the telephone on Saturday and the confirmation copy came this morning. Jennifer was thrilled with it.

This morning I washed your sister's cupboards and drawers out, and the spare room with Jeyes.

I have finished Jennifer's petticoat and have just got the knickers done.

'Jennifer has been sorting out some toys to take to school, and saying to herself, 'I mustn't give that away mummy gave it to me when I was three, and I must keep this Taid gave it to me and he wouldn't like me to give it away and I can give this away because I bought it with my very own money.' The Woolworths teddy was put out but half an hour afterwards he had to go back in the cupboard, he looked so sad. Bardy is still in the cupboard.

We have not been able to get Radio Normandy for nearly a week. Stratton said the accumulator was worn out, and so he is ordering two new ones.

I went out in the car with Mrs Dyer this afternoon while Jennifer rested. Mr and Mrs Dyer came to tea and Jennifer was so pleased she said she wished she had a cold more often.

Do you get letters any quicker if they are air mailed? ...'

Sometimes there was a reference to her own personal concerns, and farm news, but mainly the letters were filled with details of Jennifer's daily existence. There were frequent references in her letters to Elizabeth Mary and the shared activities of the girls. Elizabeth Mary was the daughter of Frances's old friend and lawyer, John Morris, and his wife Elsie. Elsie had been divorced from her first husband and therefore, like Frances, had not led an entirely conventional and respectable marital life. Her second marriage and second child came more than twenty years after her first and it suited Elsie to allow Liz to spend a great deal of time with Jennifer. It also suited Liz and Jennifer. They became as close as sisters. They also encouraged each other in scrapes and, like ordinary sisters, frequently got each other into trouble. This did not lessen their affection for each other one jot.

Frances never felt that Jennifer needed more family than she herself provided, but she was happy if Jennifer was happy and was therefore pleased to encourage Liz to stay whenever she could.

She was working hard with Lloyd George on the memoirs. Progress throughout the year had been continuing and for the most part Frances was leading a busy and satisfying life – but moments that reminded her of past glories did give her a pang. On the 10th June they lunched with another member of the old War Cabinet and memories of office were brought back. More spectacularly, Lloyd George made a superb speech in the House on the 18th June, attacking the government on the failure of their Abyssinian policy. Frances described it as 'a real resurrection of his old fighting days. The House was almost hysterical and so was I.'[13]

With Lloyd George she shared all her impressions of Germany and how terrifying she had found the general atmosphere. He would be bound, however, to have had reservations about her judgement in this area, because he knew she still felt antagonistic to the people who had killed her brother. Doubtless he remembered that in the build-up to the First World War she had been far quicker than he was to see war as an acceptable option. Still, her reports, combined with the fascinating information he received about the progress of Hitler's programme of recovery, interested him enormously.

Rumours of German rearmament he refused to take seriously at first, and the reoccupation of the Rhineland, which took place on the 7th March 1936, Lloyd George dismissed as an understandable result of Franco-Russian provocation in the 'Pact of Mutual Assistance'. In 1935 Lloyd George had told Thomas Jones that, if he were in office, he thought he would be able to placate Germany. With this in mind and with an overriding desire to see German achievements for himself Lloyd George accepted Hitler's invitation to visit him at Berchtesgaden in September 1936.

Frances did not go with Lloyd George to Germany. This trip was far too public, so she did not meet Hitler for herself, but she understood Lloyd George's feelings about him. As she put it in her autobiography, 'it is not surprising ... that he was full of admiration for one who had done what he had failed to do,' and 'surmounted Germany's economic difficulties in the process.'

Neither Frances nor Lloyd George believed that the persecution of the Jews was as bad as some suggested. They had known the exaggeration and false imputation that had been levelled against the Germans during the First World War, when they had been accused of eating babies and raping nuns in Belgium. They doubted atrocity stories now.

Lloyd George returned to Churt, very impressed with the quality of leadership he perceived in Hitler. In the throes of writing his war memoirs, Lloyd George could not fail to be reminded of just how close

[13] Diary FLS op cit

defeat had been for England at times during the First World War. It struck him that Hitler had achieved so much and come so far that he was a far more awesome leader than the Kaiser had been. It was therefore vital to avoid confrontation.

When he wrote the article about his visit, Lloyd George described Hitler as the 'George Washington' of Germany and stressed that he believed Hitler wanted peace for reconstruction. He announced that Hitler was 'no more militarist than any other leader who relies on an army to defend his frontiers'. He also believed that Hitler would hardly want to expand into non-Aryan territory.

Hitler's ideas about racial purity did strike him as absurd. Phipps wrote to Eden that 'Lloyd George flatly refused to keep to programmes or play up to local bigwigs' and he had said that the treatment of the Jews was 'a grave and deplorable thing', but that it was understandable in the context of revolution and would disappear when Germany was re-established as a European power and thus no longer a resentful and humiliated state. It should be added that he had no idea of the extent of the maltreatment of the Jews. Jennifer remembers Lloyd George explaining to her on a car drive that Jews had more loyalty to their own people in different countries above their loyalty to the country they lived in and that it was believed in Germany that they had not been helping the country to recover from the devastation caused by the First World War. He told her that Hitler was only acting against rich, monopolistic Jews, who had used their finance and international contacts to obtain money that would have helped Germany prosper. To ordinary Jews, whom he did see as vulnerable and victimized, he was as sympathetic as ever and wrote in the *Strand* magazine in April 1937 of the many examples of brave, loyal Jews who 'fought bravely for the land which accorded them just treatment'.

On his trip he had seen 'work camps' which seemed to be doing valuable work of reconstruction, but none of his party realised that this was forced labour. Instead of noticing a lack of freedom, Lloyd George was very impressed by the classlessness he found. On the evening of 4th September they went to a beer garden where he was much struck to see secretaries, chauffeurs and diplomats rubbing shoulders. Hitler exercised all the charm of which he was capable, telling Lloyd George he was 'the man who won the war' and signing a postcard of himself for Jennifer, 'the little girl' Lloyd George admitted he had at home.

Frances felt that Lloyd George could have worked to handle and contain Hitler. She always believed that, had he been in power, the Second World War could have been avoided.

After his return, it was not long before Lloyd George and Frances set off for Jamaica. They set out in ferocious weather on 9th November 1936 and Frances suffered badly from seasickness. She was leaving Jennifer for more than two months again over Christmas, but there were no tears on either side. Jennifer was now just seven and perhaps did not fully realise how long two months would be, but she wrote to Frances, 'I hope you are enjoying yourself on your trip as much as you would with me.' and she signs herself, 'With love and kisses from your darling Jennifer.' No sense of abandonment came over in her letters, which were full of details about dancing, riding, visits from John Brook and Elizabeth Mary, tea with Miss Parry and many school concerns. Frances believed that Jennifer was entirely happy and proceeded to enjoy a magical holiday with Lloyd George.

When Frances had to leave him on the 8th January, her letter sounded bereft. She felt like his wife now and having to slide off and get out of the way really seemed undignified. They were living together virtually all the time in Churt, and in the sunshine and flowers of Jamaica they seem to have revived their love.

Sylvester described their devotedness on this holiday in his diary. On the 16th November he recorded Lloyd George as saying,

'Do you know that on 27th December Frances has been with me twenty five years. It is a testimony to her patience and toleration in having put up with me for all those years.' Frances said, 'It has been reciprocal.' LG said: 'You have been very patient.' Frances laughing, said: 'Why the unusual amount of humility?' LG said: 'I must be very difficult at times. Anyhow I am conscious of it, and that helps me to check myself.' He laughed and went on: 'If only you are patient with me.'

Before they had set off for Jamaica, Sylvester had reported back the gossip that the King would marry Mrs Simpson and Lloyd George had said: 'If the little fellow marries her, I shall back him. The only people who will be against it will be the aristocracy and they are the rottenest lot of people.'

The day after they arrived, Lloyd George received a bulletin saying that the Cabinet had decided to resign unless the King took their advice about Mrs Simpson. The Opposition had agreed they would not form an alternative government. Lloyd George thought they ought to go straight home to defend Edward. He had a strong affection for the new King whom, he felt, had shown signs of caring for the poor and vulnerable, and he thought it would be acceptable for Mrs Simpson to be a consort, if not a Queen. Both he and Frances had come to know Edward quite well at the house parties held in the twenties at Philip Sassoon's house and others. They felt that he was being elbowed out by Baldwin for being too left-wing.

Sylvester made arrangements for Lloyd George to return to England, but on the evening of the 8th December they heard from Tweed that the crisis was virtually over and that he would be too late to affect things. They cancelled the tickets and settled back to enjoy the holiday, but on the 11th December they sat on Lloyd George's balcony and listened to the King's abdication speech. Frances later wrote that if only Lloyd George had been there, he would have been able to make Edward remember his duty. Frances certainly lived by the code that private convenience was less important than the public good and that was why she accepted the insecurities of life as a mistress, rather than risk disgrace for Lloyd George.

She was very upset. She was very warmly disposed towards Edward who had troubled to put her at her ease sixteen years earlier. She had not liked his younger brother Albert, who now became King George VI. She had found him weak and caught him out in a lie when, having damaged his host's piano, he denied any knowledge of it. His diffidence and modesty had not impressed her and, when she returned to England, she wanted to refuse the invitation that came to her to be presented at Court. She 'phoned up with her excuses and was told that apologies were not being accepted. Apparently so many people had tried to cry off that there was a three-line whip in effect. Although it was now unfashionable to keep photographs on the piano (because it was thought to show that you were not really musical) – Frances kept one large one of the Duke of Windsor signed 'Edward P' on hers. Even when she learnt to respect George VI for the way he rose to the occasion during the Second World War, she did not remove her photograph of 'Edward P'.

Frances had left England on the 9th November and she finally left Lloyd George in Jamaica on 8th January, because Dame Margaret's arrival was imminent. She had been away for two months already but she did not rush home, instead taking advantage of her location to go to New York and stay in the Waldorf Astoria with Sylvester's wife, Evelyn. From New York Frances wrote a very long letter to Lloyd George describing the city, American politics and Evelyn Sylvester's poor state of health. Always kind and aware of how she ought to behave, though privately disappointed, Frances cancelled visits to Niagara Falls and Washington and stayed helping Mrs Sylvester. She was particularly sorry to miss her trip to Washington, as she had planned to be at Roosevelt's second inauguration. She heard the speech on the wireless and commented in her letter: 'Some of it struck me as being like your speeches, though of course his delivery cannot compare with yours. It is utterly lacking in art. I thought the ending rather fine, however.'

The time together had obviously been very special for them both.

Their letters are full of references to renewal in their relationship and Sylvester described in his diary how sad Lloyd George was that Frances had gone. She finally got back to Churt on the 29th January and slotted back into Jennifer's life bringing thoughtful presents and entrancing bed-time stories. As an adult the sound of the first carols would cause Jennifer to feel a sinking in her stomach.

Almost immediately after Lloyd George finally arrived back from Jamaica, on the 17th February 1937, he was confronted with a personal crisis. He was informed that there was a whispering campaign about his moral character and suggestions that Jennifer was his daughter. He reacted with fury. It was always his way to defend by attacking and he threatened and blustered and said that he needed Frances for his work.

> Tell them she is a graduate of London University with honours and that she is very able ... Frances was there at the time J.T. (Davies) was there. Now he is a Director of the Suez Canal and Ford Motors. As long as I am writing these books Frances is absolutely essential to me. She knows French. She knew Foch, Briand, Clemenceau, Bonar and all the ministers – Smuts, Henry Wilson, Curzon, Austen Chamberlain, Winston ...

In addition to this reference for Frances, Lloyd George said that his prostate operation six years previously made the charge preposterous. Since Jennifer was now seven and a half this defence was a rather weak one, but he did have a point when he added that there was a 'Statute of Limitations' which said that a man could only be identified as the father of an illegitimate child in the first three years of the child's life. Of course the smear might stick however little legal claim the child had. Finally he produced a strong defence and said, 'I have a letter from Tweed saying that he is responsible for the child.' No such letter has ever been found.

Fortunately, the stories seemed to fade of their own accord and, shortly after this explosion Lloyd George had relaxed enough to risk a little public teasing of Frances.

In 1931 Sir Thomas Jaffrey had apparently proposed to Frances after the death of his first wife. He was seventy then and Frances had refused him, whereupon he had turned his attentions elsewhere and was by 1937 married again. However, he invited Frances to lunch with him at the Savoy Grill. Lloyd George then took a small party along to the same restaurant and sat facing Frances. He kept his eyes on Frances and kept silently toasting her. Hardly surprisingly, Sir Thomas was upset.

He made no further reference to Tweed being Jennifer's father and continued as devoted and interested in her as ever. Frances was making no claims. As she wrote of Jennifer in the unpublished chapter of her biography: 'I was providing for my future as well as for her. I knew that in the future I should need someone to love and care for, and at every turn I tried to put the child's interest before my own.'

Chapter Seven

A War on several fronts

Due to the anti-Semitism in Germany and Poland, the flow of Jews out to Palestine had greatly increased and the Arabs resident there were actively hostile to these incomers. Palestine was a British protectorate, and the widespread disorders there were a British problem so a commission was set up to investigate the situation and try to find a solution. Lloyd George, who had offered the Jews a national home in the Balfour Declaration of 1917, went to speak to the Commission on the 16th April 1937. Sylvester described him as: 'brilliant... beseeching men like the Tory diehard Peel to keep their words and not run away from the honourable word of Britain.'

Interestingly Lloyd George also said:

> There are two people I would not quarrel with if I were running a State. They are both international forces. One is the Jews and the other is the Roman Catholic Church and Hitler is quarrelling with them both.

Clearly Lloyd George believed that Hitler was making a fundamental error.

On the 12th May George VI was crowned and shortly after this Baldwin resigned and allowed Neville Chamberlain to take over as Prime Minister. If Lloyd George had disliked Baldwin it was as nothing to what he felt for Neville Chamberlain.

During the First World War Lloyd George had appointed Chamberlain as Director of National Service, in which job he failed. Lloyd George had a high regard for the now discredited science of phrenology, which assessed people and what they would achieve from looking at the bumps and shape of their heads. He called Chamberlain 'pinhead'. Baldwin might have been prepared to listen to some of Lloyd George's ideas. There was no chance that Chamberlain would. A J P Taylor once described him as 'a meticulous housemaid, great at tidying up.'[1]

In less demanding times Chamberlain might have done quite well, but

[1] *Oxford English History Vol XV 1914–1945* ed A J P Taylor

with the menace of a Hitler in Germany he was not the man to have in office and Lloyd George knew it. He told Frances that there was now no chance that he would be invited in to take a position in the government, for Chamberlain disliked him every bit as much as he disliked Chamberlain.

Lloyd George also recognised that he might not be up to the demands of ministerial office any more. He could not face doing the job less well than he knew was necessary. He told Frances this and she agreed that: 'he was constitutionally incapable of doing a job without using his whole strength to it.' Frances herself thought he was sometimes too thorough: 'as those around him know to their cost.' She seemed to accept this, but she could not entirely reconcile herself to powerlessness. She yearned for him to step in and change the momentum that was dragging Britain towards war. She had faith that he could still do it and it was little men who thwarted him.

Christmas of 1937 was spent in Antibes. Frances and Lloyd George had both adored Jamaica but Antibes had a lot of charm for them both and it was significantly closer. They did not want to be too far away to be involved if there was another crisis. It also meant that Frances did not need to miss Jennifer's Christmas holidays completely. She was able to return for Christmas with Jennifer and be back in Antibes for the new year until 11th January, when Margaret and Megan were due to arrive.

Lloyd George's family were arriving in Antibes for the celebration of his Golden Wedding with Dame Margaret. (Quietly and privately Frances was also aware that she and Lloyd George were celebrating a silver anniversary.)

Lloyd George paid for the entire family to come out and commemorate the event, but Sylvester recorded in his diary that he was anxious that they should not stay on too long afterwards as he wanted Frances and wrote that he had said: 'It was necessary for him to have Frances ... J.T. (Davies) and Frances are the only people who know the papers.'

Sylvester was graphically contemptuous of this statement. He felt that Frances only passed reports to Lloyd George and spent her time waiting to cosset him. Sylvester shows in many instances that he believed that it was he himself who was indispensable, but Frances had shared the war years and she could give Lloyd George the benefit of her memory and her intelligence.

Having told Jennifer how enchanting Antibes was, Frances suggested taking her there, much as she had done to Portugal. Lloyd George was agreeable, but worried that this would interrupt their work. They came up with a compromise: Jennifer would go for a short holiday with them in Paris when they were en route for Antibes again in March.

Daringly, Lloyd George allowed himself to be photographed by the Press with Jennifer holding his hand, visiting Napoleon's tomb. An enterprising French photographer asked Sylvester for Jennifer's name and he managed to avoid giving an answer. He wrote that day in his diary: 'Frances looked on with evident satisfaction.'

They stayed at the Crillon and Lloyd George told Jennifer stories about Clemenceau, the Tiger, and his fierce attitude to the English. Sylvester described how at Clemenceau's house: 'Lloyd George did not want to go upstairs, but deferred to Jennifer's wishes.'

He made himself late for a meeting with the new French Prime Minister, Blum, because he had been enjoying showing Jennifer Versailles. He even introduced her to Blum.

The French newspapers published pictures of Lloyd George with Jennifer and one said that she was his grand-daughter, another that she was his small friend. It was safe to assume that his family would be very angry, but Frances did not care about that. She was glad to see Lloyd George showing the world his care for Jennifer, and they would avoid any ructions because she and Lloyd George were going on to work quietly again in Antibes.

Jennifer was brought home by Nanny Hackett who wrote to Frances:

> Dear Miss Stevenson,
> Thank you very much for a lovely time in Paris. I enjoyed every minute of it. Jennifer was very good coming home, but a bit disappointed because the sea was calm, so she is hoping to come to Antibes and that the sea will be very rough.
> Jennifer was very pleased that she did not have to pay duty on her toys. They asked if they had been used and I said, 'yes'. Jennifer looks up and says I haven't used the paints.
> I will find out over the week-end what she enjoyed most as she is sure to tell Elizabeth Mary everything.
> ...Jennifer thinks you are very lucky to have the Duke and Duchess of Windsor staying at the same hotel.

Frances also found it exciting that the Windsors were staying at her hotel. She even recorded the fact in her autobiography, but she does not say that they renewed their friendship nor indeed did she comment on their life together.

More significant for them both was the fact that, while they were in Antibes, two of the trustees who managed Lloyd George's political fund died within twenty four hours of each other, making for complications and concerns about what would become of the money. Frances wrote to Tweed saying that Lloyd George was talking about putting him on a retainer and asking him to vacate his room to save money. Tweed was very angry at the prospect of what would have amounted to dismissal, but in fact it came to nothing when a distinguished KC settled the issue and left the money safely in Lloyd George's hands.

It is interesting to see that Frances still felt so concerned for Tweed that she wanted to warn him about these developments. They had no personal contact with each other now but still occasionally met over political business.

As ever, the relationship between Lloyd George and Frances went up and down. Margaret may have been so stoical because she was saved from being expected to support and care for a very demanding and difficult man. Sylvester wrote that Frances had shown Lloyd George that she was disappointed when he revealed he would not be going away to Criccieth for Whitsun. When he questioned her about this, she admitted it and said she had been thinking: 'she could just hold out until then. This has brought him to his senses a little, but not for long. He was now always going round his orchard, counting thousands of small apples forming on the trees and making a computation of the crop. The truth is that he is after two girls on the estate.'

This was Sylvester's interpretation of events and his judgement was by no means infallible, but it is true to say that as Lloyd George got older, his lechery did not diminish and he seemed to lose control or the perception to see when there really was a need for restraint. Frances found herself often coping with distraught young secretaries or farm workers. She was later to say that at least Lloyd George always took no for an answer, but the trouble sometimes arose because young girls did not know how to say no to this enormously famous and distinguished elder statesman who was also their employer.

For Frances, a romantic and an idealist, this side of him must have been hard to accept. She loved and admired him, and as with many of the less pleasant aspects of life, she preferred to brush it away and avoid thinking about it. Perhaps at heart, her French blood gave her a feeling that 'men will be men'. Her father was not like that, but nor was he wildly successful or dynamic; and the two men she had been in love with had both been unfaithful to their wives.

She no longer considered that Lloyd George's family had any right to resent her. She knew of course that they did, but she wrote in private notes for her autobiography:

What surprises me is that not one of the children (except perhaps Gwilym) who were after all intelligent people, seemed to realise that they owed a certain amount of consideration for their father. They were prepared to use their mother against him. It was a form of blackmail. She was not unhappy. LG would have blamed himself if that had been so. He considered her – went to enormous lengths to be sure that she had all that was due to her as his wife – except of course himself. He gave her lovely presents (but this, I believe, is customary when husbands are unfaithful to their wives) and humoured her to an extent which was almost? undignified.

She put a cross through this and did not use it in her autobiography, but it shows how she viewed the situation towards the end of Margaret's life and why she found the children's hostility so hard to understand.

Sylvester, on the other hand, recorded at the time that Lord Dawson thought Margaret was far from reconciled to the situation and that in fact her unhappiness placed a great strain on her heart. All her children believed her to be very unhappy with the way things were, though children are perhaps not the best judges, as so often they believe their parents are happiest and best together. Margaret had a rich and fulfilling life apart from Lloyd George without the strains and dramas his presence imposed. She had her children and her beautiful garden, good work, the community, enormous respect, status and peace, but Frances's reluctance to believe that Margaret suffered as a result of her own relationship with Lloyd George may have been wishful thinking. However, the children did not perhaps fully appreciate that other women would have featured in Lloyd George's life whether Frances had been there or not, and she at least contained things to a large extent. Her discreet calm made sure there were no hideous scandals. Dame Margaret would also have found, if he had returned to live with her that he now not only wanted care and pampering; he was beginning to require a nurse. Frances, as ever, was prepared to fill any requirement he had of her.

On September 20th 1938, Jennifer began boarding full time at Penrhos College in Colwyn Bay. She had begun her boarding life as a weekly boarder at St Ursula's in Grayshott so that she should get used to it. Now, three weeks short of her ninth birthday, she set off for Wales. There were no tears though. She loved the new school and, half way through her first term, she became afraid that she would wake up and find she was only dreaming.[2] Nanny Hackett went on to be nanny to the Fox brothers of the film world and Jennifer was left with no nanny and no adult completely responsible for her when her mother was at Bron-y-de (though there were always adults living at Avalon). Frances was at Bron-y-de more or less constantly, though she still had to evacuate if any of the family arrived for the weekend.

Frances was distracted from worrying about Jennifer's settling in at school by the disturbing events surrounding Czechoslovakia.

On the 15th September, Chamberlain had flown to see Hitler at

[2] Conversation with Jennifer Longford

Berchtesgaden and accepted that Hitler should have the Sudetenland region along the Bohemian borders of Czechoslovakia. Lloyd George had always found the Czechoslovakian President, Benes, quite loathsome and felt that he had been greedy and stupid to take land principally populated by Germans. In principle, therefore, it was difficult to condemn Chamberlain for recognising something he had long held to be an inevitable development. However, he was by now being forced to recognise that Hitler needed containing, and easy collapse before his demands might be very dangerous. Lloyd George, along with many others, recognised that appeasement from apparent weakness failed to appease, but rather enticed. He voted against Munich. Having felt that Czechoslovakia had, to a large extent, brought this upon itself, he did not comment immediately, but on the 26th October he finally spoke out. He said Britain had shown herself unreliable, dishonourable and weak at Munich and, in the long run, cowering before a bully does not encourage the bully to go away.

On the 19th December Lloyd George spoke in Parliament, saying that the longer it took to stand firm and stop Hitler, the more powerful he would become and, in consequence, the more ambitious. He said that, if challenged, Hitler would draw back, at least for a while, and this would deprive him of yet one more easy triumph.

In Lloyd George's conclusion to his *War Memoirs* he had said there were three major considerations against any war. First that 'chance is the supreme judge of war and not Right'. He suggested that if Bismarck had led Germany in the First World War instead of Moltke, the outcome might have been victory for Germany. Then there was the personal suffering by the millions killed or mutilated to take into account. Finally there was the disruption of trade resulting in economic upheaval. These affected everyone and made war too costly. Yet on 11th September 1938 in the *Daily Express* he published the view that Britain and France should defend the rest of Czechoslovakia from further encroachments. He felt that a firm stand in time was more likely to avoid war than retreat before any challenge.

Now that he accepted that Germany was a threat again, he wanted rearmament and allies. In January 1939 he wrote an article saying that Russia would be a useful ally, as Germany and Russia were natural enemies. He and Frances often entertained the Russian Ambassador, Maisky, and Maisky warned Lloyd George that Russia might be driven, through fear of isolation, into making an accommodation with Germany. Lloyd George tried to warn the Government of this, but 'pinhead' Chamberlain was too frightened of Russia to play politics and win her over before Germany did.

At the end of March, when the weakened Czechoslovakian state finally collapsed and Germany annexed the Czech territories,

Chamberlain and his government woke up to the fact that a firm stand was going to have to be taken some time. They gave guarantees to protect Poland and Romania. Lloyd George discovered from Maisky that Russia had not been consulted or even informed of this, yet Russia was on the borders and would have been indispensable to any coherent campaign in Poland and Romania. Lloyd George questioned Chamberlain about this promise and heard that experts had shown him that Germany would not fight on two fronts, but Lloyd George pointed out that the Polish army was hardly strong enough to provide a reliable second front. Chamberlain said he thought Russia would come in ultimately, but Lloyd George knew this was a gamble, as he suspected from his conversations with Maisky that Russia might be making her own terms with Germany.

On the 3rd April Lloyd George attacked the government for walking into a trap and he tried to press them into making some kind of arrangement with Russia. Frances was present, as she usually was, in the Strangers' Gallery when he made this speech and she had, on this occasion, taken Jennifer to hear 'Taid' make an important contribution to the debate. Lady Oxford, Asquith's widow, was also there and Jennifer was startled by this elderly woman's coldness to her mother.

Frances had been suspicious of Hitler and German intentions for longer than Lloyd George, but it brought her no pleasure to see that he now shared her fears and that he regarded the present government as making a series of terrible and provocative errors. Neither of them could face the fact that another war was beginning to seem inevitable and Frances could not understand why the government did not see the truths that Lloyd George was drawing to their attention. She and Lloyd George were aghast when Chamberlain and Halifax visited Rome and toasted the King of Italy as Emperor of Abyssinia and then recognised Franco's fascist government victory in Spain less than a month later. The world was beginning to seem a very dangerous place and reports of bombing in Spain made it appear that a war would not be restricted to the armed forces. Civilians would be bombed.

Yet Frances could not quite bring herself to accept that doom and destruction were certain, although she did believe war would bring economic privation and danger for everyone. She took steps to ensure that Jennifer would be alright whatever happened, and tied Avalon up in a trust fund so that it would belong to the child for ever. Of course this did not cater for every contingency – but she hoped that it would.

Enormously distinguished and interesting people came to visit and dine with Lloyd George. A great many of them found Frances charming and some became her friends. Some of them asked her to persuade Lloyd George to make more of a stand, to try and get something done. Basil

Liddell Hart told her that weapons and training must be expanded if Britain were to be ready for a war and disheartened her by saying that the Government seemed to be ignoring his warnings. It was what she already perceived to be true – this government did not heed the warnings and she was afraid they would not be ready.

Life at home continued to be exasperating and difficult at times. She wanted Lloyd George to get up to London and change things, and though she thought the government was stubborn and that it was their fault they did not use Lloyd George, she also found that Lloyd George was ageing and had less energy and ability to influence events. As is so often the case with old age, controls were slipping, and Lloyd George's pernicious jealousy was coming out in stupid forms. He accused her of having an affair with the chauffeur and in June of 1939 there is a reference in Sylvester's diary to midnight visits from Lloyd George, who was checking that she did not have Victor Finney (the Secretary of the Council of Action) in her room.

Lloyd George was still being a glorious grandfather figure to Jennifer, however. When she was home for the summer holidays in 1939, instead of attending Parliament Lloyd George spent several days playing with Jennifer in a new caravan that had been bought as a moveable extra room on the estate, but was now given to Jennifer. Parliament had been discussing whether or not they should take a summer recess with war clouds looming, but Lloyd George was already taking his recess and Parliament could do as it liked.

Jennifer usually went to Felpham for a summer holiday by the sea and 1939 was no exception. Frances had bought a small bungalow there, and Jennifer, Elizabeth Mary, John Brook and Derek Goldsmith were there. Derek Goldsmith was a bit older than the other three and the son of an old Holloway friend of Frances who had been widowed in tragic circumstances. Her husband, a naval officer, had been drowned on holiday, swimming out to help two of his children who had got into difficulties with a boat. The older of the two children involved in this accident was John, killed himself a little later, testing a new plane for the Fleet Air Arm. Peter, the oldest son, was seriously mentally handicapped and in a home. By the summer of 1939 only Derek remained, destined for the navy (though not for an early death) but at seventeen still at school. Some adults were always at Felpham – not the same ones all the time – and there was usually a nanny or two, as well as a cook and a maid. Frances was there sometimes, especially when Lloyd George joined his family in Criccieth, but she was in Churt with Lloyd George when Hitler marched into Poland on September 1st 1939.

Jennifer remembers that they knew war must be close when the milkman told them, but the telephone was fortunately out of order and they had one last glorious swim, in a perfect sea – with a great swell. When they returned to the house, two cars were waiting to take them back to real life, and Jennifer never spent a holiday in Felpham again.

On September 3rd they were back at Avalon and listened to Chamberlain's broadcast at 11 am. The tension was broken when Jane, the Goldsmith's bull terrier, stood up with the rest of them when the National Anthem began.

Although Frances had been aware that war and probably bombs were going to come, she had not yet built any kind of shelter and Avalon was full of glass. The first warning was a false one (like so many in the early stages of the war), but it went off at 7 a.m. the following morning and the children were sent to Jennifer's small bathroom which was thought to have the least glass.

Frances had set off for London with Lloyd George on the morning of the 3rd and they heard the declaration of war on the car radio in Richmond Park. As they drove on to the House of Commons, sirens went off, due in fact to a small British aeroplane seen flying in from the coast. Lloyd George went down to the refuge carrying his gas mask and asked Sylvester to fetch Frances. Then the 'all-clear' sounded, Lloyd George came up and went into the House to offer his support and any help that was wanted from him to the Government.

He told Sylvester 'it was well worth while coming up to have had the experience of an air-raid warning'. Lloyd George had always been frightened of bombing. During the First World War, he had hurried down to the Foreign Office basement at the sound of a siren. Now he was seventy seven and not busy, so he had more time to dwell on the dangers and less self control. He knew he was physically inept (he never managed to tie his own shoe laces). He did not share Churchill's 'supreme physical courage' though his courage had never failed him during the First World War when it was actually needed. When he had visited the front, he had been nervous, but this had not prevented him from making a proper inspection.

Frances, in contrast, was astonishingly calm and faced bombing with insouciance. She probably had a less vivid imagination, but she also had an optimism that, for her, everything would work out for the best in the best of all possible worlds. (She would take sensible precautions, the prospect of bombs did not upset her – though she coped with others' fears sympathetically making Avalon a home for various refugees from the blitz: the Morris family and her sister Muriel spent most of the war years there.) She also wanted to protect her daughter as far as possible and she did consider evacuation. Her old friend Philip Kerr, now Marquis of Lothian, had become Ambassador to the United States. She admired his goodness and treasured his friendship, so she was very much touched when he offered to make a home for Jennifer in the United Stated for the duration of the War.[3]

Jennifer was now just short of ten and showing that she had a mind of her own, encouraged by Lloyd George and Frances, who both treated her from earliest childhood as a person with less experience than them, but with opinions that counted. Frances asked her what she would like to do, and Jennifer believes, without trying to influence her either way. The child chose to stay and that was agreed to, though she was packed off slightly early for term in Colwyn Bay, in case bombing started.

Lloyd George started building a deep shelter in the side of a hill in the grounds of Bron-y-de. There was an entrance near the front door, and from there you descended a long flight of steps to an underground 'home' equipped with bedrooms, a sitting room, bathrooms and a kitchen. The rooms were lined with split tree trunks, comfortably furnished and quite warm and dry. The main entrance was below the house. Jennifer found she was expected to sleep there in the school holidays; for a short time, she enjoyed the adventure. After she had pneumonia in 1942 she asked if she could stop sleeping underground and this was agreed. By the end of the war, it was not much used by anyone except for storage of all Lloyd George's papers, but it was always made available by Lloyd George to anyone who wanted to use it. Part of Lloyd George's idea in building it was that, in case of invasion, quite a number of people could shelter there, but Jennifer does not remember anyone except Lloyd George and his staff at Bron-y-de using it. When bombs did not immediately begin to fall Jennifer was allowed to return home from school as normal and spend Christmas at home.

In the February of 1940 Tweed was taken seriously ill and had to go to Hendon hospital, but it had seemed that he was recovering and was sufficiently alert to write a tribute to Lloyd George, now celebrating fifty years as an MP. On the morning of the 30th April he was sitting up in bed, smoking a pipe, when he suffered a final stroke.

Among Frances's papers is an album in which Miss Russell had carefully cut out and stuck in the centre of each page every obituary she could find. In them he was described as 'a brilliantly witty conversationalist whose air of cynicism hardly served to conceal his genuine kindness of heart. He had a host of friends who will deeply regret his passing.'

Both Frances and Muriel were very distressed. Frances had managed to visit him secretly, but made no secret of her attendance at his cremation ceremony. She dressed in deep mourning, as did Muriel. Lloyd George had not been to a funeral of any kind for some time, but at the

[3] ibid

last moment he turned up for the ceremony with his daughter Olwen. Sylvester claimed to have been shocked:

> He is always most particular about his attire on all occasions. Today must have been a studied insult to the dead, and intended to persecute the living in the person of Frances. He wore a blue suit, a blue over-coat, a blue hat, with a dark tie that was not even black. His face was white – knowing him he was het up. He sat on the front seat, well towards the left. As he looked towards the pulpit on the right, he could see Frances in the second row and watched her every movement and reaction ...
>
> Afterwards, on the telephone Frances told me that he was literally persecuting her to death. He had twitted her about being upset. He wondered if she would be upset when he died. He criticised her deep mourning. In the end, and unwisely I think, she said she had confessed to LG that she had been very fond of Tweed, that Mrs Tweed had been very kind to her and had taken her home, where they had had a frank talk.[4]

In Frances's papers there is a letter from Tweed's daughter, Wilma, but signed by herself, her brother Fred, and her mother Louise on 6th May 1940.

> Dear Miss Stevenson,
> Mother, Fred and I wish to thank you very deeply for your very charming and sympathetic letter, and also for the beautiful flowers.
> It is a great solace to us all to know that you share equally with us our grief at this time and we do sincerely trust that you will keep your promise to visit us.
> Mother – and all of us – are sorry that your sister's health is poor just now but hopes her recovery will soon be complete.
> We are happy to have had the opportunity of knowing you and trust that we will continue to do so.

Very shortly afterwards, on May 8th, Lloyd George made his last great parliamentary contribution. The spring campaign in Norway had been a fiasco and the British troops had been withdrawn. Chamberlain had to face the house with an explanation. On the second day of discussion, Chamberlain appealed to friends he had in the House and, by reducing the debate to a challenge for personal loyalty, he made a major error. Lloyd George seized the opportunity and dramatically said:

[4] Sylvester Diary op cit

He has appealed for sacrifice ... I say solemnly that the Prime Minister should give an example of sacrifice, because there is nothing that can contribute more to victory in this war than that he should sacrifice the seals of office.

Chamberlain resigned the next day and Churchill became Prime Minister just as the Germans invaded Belgium, Holland and Luxembourg, and the war began in earnest.

Frances was hopeful that Lloyd George would take office in Churchill's cabinet, but when no immediate offer came through, Lloyd George started to say that Churchill was going to be too influenced by the Chamberlain crowd and would do no better than his predecessor. Frances berated him for being negative and said she thought he almost wanted them to fail because he disliked Chamberlain and his followers so much. On the 28th May Churchill finally asked Lloyd George to join the War Cabinet, subject to Chamberlain's agreement. Lloyd George understandably replied that, since this was not a proper offer, he would not consider it. On the 4th June the proper offer came, but Lloyd George replied to it: 'If you cannot stand up to Neville Chamberlain and Margesson how can you stand up to Hitler?'

Frances and Beaverbrook carried out a campaign to persuade him to take up the offer of office. Frances said it was his patriotic duty. On the 10th June Italy declared war on Britain and France, and on 14th June Paris fell. During the night of 19th June Frances was telephoned by Brendan Bracken speaking from Downing Street and asking to speak to Lloyd George. She told him that Lloyd George was asleep and could not be disturbed. She knew by then that he would not take office, that he was determined absolutely to stay out of this cabinet. She was very unhappy. She knew people thought he was defeatist – an English Petain, and she desperately wanted him to put the rumour to rout. She felt 'he should make any sacrifice to help his country in her time of need', but Lloyd George had made up his mind.

Later Frances came to the conclusion that Lloyd George was beginning to suffer from his last and fatal illness and that he knew he would not be strong enough to do the job properly. In this way she reconciled herself to his inaction.

On the 26th July Tweed's will was published and the press discovered that he had left £2,000 to Frances, 'in partial repayment of a loss incurred on an investment taken on my advice.' He also left £1,000 to Muriel and £500 to Jennifer. The attendant publicity made it inevitable that Lloyd George would get to hear about it, so Frances informed him herself. More than a week later things were still 'so difficult' at Churt according to Sylvester. Finally, on the 22nd August, he left for Criccieth and, very unusually, stayed there for almost four months except for four days in September when he intended to go to Westminster, but did not in fact leave Churt. The reason for this long stay in Criccieth appears, however not to have been because of Tweed's legacy, but because the bombs falling in Churt seriously frightened him.

When the bombing of England began, air raids over Churt were at their most serious. Much more so than later when the bombs were bigger. It was suspected that the frequency of these raids was because German pilots, afraid of the anti-aircraft defences round London, tended to drop their bombs before reaching the capital and then turn for home. A number fell on the farm, but the only casualties were two pigs and their sty. A bomb also probably damaged one of the medieval fish ponds in the grounds of Bron-y-de – a set of three built originally by the monks of Waverley Abbey. One evening there were several people to dinner at Avalon and the guests heard seven bombs drop of the usual 'stick' of eight, coming nearer and nearer. Gwilym Lloyd George was in the middle of an entertaining story and could not understand why everybody dived under the table just as he reached the punch line. Nothing happened then, but a day or two later the bottom of the one of the big ponds collapsed. After these early problems, the German planes were fitted with cameras to record where the bombs were dropped, and they had very few more in Churt.

Frances felt that if Lloyd George had had a proper job to do he would not have had time to think about his fear. She was relieved when he took his panics and stubbornness away and inflicted them on Margaret for a while. Her letters told him all about the bombs and encouraged him to stay away.

> I do feel very cut off from you at the moment. On the other hand, I am glad you are away while things are as lively as they are, and yet I am glad that I am here in case anything should happen which should require a decision.

Sylvester recorded that:

> Megan told me that Dame Margaret had had a terrible time with LG in Wales. That he thought of nothing but air raids, that he had got them completely on his mind and that they were afraid he would make himself really ill.

It was Margaret whose health was suffering.

Frances tried to accept that Lloyd George was too old and frightened to enter the government and she took consolation from his contribution to farming. He bought a beautiful Queen Anne house in Llanystumdwy called Ty Newydd with the intension of converting the land around it into a thriving farm on Bron-y-de lines. He also wrote encouraging articles with titles such as 'Hitler cannot frighten us' in the Sunday Express on 11th August and 'Freedom let's fight for it' on 14th August in the Daily Express. In addition he declared in the *Sunday Express* on 25th August 1940 that the Channel would be as difficult for Hitler to cross as it had been for Napoleon.

In private, however, he had taken to listening to German broadcasts and in particular the propaganda put out by Lord Haw Haw. If he had to miss one, he asked that it be taken down and typed up for him to read. Sylvester said, in exasperation, that Lloyd George cared only for Wales and did not care if England was defeated, an opinion which sits ill with the man who had shown such a passion to win in the First World War. Nor does it fit his love of the land, the countryside and aspects of English literature. He loved Cobbett, and he had chosen to settle and live principally in the South East of England. In his earliest years he had sought to free Wales from English domination, but he had never wanted separation. The truth is that he would have liked to rescue Britain again, by tremendous feats of ingenuity, and he was not altogether happy to watch a younger man doing it.

He was jealous of Churchill and he believed it was quite possible that one day he would be called upon to retrieve the situation. He received reports from Sylvester, Hankey and others which supported the idea that Churchill was not able to cope. He heard that Churchill got drunk, would not listen to the advice of others and dogmatically insisted on his own way. There is every indication that Lloyd George felt he should hold himself in readiness to rescue his country when other methods failed. When Lord Lothian died unexpectedly on December 12th 1940, Lloyd George was asked if he would like to be Ambassador in the United States (far from the bombs) and he refused. He made out that he was refusing for health reasons, but to Cecil King he said he wanted to be where the war was decided. On the 22nd October he had written to Frances that Beaverbrook was 'ill and depressed over the situation' and 'Winston entirely in the hands of sycophants who feed and fan his illusions.' Beaverbrook had sent a messenger to Lloyd George telling him that he 'should concoct some plan for saving the country'

Lloyd George returned to London for a discussion with Churchill on December 15th 1940 and thereafter remained based at Churt until September 1944.

Frances rose to the demands placed upon her. She was supervising the farm, reassuring frightened employees, and she even found time to rescue her youngest sister, Muriel, and instal her at Avalon. Muriel had found the strain of the London bombing too much to bear, and had stopped eating or going to work. Her doctor had advised her to spend six months in the country. She had been appalled, but in fact six months in Churt reconciled her to life there and she never moved away.

Muriel worked in the Bron-y-de farm office, ran the household at Avalon, looked after the poultry – chickens, ducks, geese and turkeys – and cared for Jennifer, who was now eleven and more interesting to Muriel than small children ever were.

Jennifer's school had been evacuated to Chatsworth, as Colwyn Bay was thought to be so safe that government offices were installed in the school buildings there. From there she had written to Lloyd George asking why he was not joining the War Cabinet. From Criccieth, on November 11th 1940, the twenty second anniversary of his peace he wrote to her:[5]

> Darling Jennifer
> I have been thrilled by the description given by your Mummy of the beauties of that grand old English country house and its surround-ings. It must be a wonderful place in which to dwell at a time of life when one forms deep and abiding impressions. I was also glad to hear from her that you are working hard and steadily at your lessons.
> Your letter interested me very much. You put your points intelli-gently and clearly. You want to know why I have declined to join the War Cabinet when I was given the Offer. I have asked Mummy to give you my reasons when you meet this weekend. But I can give you just a hint – for yourself alone. You are not to repeat it to anyone else except of course, your Mummy.
> 1. I do not believe in the way we entered the war – nor in the methods by which it has been conducted. We have made blunder after blunder and are still blundering. Unless there is a thorough change of policy we shall never win.
> 2. I do not believe in the way or in the personnel with which the War Cabinet is constituted. It is totally different to the War Cabinet set up in the last War. It is not a War directorate in the real sense of the term. There is therefore no real direction.
> I am convinced that unless there is a real change in these two matters it would be a mistake for me to join up with the present lot. If I entered the Cabinet I should soon have to resign because of total disagreement with the plans and methods of this lot and that would do no good.
> There in brief you have my reasons.
> I had experience in directing a great war and I helped to win the

[5] Jennifer Longford's private papers

victory. I am unhappy at the way things are done today and I wish I could be in a position to alter the course of events.

Love and kisses from Taid.

On 21st November, Lloyd George still seemed to intend staying on indefinitely at Criccieth. Frances managed therefore to visit Jennifer and stay nearby in Rowsley, near Bakewell, at the Peacock Inn. Lloyd George wrote to her: 'It is good for you that you had stored away a reserve of optimism during your weekend from our inexhaustible fount of joy and delight'.

He was being a thoroughly disruptive guest in his wife's house, causing a gardener to resign and shocking the workmen by swearing in Welsh.[6] When Lloyd George came back to Surrey to deal with Churchill's offer he stayed on over Christmas and into January, but he had left Margaret ill with her broken hip and this was not repairing as it should. In January Lloyd George was contacted because she had become worse and the local doctor was concerned. Lloyd George said a specialist should be sent, but at that point made no plan to go himself.

Lord Dawson travelled to Wales with Sylvester to see Dame Margaret but the snow and drifts prevented them from getting further than Bangor. Sylvester recorded in his diary that he understood Dawson to say that taking office would be too great a strain for Lloyd George now.

If he entered the Government and died at his post that would be a great ending, but the danger was that he might, through lack of physical courage, become a failure and that would ruin his reputation.

Sylvester also recorded that Dawson thought Dame Margaret was suffering with her heart: 'L.G.'s treatment of her and his carryings-on had no doubt worried her and this would undoubtedly aggravate the trouble and speed the end.'

It now became evident that Margaret was very ill indeed and that Lloyd George would have to set out at once if he wanted to see her again, despite bitter weather and deep snow. In Wales the car ran into drifts and he did not manage to arrive until January 21st. Margaret had died the previous morning. He was shattered and said she had been his 'great old pal'. They had shared so much from the early days and were connected by long standing ties. No one could now fill the special place she had held.

Frances had no more suspicion than Lloyd George that Margaret was so ill. She travelled with him as far as Broadway in the Cotswolds and on paper headed 'The Lygon Arms' she wrote to Jennifer that 'Taid on his

[6] Sylvester Diary op cit

way to Wales. He had to go quite suddenly, as his wife is not at all well. If only it had been earlier in the week, I could have stayed at Bakewell.'

She had delivered Jennifer back to school and returned to Churt to be with Lloyd George for his birthday on January 17th. The letter is chatty and cheerful, saying how delighted 'Taid' had been with his 'witchball and your little note.' Gwilym and Edna, his wife, had been for the weekend and had been asking after Jennifer.

Jennifer was now eleven and Frances went on to say:

> I expect by now you have started work in real earnest. Don't forget to write me a line every week, darling, to say how you are getting on. I am so glad your new form mistress is nice. Don't forget:-
> a)   To be a good girl (as good as you can, that is).
> b)   To wash your face.
> c)   To clean your teeth.
> d)   To brush your hair (Cleanliness comes next to godliness).

The following Sunday there is another letter to Jennifer and, oddly enough, Frances does not even refer to Margaret's death. She always tried to give people what they wanted and she usually wrote jolly as well as caring letters to Jennifer. Nonetheless she would normally tell her about casualties or death among their friends and acquaintances. Perhaps she just did not know how to approach the subject.

> My little Darling,
> I wonder if you are snowed up in Derbyshire? I hear stories of huge snow-drifts in the Midlands, and people not being able to proceed along the roads; and Taid has been unable to return, as he intended to do, because of the snow in Wales. And as he got stuck in a snowdrift, on the edge of a precipice going down, he is not anxious to repeat the experience. All being well however, he is coming back tomorrow.
> I am hoping that perhaps you are having some tobogganing, or fun in the snow, as a compensation for all the inconvenience. Did the skates arrive safely? And have you been able to get someone to teach you.
> Grannie is much better you will be glad to hear, and we are hoping she will not get another attack.
> The usual send their love. Paddy is very well, but Mirren tried to take her for a walk, but instead of which she took Mirren for a walk! Last weekend Auntie Elsie was putting her back in her shed, and she suddenly leapt past and jumped out again; and Auntie Elsie and Humphry (who was here) chased her all round Well Field before they caught her.

And on to discuss gym slips and stockings and the usual concerns of a country coping with rationing for clothes.

Jennifer seems to have started to keep her mother's letters and when they came back with her in the holidays, Frances boxed them in files along with Jennifer's to her. They help build up a picture of a domestic and social life with concerns of war time very much revolving around what they cannot buy or how to travel. Little reference is made to political developments, but Jennifer rarely discussed politics with her mother then. It was always Taid who encouraged her to think and discuss events. Frances was being the gentle guiding mother who told domestic anecdotes she thought would amuse. The letters include some serious news, the occasional death or injury, and many reports of Louise's declining health. June 18th 1941 she reported: 'Granny is about the same, but still very ill.'

In the same letter she wrote, 'Taid sends his fond love. He is very well indeed – but very lazy!'

Another letter in May describes how:

Avalon is looking lovely now and this morning Taid and I walked over three new fields. They are delightful and very sheltered, and in one of them is the largest pear tree I have ever seen. It is so tall and Taid thinks it must be at least a hundred years old. There is also a spring in one of the fields where we will be able to grow water cress.

Lloyd George was frequently mentioned in these letters but usually in connexion with the farm or the countryside. At the end of March she wrote: 'Taid and I go up to London tomorrow for the day. He *may* make a speech in the House of Commons. I hope he will.'

In another letter Frances wrote how 'awful it is to say goodbye', and 'how I shall miss ringing you up tonight.' From Bron-y-de to Avalon she could say good night to Jennifer on the telephone, but boarding school did not allow such indulgence.

In addition to what she called the 'rabbit, goat and other news' Frances frequently referred to stamps or autographs she had acquired because she thought Jennifer would enjoy them. While she could not spend much time with Jennifer, she could at least devote a lot of thought to her and use her talent for generosity and thinking of appropriate gifts for people. Frequently she assured Jennifer that she was her greatest love. Many of the letters had 'no news' or mentioned how dull things were, but she was reconciling herself to this. She had been told that Lloyd George might have a growth and that he was definitely not up to ministerial office, so she settled down to the role of nurse and general factotum.

She also decided that, now that Margaret was dead, there was no need to disappear every time any of the family came to Bron-y-de. She accepted that Lloyd George should not turn round and marry her at once, but she did feel that her presence in his life need no longer be denied.

Frances had no understanding of why Megan, in particular, should continue to be so bitter towards her. It is ironic perhaps that Megan did. She had herself been having an affair with a married man for the past five years, but several things conspired to make her particularly sensitive at this time. Her adored mother had just died, and she believed that Frances had made Margaret very unhappy. She also felt that Frances had been deeply treacherous, having been welcomed hospitably by the family as an employee and then as a friend. Worse still, Margaret had begged, on her death bed, that Megan should give up Philip Noel Baker, her lover, giving her the pain of trying to fulfill her promise. On top of that, her beloved father looked very unwell and frail. As if all this were not enough, she had just forfeited political advancement and the country was at war so she was having a difficult time.[7] She certainly had reason for bitterness, but her hatred for Frances was rooted in more than that. Frances had originally come into the family home as Megan's teacher. Megan had liked her and felt she was her friend, not just as a child but right up until 1921 when she was nineteen. A letter from Megan in the summer of 1920 shows that she was still enormously attached to Frances and still called her the old nickname of Pussy.[8]

Dear Puss,

Scuse the notepaper, but the house doesn't boast any better – the family having had a craze for letter writing these last days.

My goodness me! It seems that I have been to sleep ever since I came here. – The weather's been too bad for tennis or anything else really – we have had sunshine, but then the rain in between times has made the ground too wet for play and everything else uncertain.

I have not done anything out of the ordinary or held converse with anyone out of the ordinary since I have come down here my life has been an uninterrupted hum-drum.

I spent a few days with Marjorie Brownhill and her father and mother who have been staying at Llandudno, and spent a weekend with Mair, but as to anything ... *nothing* has happened.

Still the weather has looked up considerably since Monday and I have been basking in the sun all day with my dog.

I suppose you have been working hard since your return from Lucerne.

[7] *A Radical Life* – Mervyn Hughes Hutchinson
[8] FLG Papers

By the way I'm enclosing two snapshots of 'Papa' that he might like to see – the one with Lady Greenwood is rather good, and worth enlarging I think!

It has relieved me considerably to let off steam about the weather and people in general to you. Thank you for being – I hope – a patient – and sympathetic listener.

Cheer up – (unreadable) Au revoir, Megan

It was because Megan had trusted Frances and genuinely liked her that she felt so betrayed and that her loathing went so deep. Apart from Gwilym, all Margaret's children hated Frances believing she had caused their mother so much pain. They felt she had been kindly treated by their mother and had repaid her by taking their father away. Her soft, gentle manner and calm only served to antagonise the lively and ebullient Lloyd George children, but the others were not as vitriolic or persistent in their bitterness as Megan.

In Frances's preparatory notes for her autobiography, she had a page written about Megan.

It was not until after LG took over Chequers in 1921, that a difference occurred in our relations. Dame M. did not go there very much and I think Megan expected to play hostess when she was there. But as her appearances were very uncertain, the staff relied on me for instructions. One Sunday at lunch time the butler came to me with a message from Lord Riddell asking if he could come down for the night. I naturally referred to LG who gave the reply that Riddell would be welcome. I noticed the look on Megan's face when she was not consulted, and after that our relations became much more strained and she was often quite rude to me. Some of her friends had been present on the occasion of the butler's gaffe, and I realised that she was being influenced by them, some of whom resented my position with LG.'

For Frances to suggest that Megan disliked her purely because she had wanted to play hostess at Chequers reflects her own animosity to Megan. When Sylvester was interviewed in 1989 he said that, in his opinion, no one would ever have suspected Frances of conducting a sexual relationship with anybody: 'You would take her to be a prim school teacher,'[9] and Frances could be puritanical and rather judgemental. At first Frances found Megan an 'enchanting child' but in her diary, before the rupture in their relations, Frances began to write critically of her. In 1917 she

[9] Interview with A J Sylvester in 1986

wrote that Megan was 'getting rather artificial' and in 1920 recording that Megan had sent a 'scrappy wire' to LG for his birthday and failed to keep her promise to return to school.

Once Megan realised the true state of affairs between her father and Frances, she used all her ingenuity to try and break things up, or at least make things harder for them. On one occasion she persuaded her mother to go down to Chequers from Criccieth, saying that Lloyd George needed her there to entertain the Crown Prince of Japan. Margaret had not intended to go and Lloyd George did not expect her, but Megan persuaded Margaret to leave Criccieth, much to Margaret's inconvenience, to go and play hostess for the Whitsun weekend.

Frances was left with nothing to do for the long weekend and wrote in her diary: 'D Frightfully angry with Megan, but of course he hasn't much of a case.'

Megan was so angry and upset that she was really something of a liability. Neither Frances or Lloyd George could be sure that she would not expose them just to show her father just how angry she was. Frances could not join Lloyd George in Geneva when he was Prime Minister in 1922 because Megan was there and was likely to leave in open displeasure if Frances turned up. On 30th April Lloyd George had written to Frances:

> Megan is getting sick of this place. Worrying her mother for permission to return to London. It wouldn't do for you to come out the moment they go. On the other hand if you came whilst they are here Megan is quite capable of taking advantage of that to say she insists upon returning because you are here. That would create a first class scandal ...

Once Lloyd George was out of power, Megan's animosity was less of a threat and gradually she had to put up with the fact that her father chose to spend most of the year with Frances rather than her mother. There was nothing she could do about it, except to make it plain to Frances that she loathed her and would work against her if she could. The opportunity had now come. Frances expected now to become Lloyd George's wife at last. Megan was determined to do everything in her power to prevent her.

In April 1941 Sylvester wrote:

> There is a terrific row in progress between LG and Megan. Since Dame Margaret's death, Frances remains at Bron-y-de during the weekend. Megan saw her the other day and as a consequence, just ignored her

father and refused to speak to him. Megan was very bitter in talking to me.

Lloyd George had promised Frances that, should he ever be free to do so, he would marry her. Naturally he could not marry her immediately after Margaret's death. It would have looked most unseemly and was not what Frances wanted. What she did want was to know that he would marry her some time sooner rather than later. Megan was implacable in her ferocious and bitter opposition to any marriage plan.

Frances told Jennifer that she and Taid planned to marry and Jennifer was delighted, but time passed and nothing further occurred. Her mother continued to be Miss Stevenson and letters continued to contain no more than domestic details of a humdrum nature. Jennifer could not realise that her mother was involved in the fiercest battle of her life.

On the surface, Frances appeared gentle and submissive, but there was a core of steel and in this battle she was fighting for what she believed was her rightful position. She had been self effacing and discreet for nearly thirty years. She wanted to claim her place by Lloyd George's side and she felt that Megan was being mean and irrational.

In the spring of 1942 Frances asked Sylvester to find out about the procedure for a Baptist marriage. There was also talk of Lloyd George taking Frances and Jennifer to his new home in Llanystumdwy for Easter. Megan announced that 'If LG takes Frances and Jennifer to Ty Newydd' it would be an insult to the memory of her mother. Frances asked Sylvester to let Megan know that marriage was planned. In July she started wearing a diamond ring on her engagement finger. By November Lloyd George and Frances were quarrelling about it. Lloyd George had been told by his son that remarriage would be unpopular with the people of Criccieth, not to mention the children. Lloyd George said that the present circumstances suited him and he saw no need to change them. Frances told Sylvester that she had reminded him of chances she had had to be married which she had given up. 'That is all done with,' LG had replied. 'Honourable people think you should do it,' Frances had said. 'There are no honourable people,' LG had said.'

Frances did not give up hope. She asked Sylvester to continue his research into 'ways and means' and he sent her information telling her about the £25 special licence and how to set about a registry office marriage.

Less that a week later, her friend and lawyer, John Morris, advised her to leave Lloyd George so he could make up his own mind. He was now so dependant on her that her absence might have been expected to bring him quickly to heel, but Frances did not want to take such extreme measures. She could not even tear herself away to visit Jennifer at half term, writing to say that she could not leave Lloyd George when he needed her.

Jennifer had had pneumonia in early 1942 and it had been decided that she should go to school further south and nearer home. In September 1942 she had gone to Headington in Oxford, where she had a fresh start and found that she made friends with the girls much more easily. On the other hand she was heartily disliked by her house mistress, but as usual did not tell Frances.

Frances had problems of her own. She said, 'LG is an old man. I do not like to bring pressure on him.' and she did not resort to the powerful threat that she might leave him, but quietly and determinedly she did continue to work towards being married.

Lord Dawson was brought into the troubled arena. He interviewed Frances, rather as if she had been applying for a job, and reported that, 'She was an extremely well preserved woman who would be acceptable in any place or circumstance.'

Unfortunately he also found Megan 'Irreconcilably opposed to the idea' and saying that 'it would sully her mother's memory'. If the event took place it would mean a definite break between Megan and her father.

Two full years after Margaret's death was Lloyd George's eightieth birthday and he had said he would celebrate it by marrying Frances, but just as he had already shown himself too old to relish political battles and enter the government for the duration of the war, he was now too old to confront Megan. She made such a fuss at the prospect of sitting with Frances at his birthday lunch that she allowed her to believe the marriage plan was dropped. Lord Dawson wrote to Megan:

> The birthday would seem to offer an opportunity for a gesture – because other members of the family will be going down – there will be the occasion to carry off any difficulties. And if the gesture were made it cannot be doubted it would make a great difference to your father's comfort and happiness. If you make the gesture, as I hope you will, it must be warm and really friendly in its quality. It need not last long, but you could make the short time Miss S. was there an occasion and then as it would be a family party she would probably go from the room on her own.
>
> Now I want you to listen to me. I both understand and sympathise with your feelings and especially those which surround your mother's memory, but I am sure she would wish nothing but that the evening of your father's life should be made as smooth as possible. He is in need today of physical care and is likely in this respect to become more dependent in the future. Miss S. fills this role and there is no one else at once fitted, available and acceptable for this duty.

If it be a fact that what you feared is off, as it appears to be, it must in justice be said she has now made a great sacrifice and from what she said to me I think she has made things easy and put aside the bitterness of her disappointment ... You are not called upon to be a friend but only to be kindly, in the way you understand so well, when you meet her in the capacity as a necessary helpmate for your father today.

Knowing that you were brought up a Christian there can be no question that you should make this gesture ... For it is a matter of Christian charity for your father's sake. He has changed his intention mainly for you. From my deep attachment to you I do urge you on the next suitable occasion to make that gesture and make it generously and you will never regret it.[10]

Megan responded to this appeal and attended the lunch – perhaps because she believed, as Lord Dawson seems to have thought, that Frances had given up any idea of marriage.

She had not.

In the Easter holidays Jennifer asked her mother what had happened to the marriage plan and Frances told her to ask Taid. She did this when she and Lloyd George were standing by the gate that led from Bron-y-de grounds to the first of the orchards. Beyond it was a long path with great cherry trees on either side, the object of one of Lloyd George's farming experiments: when the trees were in blossom and when frost was feared, round flattish braziers were lit at the bottom of each tree.[11] Lloyd George roared with what sounded like very embarrassed laughter at her question and said something fairly non-committal, but the marriage did finally take place six months later.

On Friday the 23rd October the wedding was arranged in a registry office, very quietly to avoid attention. The night before, Megan telephoned and insisted on talking to Lloyd George, threatening to arrive in person if he would not talk to her. He was such a long time on the telephone that Frances went to see if he was alright and returned to fetch Sylvester, saying she thought Megan would make her father ill. Sylvester realised that Lloyd George was agitated and exhausted and relieved him of the telephone. He quoted Megan as having said to him, 'People will laugh at him. I couldn't bear people to laugh at him. He says he'll see me next week, but he doesn't realise he wont, he will absolutely break my heart if he does it.'

None of the children attended the ceremony. Jennifer came home from school for the weekend and was allowed to answer telephone calls from

[10] 15 January 1943; in National Library of Wales
[11] Jennifer Longford memories

the press, providing she pretended to be a secretary – she was on no account to say she was Frances's daughter. Gwilym and Edna did come down in the evening for champagne and a quiet, very subdued celebration. Sylvester and Muriel were the witnesses. Frances described how she felt in her autobiography:

> The whole countryside was bathed in sunshine, as was my heart, and a deep contentment possessed me; contentment, but not the thrills of the usual bride. Our real marriage had taken place thirty years before.

Jennifer, now fourteen, acquired five nephews and two nieces, all older than she was and all invariably pleasant to her.

Frances wrote to Megan shortly after this victory:

> My dear Megan,
>
> I hope you will read this letter through as it is written in all sincerity to ask if you will not reconsider your attitude towards your Father's marriage with me. I am so anxious that you shall not commit yourself to a permanent and irrevocable estrangement from him, both for the sake of his happiness and your own, and that is why I am sure you would not forgive yourself if you were to be the cause of any sadness in his last years and I know you would never regret it if you could bring yourself to put your own feelings on one side in this matter and to act generously as I believe you are capable of doing.
>
> I am depriving you of nothing in becoming his wife – neither of his affection, nor of any material benefits now or in the future. You must realise how much you owe to him, and how an estrangement would hurt him. Even if you cannot see your way to burying the past as far as I am concerned, I hope you will make this concession to him and so establish yourself even more firmly in his heart.[12]

Megan did not reply. Nor did she forgive.

Frances, however, was Mrs Lloyd George at last and she was proud and happy to be so. Of course not everything was perfect. The family's hostility was unpleasant but she was safe in the harbour of marriage at last and felt they could not hurt her there. Worse than the problems encountered with his first family was the fact that Lloyd George was now clearly ageing and unwell, but he was not in great pain and both Frances and Lloyd George seemed entirely contented in their new marriage.

Ty Newydd had been renovated but was still sparsely furnished and not quite a home. Jennifer spent a couple of weeks in the summer of 1944

---

[12] 7 November 1943; in National Library of Wales

with Muriel and her Canadian lover, Walker Kayes. Major Kayes was a in the Canadian Army, stationed near Churt. Muriel was sure he would divorce his wife and marry her as soon as he returned to Canada; he did not. He was a delightful companion, good looking and gifted and had been spending as much time as he could at Avalon, long before Jennifer moved out. She once told Frances, in a rare confidence, that she looked upon him as a substitute father. Frances was angry – not (Jennifer thinks) because she saw anyone else in the role, but because she thought of herself as being entirely adequate.

Finally, in the autumn of 1944, Lloyd George, Frances and the secretaries Ann Parry and Sylvester went up to Llanystumdwy to stay at Ty Newydd. It was intended that it should just be a fortnight's holiday, but Lloyd George was very sad to say goodbye to Bron-y-de and kept delaying his departure. He did not at any point acknowledge that he might be dying, but perhaps he did know in his heart that he would never return. Eventually, on the 19th September 1944, he managed to set off for his homeland.

Dame Margaret had left Brynawelon to Megan and she was therefore living just a couple of miles away. Sylvester telephoned her to ask if she would see Lloyd George. She replied that he could come and see her, but that he must come alone. He did so and they had a delightful reunion walking around the garden together, but Megan would not visit Ty Newydd.

While this personal war continued with no obvious end in sight, the second World War was clearly drawing to an end, and discussion was rife about what should be done in a post-war world. Lloyd George felt strongly that he still had a contribution to make with lessons learnt from the First World War – but he also had to recognise how frail he had become. He now realised that he would not be up to fighting another election.

Initially he sent Sylvester to London to sound out the Tory and Labour parties about the possibility of his standing unopposed. Locally the parties were against this idea, so Lloyd George recognised that if he wanted any kind of political platform he should accept a title and sit in the House of Lords. Had life peerages then existed, one would have been ideal for him. He did not want to start a dynasty of aristocrats and Frances had obtained the title she wanted when she became Mrs Lloyd George, but since he needed to be in the parliament somehow, they accepted that the House of Lords was better than nothing. Lloyd George did have his reservations. He had been so scornful of the House of Lords and he had liked being the cheeky outsider, but he could not face life without a political future.

Jennifer arrived home from school on the 20th December. She had been given a Father Christmas outfit to bring down with her and a goose for

Christmas lunch – each of these in large cardboard boxes handed over by Bartling, who worked for Lloyd George as a messenger in the House of Commons. Luckily for Jennifer Bartling went with her to the station. Everything was late because of fog and Bartling and Jennifer stood on the platform at Euston station listening to the occasional crash of a V2 for more than two hours. When the train arrived, Bartling leapt on the train before it stopped to get Jennifer a seat. There was such a crowd that there was considerable difficulty in getting him off and Jennifer (with her suitcase, Father Christmas outfit and goose) on. In the end there were seventeen people sitting and standing in a compartment for eight. They compared notes as to where they were going, Jennifer found that the train was going to Manchester, not Chester. However she was able to change at Crewe (with her suitcase, goose and Father Christmas outfit), and Dyer the chauffeur, met her with the car at Chester. She was by then seven hours late and they then had to find their way over the mountains in the dark and thick fog with no signposts because of the war. Dyer relied on the wind blowing the fog to tell him he was going in the right direction. The Father Christmas outfit was worn by Sylvester at the school party. Lloyd George made a little speech and totally forgot what he had been going to say in the middle of it. Frances found it a dreadfully sad occasion.

Settling into the Welsh community was not proving too hard for Frances at this time. A letter from her sister Muriel in October for her birthday on the 7th ended by saying, 'I am so glad you are having such a pleasant time in Wales. It will do you good. You will probably decide to spend the winter there.' Everyone was aware that Lloyd George was very ill and they were kind and helpful. Megan was aloof at first but eventually she was persuaded by the local Doctor Prytherch that it would distress her dying father very much if she continued to refuse to enter the house while Frances was there. She therefore behaved with reasonable courtesy and restraint, visiting her father regularly. Jennifer who had never met her before and had never heard a single nice thing about her, was charmed and amazed.

Sylvester told Frances he wanted to return to London. He recorded that she appealed to him to be loyal. 'She thought it would be to my advantage to do so. She wondered whether it was not my duty.'

He exploded and said that he did not think it was his duty to give up all his 'contacts and my parliamentary position' to run a 'thirty-seven acre farm' and as to loyalty and duty, his friends had told him he was a fool 'to stand so closely by a man whose attitude to the war was doubtful and who had long since shown that he was gaga and politically finished.'

A compromise was reached, with Frances assuring him that 'things would be all right for me later.' Sylvester commented bitterly in the notes to his 'Diary' that 'she did nothing to keep this promise!' In fact, among her papers is a request from Lloyd George to Churchill for a knighthood for Sylvester. It is with a letter from Churchill written on the 12th December, asking Lloyd George if he wanted Lewis Davies Lewis on the honours list, because competition was strong for knighthoods in wartime and he felt that there should be an especially good reason for giving it to him. The copy of Lloyd George's letter is attached to the back and contains the request for Sylvester: 'There has been on my conscience an earnest desire to obtain a knighthood, and that is for Sylvester, who has served me so devotedly for over twenty years'

This came to nothing, but it is clear that Lloyd George felt he could not dispense with Sylvester's services. It is not surprising, however, if after Lloyd George's death Frances did feel that she could. His hard work and apparent loyalty made him a valuable servant, but his vanity and ambition made him touchy. Frances had never liked him much since he first came and insisted that his secretarial status should be superior to hers. She would laugh at him and his voice which had a strong nasal twang overlaying a Staffordshire accent and his hand-rubbing outward subservience which made him seem like a modern Uriah Heep. He thought her prim, and stiff and only providing comfort for Lloyd George: she thought he was efficient but difficult. He was left a thousand pounds in Lloyd George's will.

On the 18th December Lloyd George heard that he had been offered an earldom in the New Year's Honours list. He said 'That is very nice'', but asked if he could sleep on it. The next morning he sent his acceptance, but he was quiet and not a little apprehensive. He knew that Megan would be appalled, and indeed she usually refused to use the title she acquired as daughter of an earl, but her father was so obviously unwell that she did not berate him. On New Year's day those who were at Ty Newydd drank champagne to celebrate at 11 o'clock in the morning and Lloyd George seemed enormously restored in spirits, even excited at the prospect of what he could achieve in his new position.

Congratulations poured in, as did criticism. Some of the letters sent to him were extremely unpleasant, but these were not shown to him. Frances was also sent quite a bit of hate mail, accusing her of influencing the 'great commoner'. Jennifer, who opened a lot of her mail, put most of these straight on the fire. A number of people suggested that he accepted the earldom as a kind of present to her, or to make things easier for her after he died. Jennifer is sure that this is not the case. She had been entirely contented with her status as Mrs Lloyd George and neither wanted or needed anything more. It was done in order to save him from being out of politics and he got a good deal of fun choosing the title, the coat of arms and so on. He had no idea that, not only would he never take his seat in the Lords, but that the General Election would not happen until after he was dead. Even the by-election in his old constituency had not taken place when he died. The list of candidates was published in the same issue of the local newspaper as the account of his funeral.

Shortly before the end of the holidays, Jennifer needed to have her appendix out. Lloyd George's eldest daughter, Mair, had died after an appendectomy; although that had been more than thirty years previously, he was still anxious that Jennifer should convalesce properly. By the time she had fully recovered, Lloyd George was so ill that it was decided she should not make the long journey back to Oxford, when she would probably have to return almost immediately for the funeral.

Frances arranged for Jennifer to be coached by outstanding tutors in her two weakest subjects, so she did not suffer, (rather the reverse) by missing a term in her School Certificate year. Sadly, the long decline in Louise Stevenson's health also accelerated at this time. Muriel telephoned to say that their mother was asking for Frances, but it was impossible to leave Lloyd George at all by this stage. Frances wrote to her father:

> I can't tell you how desperately sorry I am not to be able to come to you but the Doctor said it would have a very adverse effect upon LG if I went away, so that I clearly cannot leave him. He is not so well today and the Doctor fears that the end cannot be far off.

Not even to be able to attend her mother's funeral upset Frances very much, but it had been confirmed that Lloyd George was now dying and she was nursing him day and night. As ever, she did not break down or make a fuss and Jennifer, who had been very fond of her Granny, felt that she did not care and made some very rude comment to her mother. For the only time in her entire life Frances hit Jennifer. It was so entirely surprising Jennifer at last began to realise the enormous strain that her mother must be under and felt ashamed rather than resentful.

In a letter from Doctor Prytherch to Lord Dawson Frances is described as

> doing a grand job of work. She has done so for the last six months and latterly, with his loss of control, this is no easy task, but she is doing it with all the devotion he deserves and she is doing it unstintingly and extremely well, and he calls for her constant presence. One cannot say more than that he is one of the best cared for patients I have ever had. [13]

He also described how he had 'escorted Megan there twice this week (this still requires patience, diplomacy and time.)' Hostilities may have

[13] Sylvester Diary op cit

been suspended, but the ceasefire was only temporary and a call to arms was never far off. A letter from Muriel in January 1945 begins,

> I was so furious when I heard your talk of Megan's visit to-night that I felt I would explode. Do for goodness sake, put her in her place. It really is Time she was annihilated, and you could easily do it. She no doubt thinks you are afraid of her as everyone else has always been.[14]

The truth was more that Frances wanted to keep the peace for Lloyd George's sake.

As the end approached Megan came every day and, in the final hours she held one of her father's hands and Frances held the other. For several hours on Monday 26th March 1945, Lloyd George lay dying in the library which had been converted into a bedroom so that he could see the beautiful view out to the sea from his bed. When he died, Megan was distraught for some minutes and was comforted by her sister Olwen, but Frances was quiet and serious. She was sharing a room with Jennifer at the time because so many people were staying and that night she told Jennifer that she felt as though she had been 'knocked off her perch'. It was horribly true. She had been needed and her life had revolved around Lloyd George. What was she going to do now that he no longer needed her?[15]

Without drama or fuss she functioned. A funeral was arranged for Friday April 1st – Good Friday – which being a general holiday meant that thousands of people were able to get to the service. The local newspaper said there were five thousand people there, others said seven. They covered the hillside where the grave was to be and massed in the fields on the other side of the river. They sang magnificent Welsh hymns, thundering above the sound of the river.

The days before the funeral were uncomfortable. There was of course, a great deal to be arranged in a short time and this left no time for grief. The most unpleasant thing was the 'fighting over his body' by various Baptist ministers and the local rector of the Welsh Anglican church (disestablished long before by Lloyd George), as to who would do what at the funeral. The Anglican rector, a pleasant but rather lazy man called Davies, could be considered to have come off best in the fight. The place where Lloyd George was to be buried had been decided well in advance by himself. His grave was to be on a sloping bank of the River Dwyfor which he had loved as a child and from which he had taken his title. He had no intention of being buried in the Criccieth churchyard alongside

[14] FLG papers
[15] Jennifer Longford's memories

Dame Margaret and he very strongly did not want to be buried in Westminster Abbey which he thought might be suggested. There was a memorial service in the Abbey later in the month, and several years later a memorial plaque was put on the floor, but Wales was where he wanted to be. However, in the opinion of the Rector Mr Davies, the ground would have to be consecrated, in accordance with Anglican practice, before Lloyd George could be allowed to take up residence. Davies, in billowing white surplice – an effective contrast to the Baptist ministers, all in black – therefore had to start proceedings. The Baptists had no order of service for something they never did and Davies made the most of it. After him, the Baptists, who had settled with some difficulty who was to say which prayers and who was to preach, took over. The sermon, on the text, 'And David's place was empty' (1 Samuel 20.25) was moving, the prayers impressive; but it was the singing that swept all before it. Afterwards, many people leapt on the flowers and tore the wreaths to bits to take home a souvenir almost before the family had turned away from the grave, certainly before they were out of sight.

The coffin had been brought down from Ty Newydd on a farm cart, full of flowers and accompanied by four of the grandsons – William was at school. The presence of the four had been arranged by Churchill which, as they were all in the armed services and it was within six weeks of the end of the war in Europe, was quite a feat.

After the funeral they went back to Avalon to prepare for the Memorial Service in Westminster Abbey.

The period at Avalon was very tense and unhappy. John Stevenson had been brought over to stay there now by Muriel, at Frances's request, and Muriel had had the miserable business of dealing with Louise's death and John's grief so she was also feeling extremely low and was unable to support her sister. She felt upset about this and wrote on 1st May,

> Darling Frances
> Here are a few oddments which you left behind! I may find more in time.
> The house seems very lonely now that you have left, and I miss you very much. It has been lovely having you here. I'm afraid I am not all that you would like me to be and am very often a pig, but you do mean such a lot to me, even if I do not always show it. You have been very sweet indeed to me, and long suffering.
> I do hope your return to Ty Newydd has not been an ordeal for you, although there must be some sad moments there. But at any rate your memories must be of happy times.[16]

[16] FLG papers

In Lloyd George's will Gwilym inherited Bron-y-de and about fifty acres with it. Megan had the rest of the farm. She already owned a small cottage at the edge of it which she lived in for a time, though not immediately. Frances was left Ty Newydd and its farm and she already owned quite a bit of land in Churt. She had bought fields as they became available, which could be farmed as part of Bron-y-de while Lloyd George was alive and form a separate, compact farm after his death. Dick was left nothing. There had been a bad relationship between Dick and his father since childhood and he was fonder of his mother and naturally took her side in the estrangement between his parents. Dame Margaret had left a lot of money to Dick, and Lloyd George stated in his will that this was the reason for not leaving him anything else. He added, more privately, that Dick had immediately wasted the inheritance from his mother and he did not want his money to go the same way. Dick was an alcoholic and had suffered a serious attack of delirium tremens not long before Lloyd George's death and he was also diagnosed as having TB and was in a clinic at the time of Lloyd George's death and funeral. He brought a court case saying that by the time the last Will was made, his father had been of unsound mind and that Frances had influenced him. Dr Smith, the doctor in Churt, gave evidence that Lloyd George was perfectly sane right up to the time he left Churt and Dick dropped proceedings before they actually arrived in court.

It was all part of the nightmare beginning for Frances now that she had been 'knocked off her perch'.[17] Megan left Ty Newydd after the funeral and never spoke to Frances again. She 'cut' Jennifer very publicly when they encountered each other in Criccieth later that summer. The Criccieth town hall showed a film once a week and it was at one of these performances during the summer holidays that Jennifer and Megan came face to face. Jennifer innocently greeted her and felt shocked and embarrassed when Megan turned and walked straight past her.

Megan and, to a lesser extent, Olwen waged a guerilla war against Frances, and the entire neighbourhood began to be drawn into one camp or another. The butcher would be told he would no longer receive business from Brynawelon if he served Ty Newydd and apologetically he would say that it was too awkward to continue serving Frances. Even Dr Prytherch was told that he could not continue to be Megan's doctor and Frances's, but he had the courage to ignore the threat and it came to nothing. She told Olwen's boys that they should never speak to Jennifer again – they were very apologetic to Jennifer about this, and said they

---

[17] During the funeral there were so many people staying at Ty Newydd that Jennifer and Frances had to share a bedroom and that evening, after the ceremony, Frances told Jennifer that she felt that she had been 'knocked off her perch'.

would have to concur if Megan or their mother were present, but that if they weren't they would be as friendly to her as before. Jennifer remembers a wonderful evening at a party given in August by Rupert Williams Ellis – (Clough's brother) at Penrhyndeudraeth, to celebrate the end of the war in Japan when the boys were present and friendliness prevailed.

It was during this summer that she met Bertrand Russell, Kenneth Clark and Arthur Koestler and his delightful mistress among others, and many old friends came to stay, but for the most part the interest and enjoyment of the summer had the nightmare background of Megan and Olwen's hostility. Frances's friends, especially the secretary Ann Parry, felt it showed their loyalty to her if they reported every nasty thing that anybody had said about her. Jennifer had never known anything like it and wrote a passionate and detailed diary describing the horror of it all – and then destroyed the diary in case anybody found it.

Chapter Eight

A new world

Lloyd George was buried on April 1st. It was apparent by then that the war was very nearly over. All would face considerably changed circumstances and Frances could not foresee the pattern of life without Lloyd George. It had been her satisfaction to serve him and fulfill his aims so no longer to be able to do so was unimaginable. Within a very short space of time she was discussing with Ann Parry the possibility of building a grand memorial college of agriculture in his name in Llanystumdwy on the land he had left her there.

In the immediate future she hoped she might be able to live on in the beautiful Queen Anne house that Clough Williams Ellis had now made so comfortable. She did not plan to let the family drive her out. In September 1945 Jennifer began another new school. She had persuaded her mother that if her School Certificate results were satisfactory she could go to Chatelard, normally based in Switzerland, but for the duration of the war, quite close to Llanystumdwy in Aberdovey. While she was there Frances wanted to have a home nearby, but in an unbelievably short time, the formidable headmistress, a Miss Braginton, managed to get the school back to Switzerland.

Bron-y-de, the Churt home she had shared with Lloyd George had now been left to Gwilym. She now felt closer to him in Ty Newydd near to his grave and his childhood roots. Muriel was running Avalon quite satisfactorily while she waited to find out what her Canadian lover, Walker Kayes had planned for their future.

On 3rd June 1945 Jennifer wrote from school to Frances:

Has Moo [Muriel] heard anything about Walker yet? I do hope that nothing has happened to him, though I can't believe after promising to write every day he would not have written for three weeks unless something had happened. Unfortunately the posts are very good now.[1] I suppose that any bad news about him would go on to Canada,

[1] Jennifer meant that since posts were now becoming so much more reliable the reason they had not received a letter must mean in all probability that a letter had not been written and that might mean that something more serious than just that a letter had gone astray.

and Moo would never hear it. The suspense must be awful.... After you, I love him best in the world. I love him like I would a father if I had ever had one, and so all the love that I would have given a father in fifteen years has been compressed for him into three and a half years.

Frances replied on the 6th June.

Moo is just a little jealous to know that you love Walker so much! But I know he loves you and I am sure you can always rely upon his acting as a Father would to you. I always regard him as a brother myself – he seems to fill the gap which Uncle Paul left when he died. I have always felt the want of a brother and now Walker seems to have supplied that want, for I do feel that he identifies himself with all of us, and it is a great comfort.

Walker turned up very soon afterwards and everything continued as before, with Muriel running things at Avalon and Frances trying to cope with the animosity in Llanystumdwy while continuing to work for Lloyd George's best interests. Her first two jobs were to acknowledge the wave of letters she had received in sympathy and to organise the building of a beautiful grave on the little plot of land known as 'the spinney' by the river. She employed Clough Williams Ellis, who had become a friend during the reconstruction work at Ty Newydd, to design a beautiful memorial. Then she turned her attention to two other concerns, the first being, who would be designated to write the so-called 'official biography' with access to her papers and her help. Secondly, she wanted to set up some kind of museum to him straight away and make it a home for the stupendous 'freedoms' he had received from many towns and cities and had left to her in his will. She decided that a small cottage which was part of the bequest left to her in the village would make an adequate museum for the time being.

Her choice of biographer was Malcolm Thomson, who had the advantage of being an old friend who had worked with her for Lloyd George, particularly on the *War Memoirs*. With that begun she turned her attention to creating a Committee to run the Museum and to plan for the creation of the Lloyd George Agricultural College. David's brother William agreed to be on the Committee as were the Williams Ellises, Mr Davies, the rector, with Ann Parry as secretary and herself. One of their first concerns was with the dedication of the newly finished grave. The children were all invited and given their own keys but these were not acknowledged, and the only one who wrote was Gwilym who said he did not feel he could tear himself away for the service. He began by saying that he was too busy with Mining Committees, but went on to say that he would find the occasion too sad and would rather visit the grave privately at some later date.[2]

Gwilym was at this stage still making a small pretence that relations with Frances might continue as before. He had, after all, been a friend and a frequent visitor to Bron-y-de dining, and staying with his father quite happily while she was there. It became clear, however, that Olwen and Megan were badgering him to take sides and he much preferred to forgo relations with Frances. Jennifer was not totally surprised at this betrayal. She had been rather humiliated by him already when she and her mother had been packing their possessions to remove them from Bron-y-de. Jennifer had put her books in piles on the floor and without telling her Gwilym removed the Aldine collection of Poets that had been published in 1831 and put them back on the book shelves. She noticed because it was a considerable set and very beautiful and she knew that Lloyd George had been so taken with the edition that he had bought two, one for her and one for himself. As Gwilym was no longer there she explained to the Housekeeper that she was taking her books back again and no more was said, but she was very hurt that he should have assumed she would try to take what was not hers and that instead of suggesting she had made a mistake, had just removed them. The impression was clear: the Lloyd George children regarded Frances as a grasping wicked step-mother likely to encourage Jennifer to take what she could. The incident made Jennifer feel very uncomfortable.[3]

By Christmas 1945 Frances was spending more and more time in the beautiful home she had built at Avalon, with a view to taking over more of the running from her sister Muriel. Moo still had high hopes that she would soon go to Canada. However, Frances was already beginning to worry that perhaps Walker was not going to stand by his promises to Muriel as she wrote on 13th January 1946.

> Walker came home on Thursday and he goes off tomorrow. Of course, Moo has been very happy these days, but I am trembling to think what will happen when he is gone. Walker sends you his love and says he will write to you. I think he is very worried about getting a job when he gets back to Canada, so it is a good thing that he will soon be on his way there to get his future settled.

Frances had heard that Dick Lloyd George had taken out an injunction to contest the will Lloyd George had made leaving him nothing and claimed that Frances had put unfair pressure on an infirm old man. It was

[2] This was the beginning of a severing of relations.
[3] Jennifer's recollections.

made plain to him that he would lose. Both the doctor in Surrey and the doctor in Wales agreed to testify that there was nothing wrong with Lloyd George's mind when he made this will and on the 25th January Frances wrote to Jennifer to say that Dick had withdrawn the action which was 'a great relief to everyone.' A month later she wrote,

'Dick has got himself into further trouble and has to appear in the Bankruptcy court this week. He really is hopeless and a complete disgrace. Gwilym and Megan don't seem anxious to help him and I can't possibly take it all on myself.'

It is extraordinary that she should even have thought to do so. Of course she was Dick's stepmother, but he was older than she was and he would not have relished her help.

Back in Wales in May 1946 Frances wrote to Jennifer that she was having the Williams Ellis's to lunch to meet the Director of Education on the question of a Rural College at Llanystumdwy. On May 14th she wrote 'The Malcolm Thomsons are down here this week going though the papers for the Biography so we have been very busy and shall be for some time now that we have started the book in real earnest.' On May 22nd she informed Jennifer that 'the project is to be formally announced by the Education Committee on July 6th' and on May 26th she excitedly reported, 'Everyone is very excited about the prospect of the Rural College ... Old Evan Elias in the Village is informing the Criccieth people, "Now the address is Llanystumdwy near Criccieth. Before long it will be Criccieth near Llanystumdwy".' By the end of the year articles were appearing in the press about the intended 'Ll.G Memorial College' which announced that

A plan designed by Mr Clough Williams Ellis for the Earl Lloyd George Memorial College at Llanystumdwy, North Wales, has been approved by the executive committee. The Dowager Lady Lloyd George has given the site and an appeal is to be made for public support.

In her letters to her daughter in May Frances, always loving, put in that 'I realize that you are the only thing that really matters to me,' now that Lloyd George was dead. Jennifer was not inclined to be very responsive to such outpourings. She was sixteen and wanted her own life and she found it inappropriate to have a passionate 'Mummy' around now at last when she was almost grown up. On the 27th January 1946 Jennifer had written to her mother,

Very little has happened this week, but that is your fault, for I was intending to go to Aberystwyth yesterday, but I wasn't allowed to go, although I had no cold or cough, because you had insisted that I shouldn't be let out for some days. Naturally I am very annoyed. When

I heard, I wrote you three letters, each one worse than the last, but I didn't send any of them. I'll show you them one day, and perhaps they will make some impression on you. I didn't have a very bad cold and it has completely gone now.

While Jennifer's growing up and fierce independence provided Frances with a constant source of interest, she never understood that she had not built up the sort of mother-daughter relationship where advice and interference could be tolerated. Nonetheless her regular long letters, at least twice weekly, were a source of pleasure to Jennifer. She enjoyed hearing her mother's news and opinions. Frances also often inserted presents or projected treats and at the end of August 1946, when her beautiful house converted from an old barn was between lets, Frances decided to take advantage of its glorious hall and minstrel gallery, and threw a dance.

A band was booked to play for five hours from 8 p.m., and caterers brought sandwiches, bridge rolls, lobster patties, small jellies, cheese straws, fancy cakes, éclairs, meringues and cream, ices, lemonade and coffee. Frances added cider, ginger beer, a claret cup and 'something stronger for the grown up men'. Cheering people up was one of Frances's favourite hobbies, like opening a bottle of champagne as a 'pick me up'. Spoiling Jennifer was one of her greatest pleasures, just as was sharing any interest her daughter might discover.

During 1946 Jennifer became finally convinced that she was a Christian and that the Anglican Church suited her temperament as the best means of worship. Part of this came about because Churt had a new incumbent, quite unlike any other priest the parish had known before. Harry Edwards had felt that his vocation was for work among poor city dwellers but during the war he had been a naval chaplain and afterwards the Church decided it would be good for him to go to a quiet and prosperous country parish. For Frances and Muriel his brand of Christian socialism was a revelation. Frances was already confirmed but she had been a most irregular Church-goer while living in an adulterous relationship. Muriel was not confirmed and Jennifer not even christened. With the help of Harry Edwards they set about putting this right.

Walker Kayes returned to Canada and Frances wrote to Jennifer, 'Moo seems to be pretty miserable as she has had no letter from Walker yet – though he has sent her a Bible'. Jennifer remembers that he also sent her a record of the 'Lord's Prayer' and a pigskin brief case – but no letter, ever. Maybe he hoped religion would bring her solace for his defection, but long after it was clear to Frances that Moo would not be making a future in Canada she still clung to her hope that he would send for her.

Frances was quite happy that Muriel should continue to make her home with her. Certainly she could be difficult and very moody, but

Frances was used to being calm and dealing with bad tempered and demanding companions. Initially it was Muriel who satisfied Frances's yearning to be needed and useful which Jennifer would not do. Providing a home for her youngest sister was by no means all sacrifice either. Muriel could continue to help administer the farm and drive the car and apart from these considerations, when Muriel was not in a depression or feeling angry she could be sparkling, funny and intelligent. Such an arrangement seemed sensible and satisfactory.

In fact it was not. Muriel never had to cope on her own and as is so often the way, loathed feeling grateful. Moreover she felt she worked pretty damned hard in their shared home. If Frances had been the obviously dependent one, Muriel might have been kinder, but it was so galling to be her protégée. She sometimes had to exercise power just to show that she was essential. She would claim it would be too tiring to drive all the way to a wedding Frances had hoped they would attend. She would take against mutual friends or complain about the demands made by visitors and refuse to cook for them or make witty comments at someone's expense. She was not difficult in the way Lloyd George had been difficult It was a new kind of minefield Frances was entering. Muriel loved Frances, but she was moody, possessive, and very jealous. She had wit and elegance, and wonderfully good taste and she could be loving and enormously kind, but she could also be hostile and unco-operative.

A conversation with Walker led Jennifer to believe that he knew he was not going to divorce his wife and send for Muriel even before he left for Canada. He told Jennifer she must always respect Muriel for what she had given to Walker as she had sacrificed so much in the face of convention and Jennifer picked up on the direction Walker seemed to be moving in and asked him if he was saying this because he did not intend coming back. He quickly denied such a thought, but Jennifer felt that he was in fact indirectly telling her this. She wanted to believe his words, so much that later when Muriel was beginning to despair, Jennifer reassured her that Walker definitely intended to come back: she had asked him as much. In May 1947 Muriel discovered for certain that he would not return and had probably never intended to.

Frances swept Muriel off to the Hotel du Cap in Antibes where she had worked with Lloyd George before the war. Monsieur Sillon, the proprietor made special arrangements so that the money restrictions did not prevent them from going. Anyway, contravening petty rules and restrictions was her delight. She managed to get Muriel to the pampering comfort and kindness of the Hotel and to enjoy the sunshine, blue skies and blue seas of the Mediterranean.

Muriel wrote to Jennifer when they got back,

Just before we went away I had some upsetting news of Walker, which has made me realise I must do my best to forget him. I should have realised it long ago, I'm afraid, but it hasn't been very easy to accept it. I must now try to foresee other things for my future ...

One of those things, as she mentions in the same letter, was religion.

I went to Mr Edwards this evening for my first instruction of Confirmation. He takes his religion very seriously and I think he is very helpful. He told me he had a letter from you and is glad that you are going to receive your confirmation over here.

But whereas Frances found religion a source of comfort and delight, Muriel, rather typically found it a source of frustration and worry. Still, it was another area of life in which they had a shared interest, and the Church with its committees and demands became an ever more important part of the sisters' existence.

In addition to the Church Frances found that as Lady Lloyd George, she was now a distinguished pillar of the community. She became Chairman of the village Horticultural Society; she was asked to address the P.C.C. and open fêtes; she was invited onto the Committee running the local children's home in Hindhead, Twizzletwig. One morning she received an invitation to open a fête in aid of the League of Moral Welfare! She thought she ought to decline but finally accepted.[4] For the most part she completely forgot that anyone might disapprove of her past. She talked about Lloyd George either as LG or as 'my husband' even when referring to periods long before they were married. Most extraordinarily, when an unmarried couple set up house together in Churt – unable to marry because he had a wife in a mental hospital – she did not want Jennifer to meet them because she felt it would be unsuitable. She was becoming as strict a parent as her own mother had been. She very much did not want Jennifer to follow the path which she had taken. Her friend Elsie Morris was much amused when she said she hoped that the first man ever to kiss Jennifer was the man Jennifer married. Elsie may have thought it was funny, even hypocritical, but it was quite seriously how Frances felt.

The holiday in Antibes had been a tonic that Frances felt she needed after the publication at the beginning of the year in the *Sunday Dispatch* of A J Sylvester's book in serial form *The Real Lloyd George*. On February 18th Frances had a letter published in the paper.

---

[4] Jennifer remembers the invitation because it did spark a breakfast of general hilarity, but Frances did not find it quite as funny as Muriel and Jennifer and saw no reason not to accept.

I have refrained from commenting on the previous articles which have appeared in the columns by Mr A.J. Sylvester purporting to give the private life of my late husband. I thought they were beneath contempt and so beneath comment. Decent people will form their own opinion of a man who, after his master is dead, betrays intimate, if inaccurate details of his private life.

I must however protest against the article which appeared yesterday giving an account of an interview between my husband and Hitler. It is true that Mr Sylvester was of the party that visited Germany and I was not; but, on his return my husband gave me a very full account of what took place, an account which does not tally with Mr Sylvester's version.

Mr Sylvester, by exaggerating certain incidents and ignoring others, presents a distorted view of events, as indeed he does of my husband himself. To give two instances where I could cite many, he does not mention the fact that my husband took Hitler to task for his treatment of the Jews and attempted to influence him on that matter, nor does he mention the fact that my husband did not conceal from Hitler his opinion of Germany's action in breaking the naval clauses of the Treaty of Versailles.

Sylvester replied to this attack by saying 'My account was written from day to day in Germany and is accurate' – but quite possibly not complete and coloured by his own interpretation. Others were on the trip and Tom Jones who also published his diary covering this visit, showed Lloyd George as more critical. Frances was bitterly upset by Sylvester's portrait of Lloyd George, concentrating on petty domestic failings and his more awkward side while ignoring his charm, humour and inspiring qualities.

Dick Lloyd George appeared to enjoy seeing his father revealed for the difficult man he had been. On the 16th March he published a letter in the *Sunday Dispatch*.

Mr Sylvester I have known for over thirty years and no more loyal, efficient and hard working private secretary could any Minister wish to have. Knowing his methods and his careful note-taking, I can vouch for the accuracy of everything you have printed.

To put it mildly, my father was, as Mr Sylvester says, 'a very difficult man'. You could never pin him down to anything, whether to a decision or an opinion –he was as slippery as an eel, more particularly during the last twenty-five years of his life. That is why this story of his wobbling about retiring from the House of Commons and accepting a peerage makes such extraordinary reading to those who know the old Radical in the heyday of his great powers.

He was never the same man after my mother's death in 1941, and during the winter of 1944–45 he knew he was a dying man, and yet he, the great follower and admirer of Gladstone chose that belated moment to enter the House of Lords, upon which august assembly he had so often poured the vials of his wrath, ridicule and scorn. No – it doesn't make any sense. I hope one day to publish the truth, which at present is known to comparatively few.

I was ill at the North Wales Sanatorium with lung trouble, during 1944 and until the time of his death. Denbigh is sixty miles distant from Llanystumdwy, yet I was never consulted about the proposed peerage or his first title; eventually I myself chose the second, or courtesy title, Viscount Gwynedd, which my son holds to-day.

The same mystery attended the preliminaries to his accepting a peerage as preceded his second marriage. The Caernarvon Boroughs' Liberal Association, as well as myself, got the news on opening the papers on January 1 1945.

Actually he was a peer for six weeks – sic transit gloria mundi.

Dick was plainly implying that Frances had some undue influence just as he had suggested when he had originally planned to contest the will. The sad fact was that Lloyd George had not had much time for his oldest son and he accepted the title to have a voice in the peace – he did not think that his heirs would feel they needed wealth to maintain the supposed dignity of an Earldom. Had a life peerage been possible there is no doubt that this is what he would have preferred. Yet it is true that Frances enjoyed being a countess. She had been a self effacing spinster for long enough. Who can blame her if she rather gloried in her title and position as his widow? Though indeed difficult he had also been a great man and she had long before looked above the feet of clay. She hated this public attention being drawn to them alone.

It was not proving a good year. Jennifer had resolved to study French at Oxford. On the morning she was due to begin her exams she heard that one of her teachers had slipped while out climbing the previous afternoon and had fallen to her death. She had known death before. She had seen Lloyd George die, but this was the first time she had encountered someone strong, attractive and vital, alive in the morning and then through a silly error wiped out in the afternoon. She described it to her mother:

I liked and admired Miss Stanham, but I feel little grief at her loss. I can only feel numbing paralysing horror. She was so very active and it was such a terrible way to die. I have thought of nothing else for two days. If I fail my exam, which I shall, it will mean nothing to me. Had I passed it would have meant just as little.

Jennifer was right about her failure, but she had second thoughts about her future. She found that she thoroughly enjoyed being a prefect and it made her realise that she might enjoy teaching. She did not want to teach a subject which she would never speak perfectly and she decided to make another attempt at Oxford, but this time in English. Frances was immensely surprised that Jennifer should want to teach. She had found teaching restrictive and there were now so many other opportunities open to women, but she made no effort to sway her strong-minded daughter, apparently only anxious to help in any way that she could. With little time available for this change in direction she decided that Jennifer should attend a tutors in London for intensive training for the English exam. She had rented a flat in West Halkin Street and looked forward to having Jennifer back.

Muriel had now heard finally that Walker had returned to his wife, so she was planning to remain at Avalon and Frances could safely leave her to run things while she took the chance to stay in London, taking Jennifer to the theatre, out for meals and shopping. Unsurprisingly with such a hectic schedule Jennifer did not succeed in the English exams either. Frances chose instead to suggest that she went to Scotland's oldest university, St Andrews. Frances never seemed to realise that there are things it is more satisfactory to know that one has achieved alone. She wrote to Jennifer and said that she would have a word with her old admirer Sir Thomas Jaffrey about getting into St Andrews. Jennifer was accepted and in due course took a good degree there, but she hated the fact that she could never be certain that she had got in solely on her own merits.

An extravagant London life together with occasional failure to get rent from 'Old Barn' made Frances realise that she could not afford to keep up both Avalon and Ty Newydd. She had not run away from the hostility she encountered in Wales. In fact on occasion she positively enjoyed a small skirmish,

> They have asked me to preside over the Sheep Dog Trials on the Criccieth Golf links and I accepted... I very much want to do it because 1 the sheepdog trials are very thrilling and 2 it will put certain people's noses very much out of joint. (I expect I ought to have put 2 first.)

An occasional triumph was invigorating, but the constant consciousness of hatred and sides being taken was depressing and Frances decided to sell Ty Newydd and accept that her real home was in Churt.

In the spring of 1948 she went there for the last time to pack up their possessions. She retained land and the small house where the collection was being displayed and she planned to have a beautiful museum built to a design by Clough Williams Ellis. Initially she thought that since the collection was housed she would work to establish the memorial college and then move on to the museum. Together with Ann Parry she sent out charming letters to practically every distinguished person she knew and enclosing a draft of the plans for the college. They asked for support either by adding their names to a list of sympathizers or by donating money. An enclosed pamphlet explained their plans and who was on the committee. They had more rejections than success, though everyone said that they thought a memorial to Lloyd George a good idea. One objection seemed to be that his memorial should be national and not strictly Welsh. That none of the family appeared to be serving on the committee evoked much disquiet.

> I would, as I have indicated be distinctly predisposed to lend my name in connection with an effort of adequate national character but I would also like to be satisfied that other members of LG's family, in particular Gwilym and Megan as two of my Parliamentary colleagues, were associated with the effort. I am not clear from your letter if this is so, but if you would care to give me assurances on the points I have mentioned I will be happy to consider the matter again.

This reply from Herbert Morrison, Lord President and Leader of the House of Commons at the time, was typical. In fact the family were heartily disposed to scupper any plan Frances might have come up with. Not one of them attended the consecration of the grave, and not one of them acknowledged the receipt of the individual key to its gate that she sent them. On hearing that Olwen castigated Dick's estranged wife, June, for having anything to do with the memorial Frances wrote that, 'there is no doubt that this wicked persecution is still going on, and that they have a definite system of getting at anyone who they think is giving any help.'

In the autumn the 'authorised biography' by Malcolm Thomson came out to rather poor reviews. On 19th February 1949 Frances wrote to Miss Parry that she thought Megan 'is telling people about the Biography that "the family were never consulted" and that explains some of the reviews – certainly the one in the *Spectator* by Dingle Foot ...' She went on about the future of the Appeal:

> I saw Miss Scott and had a long and frank talk with her. She thought the fact that the family would not support it a very great handicap ... She suggested ... that Camrose should be asked to sponsor an Albert Hall Concert with a big artiste... The trouble is I fear that immediately the family will be asked to sell tickets or take tickets and then the trouble starts. It is damnable.

She concluded by telling Ann Parry that she was working hard on a volume of letters due to be published by Hutchinsons in May.

On March 24th she wrote to her again saying that since

> the attitude of the family to me is the stumbling block ... I was
> wondering if it would make any difference if I were to resign the
> Chairmanship and someone less controversial were to take my place. I
> would of course still give the site, but would leave the field free to
> others. Of course it would be no use my doing that if the family
> continued to take the same attitude ...

Persuaded that they would she continued as before not really wanting
to give up her involvement. Just as she had spent the first thirty-four years
of her life working for Lloyd George she found continuing fulfilment in
doing things for him and his memory. She filled the place his death had
created by working for him still, replying to historians, defending his
reputation, establishing the museum and ultimately trying to achieve her
idea of a splendid memorial college of agriculture.

On June 23rd she wrote,

> You will have heard that Megan has sent four of the freedoms back. I
> heard from John Petts: who says he is going to write to her and say
> how pleased he is to have them. Will you tell him, if he has not already
> written, that I think this is unnecessary, as John Morris had to threaten
> legal action before she sent them and also told her solicitors that she
> would not get her residuary legacy until she gave them up. Even now
> she has not sent them all, and in any case they should have been handed
> over to me in the first place ... I do not see why we should pretend
> that she has done something wonderful.

Having finished editing the letters for Hutchinsons, she was told that
they were very useful and would 'supply all the deficiencies of Malcolm
Thomson's book.' She continued to write to anyone she could think of
about the College but its attendant frustrations did not fill her life. She
wrote to Miss Parry on October 19th.

> I must travel back on the 20th – the day after the Memorial
> Committee Meeting. I have been invited to a dinner in London on
> the Tuesday, to Dr Weizmann. Smuts is going to be there and I imagine
> it is going to be a big affair and I should like to be there. And the next
> day we have our Annual Sale for the Women's Institute here, at which
> I must be present as I am on the Committee.

Six months later a further letter explained that she must get back to

Avalon in time for the Flower Show as she was Chairman of the Horticultural Society. Her life was now centred in Churt and she was pouring her energy into village life.

However these were difficult years for Frances. Jennifer still adored Avalon but she had begun to find it a depressing place to return to. Frances's sunny nature still appeared evident to acquaintances, but she was struggling in murky waters. Unfortunately, Muriel, now her constant companion, always looked on the black side of things and their discussions encouraged Frances to believe the worst.

Writing to Ann Parry Frances wrote that she heard that

Olwen launched into her stock tirade against me pretending that LG had changed his will through my influence and that the family had suffered in consequence ... I wish I could publicly state what really happened – that Olwen and Gwilym were far better off than in previous wills. How wicked they are!

Early in June 1950 Frances lunched with Max Beaverbrook on the balcony of his roof flat at Arlington House, looking over St James's Park. He persuaded her to cancel her book of letters and help him to produce a:

very important Biography of LG to be written by Frank Owen and Robert Sherwood to be serialised in the Sunday Express (for which I get a large sum of money!) and eventually Beaverbrook is to acquire the LG papers. In return for which he starts a new Committee for the Memorial Fund consisting of people who served in LG's government, himself, Winston, Lord Maclay and one or two others, and he says we shall then get the money we want for the College. None of the family would be on the Committee, but that I don't mind at all.

Frances seems to have been swept away by Beaverbrook's persuasiveness. She handed over her enormous collection of LG's papers, even her diaries, and wrote on October 22nd 1950:

Beaverbrook went to America this week. He left instructions about the Memorial, but of course I would never have got this if I had not let him have the papers. I am sure I have done wisely, but am trying to get him to let me have a photostat of them for Wales – for the college.

Since the College did not materialize the fact that no photostats were forthcoming was all of a piece. But Frances was so sure all would be well and when Clough Williams Ellis told her about a beautiful pair of eighteenth-century gates that were available for sale she bought them and placed them at the entrance of what were to be the grounds of the College. To try to raise publicity and support they had a ceremony to herald the foundation of the College with the gates. This took place on 17th January 1951. Megan, Olwen and Gwilym were invited, but of course did not come. They missed a very cold occasion which left Frances frozen to the bone. Her misery was compounded by attending a Committee meeting at which she asked for accounts in order to check that a share of the profits had been sent to the Churt village hall which had also been built by Lloyd George. The Rector, Mr Davies was supposed to be Treasurer but Frances found she had to badger him to get any accounts and on this occasion he exploded.

Frances wrote to Ann on Friday 19th January 1951

> I was very much upset and very hurt by the Rector's outburst last night. I can't make him out at all. At all other times, he is so genial and friendly I think that at the bottom of the trouble is the fact that they resent Churt having any of the money. But even that doesn't excuse him from producing a proper balance sheet ...

She later wrote, 'I went away feeling I never wanted to come to Llanystumdwy again.'

It was becoming very clear to her that as she severed links with Wales and got older she must secure the future of Lloyd George's grave. It was still her property and up to her to see that it was properly maintained, but, she wrote,

> I should be willing, happy, as you know equally well, to listen to any suggestion that the family might have to make as regards the future maintenance of the grave and to co-operate with them on such a matter. But as they replied to none of my communications regarding the building of the Grave and the inscription which should be put on it, nor did they even acknowledge the keys which I sent to each one of them individually, I have no reason to suppose that they will wish to co-operate with me now. I certainly should not hand it over to them with any confidence that they would look after it or spend penny on it themselves. You might tell T.O. that all the expense has been and still is mine. Indeed, I think you ought to tell him all this and stress the point that I am willing to listen to any suggestions.
>
> I should indeed be very glad if one of them – say Gwilym or Olwen (failing Dick) would consent to join the Trustees of the Museum for the purpose of helping in the Administration (which would then include the Grave) though I must say that they have all, up till now, done their best to prevent me from getting the freedoms which are in

their possession, and which were my legacy! Megan still has some, and Gwilym has one and they refuse to give them up. Since seeing T.O. I have communicated to them through John Morris asking their views about an inscription on the grave, but they do not reply.

Please tell all this to TO ... I shall think that if they – the family – have anything like this in mind, it is that I should hand over every-thing to them and this I certainly will not do. LG himself knew what he was doing and he had no confidence in them either. But on the other hand, if they would institute a Fund for the maintenance of the Grave, I would consider handing it over to the National Trust who would accept it on those conditions. I am looking after it now because I consider it to be my trust, but, I repeat once more, I would welcome the co-operation of the family, if something could be arranged in perpetuity, for that is what is needed.

She was feeling more than usually aggrieved because of the unpleas-antness at the Committee meeting. She would have liked to hand over responsibility for the Grave, but she wanted to ensure that it was safe. She had returned to rather fraught conditions. Her second sister, Janet, had come to stay at Avalon while recovering from a slight stroke. In addition to helping with the invalid, Frances and Muriel were without domestic help and as she described, 'now we are doing our own cooking I find there is very little time for anything else.'

Their great friends Bill and Robin James [Admiral Sir William and Lady James] had suggested that they should join them for a holiday in Teneriffe, but Jennifer had developed nasty headaches at university and Frances wanted to be around in case she needed an operation on her septum. When her doctors decided she did not and that she ought to relax, Frances decided to book a three week holiday in Italy to extend Jennifer's holiday as she was already planning to be out there.

At the end of May Beaverbrook persuaded her to go to Canada for the opening of the University Library where he was placing the Lloyd George papers. Initially Frances was loath to go, as she felt she had too much to do in the village and on the farm, but he persuaded her that by flying she would not be away for long and she had a glorious time.

It seemed to recharge her batteries. Writing to Jennifer just before dashing off to dinner with Beaverbrook she described the dinner party she had been to the previous evening. It had been held by old friends the Brett Youngs in order to celebrate the publication of C P Snow's new book *The Masters* and L P Hartley was also there. She described how they had teased her for using platitudes and promised to collect a few more for her. She had enjoyed it all enormously and had sufficient energy to race down to Churt for the Flower Show the next day, and write one of her long letters to Jennifer before going back up to London for her dinner with Beaverbrook. Though now sixty-one her zest for meeting people and enjoying herself had revived. 'I was only in Canada 2 days, but in that time I met so many nice people, did very much and was very spoilt. I loved it all.'

When Jennifer arrived in Italy Frances and Moo set off to join her there. Initially they spent two weeks in Florence and then went on to Portofino. While there they visited Genoa and met a member of the Armenino family and his wife. They never quite discovered the degree of their relation to the couple: they spoke no English and Frances, Muriel and Jennifer spoke no Italian, but they were amiable and it intrigued them all to meet distant relatives. The meeting had been arranged by a Major Canali (or Canale) to whom Frances had been given an introduction. He was a rich man – he owned a shipping fleet – but was critical of English behaviour after the war because when he went to a British officer to ask for the release of his ships the man refused to shake him by the hand and did not even ask him to sit down – and the war had been over THREE DAYS!

Frances was thoroughly rejuvenated by her holiday and up to facing challenges again. John Pett, who had been organising the collection of the freedoms, had been offered another job, so now Frances asked Ann Parry to take on the enlarged job as official 'Curator of the Lloyd George Museum.' Frances had decided, along with the committee, that the freedoms and the rest of the collection must be better housed and plans were under way to build a proper museum.

Meanwhile life in Churt continued to be engrossing. Frances's sister, Ninette and her husband, Vernon had two daughters and a son. The youngest Elizabeth had become engaged to a Roman Catholic whose parents had disapproved and put so much pressure on him that he had broken the engagement. Elizabeth had sought to ease the pain by entering into a whirlwind of gaiety and had consequently become very exhausted. She was so tired that she had not been immediately aware that her exhaustion was more serious than normal over tiredness. TB had taken a firm grip by the time it was diagnosed. She spent a year in hospital and emerged much weakened. Frances, as ever, wanted to help and offered Ninette a cottage on the Avalon estate so that Elizabeth could recover in the country.

Frances eventually brought all her sisters to live with her or close to her, seeking to help them as she thought best. This was not always ideal. Ninette's oldest daughter, Nancy, was passionately in love with her husband, almost to the exclusion of her children and by the age of eight her son Christopher was clearly so unhappy that Ninette and Frances decided between them to pay for him to go to boarding school. This seemed a happy move, but when Frances tried to place Elizabeth in a job through her contacts Elizabeth was furious. Frances just could not understand these independent young women and their need to know that they had earned their position. Elizabeth got herself a job in the 'Legal and General' in Farnham. Perhaps her anger gave Frances a signal that she should not interfere too much in Jennifer's plans.

She did however whisk Jennifer off for a week to Paris in her last holidays before finals because she felt 'a little frivolity' would do her good. Refreshed, Jennifer went back to take her finals. Her plan had been to apply for a post graduate teaching course but she had a year to fill. Initially she worked voluntarily in the Africa bureau. Frances admitted to Ann Parry that she hoped this might persuade Jennifer that there were more exciting avenues than teaching.

For all her energy and determination Frances had to reconcile herself to the fact that she could not always organise people to do what she wanted. No matter what she did she could not persuade Lloyd George's children to forgive her and they continued to be a block to her plans for the Memorial. On July 10th 1952 she wrote to Ann Parry

With regard to the latter [the memorial fund] I have had a great disappointment. I wrote to Beaverbrook pressing for something to be done, in view of what is being done for Smuts, and I received the following reply:

'It is my view that the Lloyd George Memorial cannot be launched at the present time. Owing to difficulties and disputes the Memorial must stand over until it can be launched with certainty of success. It may be that Frank Owen's biography will set things right, but there are too many disputes now, there are too many recriminations, far too many criticisms aimed at one person or another'.

You can imagine how disappointed and furious I am in view of what he promised. I don't know what he has at the back of his mind, but I imagine he has been influenced by the family and now that Gwilym is in office he has got Churchill's ear. But there may be a little more to it than that. We can only hope that Frank's book will alter things. In the mean time, I feel that our plan is to cut them all out, to try and intensify the interest wherever we can, to collect as much as we can for the Museum, and not to let the thing drop. We might have an unexpected windfall, and at any rate the College will be built!

Brave words. She just could not allow herself to admit that she might fail in something she considered so important, but for a while it had to be allowed to slip and she concentrated on helping Frank Owen with his book *Tempestuous Journey* due out in the autumn of 1954. Helping Frank was something of a trial, as she wrote to Jennifer on August 11th 1954.

Frank, I have come to the conclusion, is really not adult. He behaves all the time like a naughty boy, but the trouble is, that you cannot treat him like one, and spank him, which is what he really needs. However, I suppose we shall work through our troubles, but he makes them so much heavier to bear!

The comment that he was not really adult sounds rather like something Muriel might have said. Muriel allowed herself to criticise Frances but she would spring to her defence if anyone else was imposing upon her. When Frances came home tired and dispirited Muriel was angry on her behalf and would add more biting comments only making such situations seem more extreme. In her year off Jennifer managed to get a teaching job at a nearby girls' private school to see if she would indeed like teaching. She would walk up the drive to Avalon and feel her spirits sink as she entered the house. Although she had a greater respect for Muriel than for her mother and found it easier to love her unreservedly, home life was easier when Muriel was not around.

Moo's memories were often influenced by her emotions – her likes, dislikes, contempts, and sense of inferiority. Once she had 'fixed' a version of events in her mind, then she would repeat the story regularly; but it may not have been accurate in the first place. In the autumn of 1952 Jennifer heard a conversation involving a group of well-dressed women who were having coffee in a New Forest hotel. The subject was nannies. One woman said she had to get rid of her nanny because the child had become fonder of the nanny than of herself. Another said she had a very efficient nanny – unfortunately the child was terrified of her 'but you can't have everything can you?' Jennifer repeated these conversations to Frances and Muriel. Years later Muriel said that Frances had once got rid of a nanny because Jennifer became too fond of her. She had never said this before and Jennifer knew the source of the story. Jennifer found that Muriel often had her own version of visits from distinguished and interesting people. Moo would work like a slave in the kitchen and produce marvellous meals, or oversee all the arrangements and serve the drinks. When, because she had been so self-effacing, a guest might fail to notice her, she would become angry and declare them ill-mannered or disappointing.

Jennifer needed escapes from this intensity and the spitefulness. Although she adored Avalon and appreciated her home and the love and thoughtfulness showered upon her but she had to get away. She needed to make a life of her own away from interference (however well meaning) from her mother and free of her aunt's bitter observations. She took her Post Graduate Certificate at Bristol and spent some time doing research in a deprived area before leaving for a teaching job in East Africa.

Frances was extraordinarily calm at the choices her daughter was making. She tried to help, but she did not rail and rage. When Jennifer was exposed to fleas through her research, Frances merely commented in her letter that she hoped the sunny weather was not encouraging 'the livestock'. While Jennifer was still at Bristol, Frances arranged that her piano should be part exchanged for one that would cope better with the temperature in Africa. Muriel later told Jennifer that Frances wept all the way back from Tilbury after they had seen her off in January 1955, but she did not weep at all in Jennifer's presence and put no obstacles in Jennifer's way. Nonetheless she started making plans to visit Jennifer the following Christmas and took a passionate interest in all things African.

In 1955 she managed to persuade the Caernarvon Council to accept her gift of the land she had designated for a College on the understanding that they were then committed ultimately to its building. She took comfort from this, but again she seems to have misjudged the level of commitment as nothing happened. At the same time she was turning her attention to more satisfying projects. She was looking forward to her visit to Africa and fell back into her practise of writing to Jennifer every Sunday and Wednesday and sending her parcels. Whereas at school these parcels had tended to be full of food they now contained magazines and books and the occasional item of clothing or length of material.

On December 2nd 1955 Frances boarded the *Uganda*, then still owned by the British India Line, and set sail for Tanganyika to stay with Jennifer over Christmas, first in Lushoto and then in Tabora where she worked. She wrote to Ann Parry on the 15th January 1956,

> We have only just reached Tabora, much later than we expected as things happened most unexpectedly – almost like a Fairy tale. We were invited to lunch at the Governor's holiday lodge [in Lushoto], near where we were staying and Jennifer, and his Private Secretary proceeded to fall in love. They became engaged after ten days, and then the Governor and Lady Twining (who thoroughly approved and encouraged the engagement) insisted upon our going to stay at the lodge for a few days. We had a heavenly time, and now have to make plans for the wedding, which will be some time this year, probably out here. Michael Longford, the young man, is completely charming, very clever and they seem to think he has a future. He is something more than a P.S., as he is a permanent Colonial Officer, and will get a district very soon, so they will be living out here. I like him so much and could not think of anyone I would prefer Jennifer to marry. She is blissfully happy as they are both interested in the same things. He is twenty-eight, his Father, now dead, was in the navy and his Mother is a doctor.

Frances was delighted, but all was not quite so heavenly as she claimed. Jennifer recalls being absolutely astonished to discover that her mother hated staying at the Lodge where everything revolved around the 'great man' (in this instance the Governor, Lord Twining). For thirty-three years Frances had seemed happy to pander to Lloyd George and she had appeared her normal serene and happy self in the Twining household, but the truth was that Frances had come to savour her freedom in her eleven years of widowhood. Jennifer was amazed that being part of another household revolving around a great man displeased Frances.

The other blot on the picture that she painted for Ann Parry was that Michael Longford, as a career Colonial Officer, was very likely to live in remote parts of the world all his working life. She would very much have preferred Jennifer back in England. No husband or career could possibly have matched up to her secret hopes for Jennifer, but she did have the intelligence to recognise that her daughter had a very different character from herself and hero worship was not what she wanted.

Returning home she set about the happy business of buying a beautiful wedding dress, organising flights (with Muriel this time) back to Africa less than six months later. She sold her beautiful grand piano to pay for it all.

Frances should have been quite a wealthy woman but her outgoings were considerable. Her farm ran at a loss, she had rented a flat in London, and then another on the South Coast. This when not being decorated she often lent to friends rather than spending much time in it herself. Generous to a fault in her years with Lloyd George she had also developed a taste for luxury. Despite her regular pension from the Carnegie trust and considerable assets she did not receive an income equal to her expenditure. She saw on paper that she was rich, so she spent richly. Her outgoings were enormous and intermittently the bank would call a halt – tell her that her overdraft was too large and she would have to do something about it. This usually entailed selling something. Her optimistic nature always led her to believe that she would obtain money somehow, that next year the farm would be more successful, that someone would pay her vast sums for her knowledge, or even that she might receive a legacy. This happened just often enough to sustain her hopes and when it did she always spent the money twice, by thinking it would both pay off a debt and occasion the excuse for a celebration. It usually left her even worse off than before. She never learnt to be careful with money and gradually she disposed of most of her assets, her property, her works of art and beautiful possessions. She never seemed to repine when her latest redecoration scheme or lavish planting in the garden meant that she had to sell a treasure she had had for years. The Bluthner went and for five years she was without a piano until her friends, the James's moved to a house in Scotland and sold her a baby grand.

She took farming seriously and enjoyed it, but she did not know much about it. She would invest in the latest equipment, build a beautiful new dairy and buy wonderful animals, without realising how long it would take her to recoup the investments. As her fruit farming was sometimes more successful she was deceived into believing that at any moment the rest of her farming might become profitable.

Still, she did not allow money worries to blight the wedding (or anything else for that matter). The only hiccough in an otherwise wonderful day was a most extraordinary coincidence. Muriel had bought material in England to be made up for a June wedding in Africa and it was very elegant when it was finished. The material was identical to that of the dress which Lady Twining wore. The governor's excellent wife was neither svelte nor elegant and did not look beautiful in the dress so Muriel felt that she too must look as Lady Twining did. She did not of course, but noone could ever convince her of it.

Jennifer and Michael went off to the Congo for their honeymoon and Frances and her sister returned home in time for the flower show and the fruit harvest. For a short time she had no project or plan to think about. Her letters are full of concern about the Suez crisis and the reaction to revelations that in 1918 she and J T Davies had burnt army figures received too late to influence the 'Maurice affair'. Jennifer wrote full of sympathy, and on November 4th 1956 Frances replied,

> Thank you very much for what you say about the Maurice business in 1918. ...the *Express* got my diary and my autobiography by a trick. I lent them to Frank for his book, and the *Express* thanked me for 'handing them over' in a letter which I endorsed, and they now claim they own them. I asked Mr Hadfield [her new lawyer now that John Morris had retired] about it, and he says that he is afraid I did part with them. It is exasperating and most tricky. I had never given up the idea of publishing my autobiography though Beaverbrook now says I can publish it if I like. But I think perhaps later on I will do something different.
>
> I ought to have taken advice at the time but I was so busy and so fussed about Frank's book and everything that was going on that I did not bother about it -not realising then how dishonest they were.

Her autobiography did now belong to Beaverbrook and when she eventually completed a fresh one, she found he owned the copyright to that also. He allowed her to print it and receive the profit in the UK but retained rights over any American publication. He had done everything legally, but Frances certainly understood that in return for her help and papers, she would receive support in her undertaking to build a memorial college. She was never a very good business woman and nothing was signed to that effect. Perhaps no-one was 'dishonest': simply cleverer.

Any dwelling on these frustrations was quickly put aside on hearing from Jennifer wrote that she expecting her first baby in April 1957. Frances was enchanted. No child in the history of the universe, with the exception of her own could have been more beautiful or more intelligent than her grand-daughter. Ruth was born as the new moon was sighted signalling the end of the long fast of Ramadhan and the beginning of the Muslim festival Id-el-Fitr. Most of Jennifer's household servants were Muslim and they called Ruth 'Mwana Iddi' – Child of the Festival. Frances wrote about this,

> 'It is wonderful that she should be blessed with this special aura, the more so that you are living among Muslims ... I know you are sceptical of the moon and the stars having any influence in our lives, but I have a strong feeling that they do.

Michael had six months leave every three years and his next entitlement was due to begin in the autumn of 1957. Frances met Ruth when she was still only six months old, without the disturbance and expense of going again to Africa.

Jennifer describes that first leave as 'rather difficult' as they divided their time staying with two 'possessive mothers'. Frances, who had not been a full-time mother to Jennifer nevertheless had a great many opinions on how little Ruth should be cared for. She was obsessed by her health and how much she ate – it was never enough – and she felt that Jennifer and Michael were mad to keep the baby with them so much of the time. On one occasion when they did leave her with Frances while they went to the opera she lay down beside the cot to be available if the infant should murmur. Ruth slept throughout but Frances was so shattered that she had to spend the next day in bed. The explosion of baby clothes and baby clutter in the beautiful surroundings at Avalon drove Muriel to distraction and concerned Frances who, to pacify her sister had a quiet word with Jennifer asking that she should be tidier.

During their time in England Jennifer and Michael arranged that Ruth should be christened at the parish church in Churt. Muriel was to be her Godmother along with Jennifer's great friend Margaret from St Andrews University, and Michael's brother Ronald (nicknamed Nibs) was to be her Godfather. Frances managed to offend Ronald by teasing him about the loudness of his jacket and saying that he would have to watch his language when his Goddaughter was older. On discovering that he had taken offence she declared they were good enough friends for her to chaff him, but that she still did think his jacket had been rather loud and his language too fruity. She did sometimes fail to charm, but in this instance, it would appear that Ronald was 'not her type' and she was not trying very hard. He was very different from Michael: rather brash and liking to shock, but evidently sensitive to criticism.

While Jennifer was packing to leave Frances wrote a letter to await her arrival in Mahenge, 'I shall only remember the happiness and pleasant-ness and not the little frictions that crept in occasionally and which I feel must occur even in the best of families.'

Jennifer took care to remember and she and Michael booked a cottage half way between the two mothers for their next leave.

When they had gone Frances felt totally desolate.

I can scarcely bear to go about the house, reminded of you and my darling Ruth wherever I turn. The Schoolroom wing, which was so warm and busy, is now empty and cold; there are no little garments airing in the cupboard, no nappies on the line, no Milton basin in the kitchen! But I must pull myself together and think of blessings instead.

Within a few days she was back in a struggle to be business-like while avoiding alienating the one member of Lloyd George's immediate family who had remained her friend. 'Uncle William' – David's brother had decided that for his ninety-third birthday he would publish a book *My Brother and I* which included a lot of letters from Lloyd George. He wanted Frances to say she approved of this. Frances had been left all Lloyd George's papers in his will and so, in effect the letters technically belonged to her. She felt that William had cleverly left approaching her until just before publication in order to rush her into giving consent. She wrote to Jennifer on February 18th 1958,

I had a pretty stiff time with Uncle William. He was determined to get me to say that I 'approved' of his book, which I had not seen, and wanted to commit me on the telephone – he tried several times over the weekend. Finally I had to write him a letter (dictated by my solic-itor) to say that I could not approve a book which I had not seen, but I was quite willing to give him permission to use documents the copy-rights of which belong to me provided he acknowledge this. Whereupon he said that was all he had asked for! The solicitors think I am taking a chance in letting him use documents without seeing them in context, but I am willing to do this, as time is getting short. He is tricky, as it emerged that the MS is already in the publisher's hands. It was obvious he was trying to rush me, and I had rather a worrying weekend as I did not want to quarrel with him.

On March 8th she wrote that they had gone round to friends in order to see Megan on television on a programme called 'Speaking Personally'. Frances thought that Megan had been

> very affected and did not make good use of her wonderful material ... I think she must have 'lost her place' in her notes, for she seemed to flounder a good deal, and at times we wondered what she was driving at ... Also she wore glasses which did not improve her appearance as they flickered in the light and gave her an odd expression. Her voice however was very good, even talking 'rubbish'.

In her letters to Jennifer along with references to the family and masses of news about life in the village with cocktail parties and committees Frances frequently commented on the political situation. In 1958 she was very concerned about the Hydrogen Bomb. Frances was very much opposed to it and felt that an end to the NATO alliance would be better than being caught up in the nuclear escalation. As she saw it she would prefer to fight communists in a conventional manner and 'die a comparatively normal death.' The idea of a nuclear deterrent had not yet taken hold and death from 'the bomb' seemed very real to her but she did not allow it to cramp her style.

On March 19th 1958 she wrote to Jennifer to say that, with regret, she had to sell the Dairy Farm and concentrate on the orchards: 'The cows are a constant worry and we have a loss of several hundreds of pounds on them each year.' But she heard from Clough Williams Ellis, who along with telling her how his part of Wales had been converted into China for the filming of the *Inn of the Sixth Happiness* informed her that the plans and site layout for her little museum were about to be submitted for planning approval and to be sent to three local contractors for their tenders. In the same letter Clough enclosed a small bill for all the work he had done for the Memorial College in what he called a 'farewell account and final discharge.'

But she did not dwell on this. The museum was being built and there was still a lot to give her cause for delight. On June 15th 1958 she wrote

> De Gaulle made a wonder speech in Paris this week, short, but it must have been a very inspiring one. The BBC reproduced some sentences in his own voice. He ended 'La route est dure, mais qu'elle est belle'. It was thrilling. He was evidently on television too, and it was one of the times when one wishes one had a TV set. I did not realise De G. had such a wonderful voice.

Her letters were also full of her latest reading and what she thought would interest Jennifer, but she still thought her daughter too innocent, or perhaps too high minded for certain books and wrote for example about Wayland Young's book *Still alive tomorrow*, 'It is exceedingly crude about physical things!' though she enjoyed it because it had a description of the same castle she had visited with Lloyd George in Marrakech. She reminisced that 'Jessica Brett Young and I were invited to tea with the ladies of the harem which wasn't nearly so exciting as it sounds.'

At the end of August 1958 she conveyed the sad news that Harry Edwards, the priest that had such an influence on them all, had died of polio. 'He did wear himself out in his selfless service'. He had moved back to a parish in Orpington and she and Muriel made the long drive, through thunderstorms, to his funeral. Frances gave his widow a substantial amount to help her through the immediate period of adjustment.

In the November Dick Lloyd George arrived back in Churt from America. Initially, the press thought he was staying with Frances or in a cottage on her estate, but he stayed in one of the two small cottages that Megan retained in Churt called Heather Cottages. Frances reported to Jennifer that,

Apparently Dick plans to attend the House of Lords regularly, as Peers now receive £3 for every time they put in an appearance, for expenses, and this, I suppose is what he plans to live on. There is also a lady living with him at the cottage – not June [his second wife] but no one seems to know quite who she is.

On November 12th she enlarged:

Dick is writing the most awful articles in the *Sunday Dispatch* or rather giving a series of interviews for which I imagine he is being very well paid. I feel sorry for the Bishops who live in the cottage next door. Mrs Bishop has been asked to cook for him (I think they have a cottage rent free from Megan or at any rate they could be turned out). Moo met Bishop in the lane yesterday and he opened his heart to her 'Excuse my language Miss', he said; 'but he's a drunken bugger!' Apparently he comes home from the pub in a taxi at 10.30 every evening, dead drunk, and the Bishops don't like to go to bed until they know he is safely in bed, as they are afraid of his knocking over the paraffin stove and setting the place alight. I suppose he will go on drinking as long as he is getting all this money, and will probably finish by having D.T.'s as he did before his father died. (He told Sylvester, who went to see him in hospital: 'The old Man came to see me yesterday: he had on his top hat a frock coat and he brought a dear little pink hen with him. Wasn't it nice of him?'

Dick is saying dreadful things about his Father in the interviews – how he hated him, and what an awful man he was. There is another interview next Sunday. I asked William George if anything could be done, and he did not seem to think we could do anything.

She consulted John Morris but he assured her that nothing could be done because 'you can't libel a dead man'.

By December 17th Dick had broken his thigh. He had fallen into a ditch on his way home from the pub and had been there for three and a half hours before he was found and taken to Haslemere hospital. The doctor told Frances that Dick was 'in the last stages of degradation' recommending that he should stay in hospital for three months.

For Christmas 1958 Frances and Muriel finally succumbed to the lure of a television set. They wanted to see a series Montgomery was giving on battles,

> though Moo does not understand battles (neither do I for that matter!) Lulu [the dog] loathes it and the first time we had it on she nearly went mad. Benny [the Siamese cat] is immensely interested and sits bolt upright in front of it, cocking her ears from one side to another as though he is taking it all in. Moo and I were weak with laughter the first time.

The television gave her the chance to see De Gaulle when he made a speach. She was very upset that the British government were on such bad terms with France as a crisis in Berlin loomed. After Christmas she described how they made full use of their set to watch the de Gaulle ceremonies in Paris.

> We locked in to his triumphal journey from the Palais de l'Elysée to the Arc de Triomphe and the tomb of the Unknown Warrior and it was a most moving spectacle ... We all agreed that on this occasion at any rate television was worthwhile! Actually we have looked in on several other very good programmes but I was sorry to have missed Montgomery's talk on Friday as we had to go to the W.I. Christmas party which was the usual tepid affair ... I would far rather have heard Montgomery explaining how we ought to have finished the war in the autumn of 1944, which is what Taid said should and could have been done.

While Frances was learning the new joys of television Jennifer's young husband was in hospital with what turned out to be undulant fever. He was dangerously ill and had to be transferred to Dar es Salaam. The capital was very hot at that time of year. Jennifer was desperately worried, away from home and coping with a baby. Her mother wrote on December 30th

> Remember that 'everything works for good for them that love God.' It must be difficult sometimes for young people to feel that, when everything does not go according to their plan, it may still be God's good will. It is only in my old age that I have come to see the truth of this, and to place complete faith in Him – bringing my difficulties to Him and waiting to see what He has up his sleeve for me, so to speak.

Just after the new year Jennifer was able to send a telegram to say that Michael was on the mend. Frances returned to writing calm letters describing the weather was bright but cold and how pleasant it was to walk around the orchards picking up prunings. There was more news of Dick.

> Valerie (Daniel) [Dick's daughter] rang me up yesterday in a great state. Dick is coming out of hospital next week, and the woman who he thought was going to look after him in the cottage (the same one I imagine who was there with him before his accident) had telephoned Valerie to say she would not come. Valerie says she thinks the woman had really had enough of Dick and he has already got through all the money he earned from those ghastly articles, there is not much inducement for her, as it would mean she would have to keep him too. Valerie's husband says he wont have Dick in the house. I did not realise that they had him there for a while last summer and Valerie says he is impossible and that it is very bad for the children.
>
> I had told Valerie about this convalescent home at Elstead and she is going to see the Matron at the Hospital and discuss with her the possibility of Dick going there for a while (the offer is free!) But I happen to know that Matron says that anyone who takes Dick on ought to be told exactly what he is like. John Morris said last night – in front of the vicar! – 'It is a great pity that when he had his fall he didn't break his neck.'

Two weeks later Frances reported that Valerie and Owen were getting permission to put Dick under restraint as he could not look after himself. It was a sad story – the bright attractive man descending into alcoholic degradation and poverty. He never came to terms with living under the shadow of his father. From the time of his school days during the Boer

War, when he had been viciously bullied because of his father's unpopular stance he found it hard to bear the weight of expectation which his name evoked.

Frances would have liked to help, but there was little she could do beyond offering advice about convalescent homes. She had become ever more involved with the Church and was on very friendly terms with the vicar and his two sisters, and when faced with a situation such as this or with Michael's illness she now did resort to prayer.

Muriel in particular, but both to an extent, had a close friend in the village, Beatrice Brounger, another formidable spinster, known as B by the sisters. On March 1st 1959 Frances wrote to Jennifer of an incident that had occurred at church.

> B has not budged in her attitude towards the Church, but she is very partial to the Vicar, and had decided she would come with us to the Service. He preached a very good simple sermon on praise and worship and thanksgiving, but apparently it didn't appeal to B. (The line she takes is that she has nothing to thank God for, and emphatically not for her 'creation and preservation'.) When we went out of Church Lady L button holed B, and said 'How nice to see you here Miss Brounger. Did you like the sermon? What did you think of it? Did you find it helpful?' B said 'No I did not; and I don't wish to discuss it with you Lady Leonard.' Poor Lady L looked as though B had slapped her face, and I must say I think it was unnecessarily rude of B, though Lady L is a fool and knows the difficulties about B, and should have been more tactful. But she is notoriously tactless, and I think a tactless proselytizer is the most annoying of all people.

Two weeks later she was doing a little proselytizing herself, writing an article in the Parish magazine on giving,

> There is to be a Diocesan drive for planned Christian giving quite soon. I have my own views on Church finance (not only Churt) but I don't think it would help much for me to air them at this time. Anyhow I am not much good at finance.

How true, but she was very good at giving. Too good as Jennifer kept finding on having to pay the duty for wonderful inessential presents. Frances was also awfully bad at receiving presents. She lavished presents on others but she did not give them the pleasure of being able to give something back. She could be so uninterested in the present that she would put it in a drawer and decide it would suit the donor and give it back to them the following Christmas. At least it showed she appreciated the donor's taste.

In March 1959 Frances was involved in a radio programme made about General Smuts.

> On the whole it was dull, and not well produced, but I was not displeased with the sound of my own voice, and even with what I said! But Moo deflated me at once by saying that my voice was unrecognisable. I'm glad it's over, as I was rather nervous about it, not having heard the recording; and I don't think I disgraced myself.

In the spring of 1959 building was begun on the new museum in Llanystumdwy and Frances booked her flight to visit Jennifer in a remote highland region in Tanganyika. She had been seventy the previous October and she now suffered from a mild heart condition for which she had to take regular medication. Undaunted she responded to Jennifer's invitation to stay with rapt and immediate enthusiasm. She wrote that she was most anxious not to inconvenience them in any way and they were not to think of driving down to meet her, she would make her own way. 'I do hope the ferry will be working again by then but I don't in the least mind crossing in a canoe.'

As ever a few little irritations ruffled the otherwise calm waters of her visit. Jennifer could not help getting cross when Frances let Ruth, by then aged two and a quarter, play with her heart pills and carry her sharp nail scissors. Frances, never having had to enforce the daily vigil of a full-time mother had not built up the strength to deny an adored child anything. Ruth found her 'Bangy' a source of delight also: Jennifer could not help being infuriated by little things. Whenever tea was brought in Frances would automatically take over the pot and pour. This was just habit and it was perhaps foolish to find it so annoying but in her own house Jennifer found her mother's habit of assuming control most irritating. At the same time she was impressed by her mother's calm particularly when a visitor was taken seriously ill. It took three hours to get the emergency equipment from the local hospital and sterilised! Jennifer noticed her mother looking a little pensive while this drama was unfolding, but she made no murmur and was more concerned that her treasured family lived here so far from medical assistance than that she at seventy should be bothered by such a thing.

The return journey began with Michael driving her to Morogoro where he had business to attend to. The car broke down. From then on Frances tried 'tactfully' to suggest that they invest in a new car. She had good reason for wanting to make sure Jennifer could travel safely. Just before she left her daughter had announced that another child was on the way. When the letters started again they were full of instructions to 'DRINK MORE MILK'. The usual sequel to a stay together also occurred with Frances writing, 'I am sure you will have forgiven me if at times I seemed to be interfering and difficult.'

It never occurred to Frances that perhaps she was not very qualified to advise a young mother. She had always wanted to be a mother and she felt maternal, but the truth was that she had not ever looked after a baby or even a child full-time. Exposed to modern ideas of child care they surprised her. Jennifer must have told her mother that she had arranged for a a sand pit to be made. Frances wrote: 'I am so glad about the sand pit. It is strange how children seem to love them. We have one at Twizzletwig [the children's home] and there we have been instructed by H.Q. to provide water play for the children – in the schoolroom! They adore it, of course and wash their dolls and their toys and everything they can lay their hands on, in bowls of water! They have to have plastic pinafores to keep themselves dry! Personally I think it is carrying things a bit too far!'

On her return from Africa Frances found that her sister Ninette was about to leave Avalon cottage and move to a bungalow in Farnham with her daughter. Her husband, Vernon, had died and Elizabeth who was still living with her and working in Farnham, found the country quiet and the proximity to all her elderly aunts, depressing. A move to a new house seemed a solution. While building was underway GCE results out. Ninette heard that her grandson, Christopher had failed every one. This caused high drama and endless discussion with the Turner family.

> Ninette seems to be heading for another breakdown and is practically paralytic in mind and body, I have had to tie up all sorts of loose ends with solicitors, agents and builders during the last few days, and Moo and I are keeping today and tomorrow quite clear so as to be able to take charge. The trouble is that she seems to resent our having to do anything (though not able to do it herself) and we have to extract information from her by a lengthy process and when you think you have got everything straight you find there is still something she hasn't told you. The truth is that she is ill and how they are going to get on by themselves in the new house (the telephone isn't in yet) I really don't know.

Ninette was now in her late sixties and had moved house before. She had a very competent daughter living with her and helping her. It is no wonder if she did 'resent' her older sister's interference. Frances seems to have behaved like the clichéd oldest sister to her siblings all her life. In some degree they accepted her implicit assumption that they could not manage without her. Jennifer, however did not accept her interference and pursued a life as independent as possible. Safely remote in Africa she did allow her mother the pleasure of running small errands for her. It was very helpful that Frances wanted to obtain specific children's clothes, nursing bras and other useful items only obtainable in England. On November 14th 1959 Frances wrote to Jennifer,

> You said in your letter that you were being a worry in asking me to do things for you, but you must know that there is nothing that gives me greater happiness than to be asked to do things for you or any member of your family.

When Jennifer warned her mother that they had decided to spend the approaching leave in a rented cottage in Hayling Island. Frances responded on January 24th 1960,

> I think I learnt a lot, my sweet, during your last leave that was very salutary. I realise how possessive I was – but I did not mean to be possessive, only helpful as Ruth was so young and you were not well. But I do know now that it will be much better for you to have your own house, and I am sure you are wise in having one equi-distant between the two mothers. I do hope nonetheless, that I shall somehow or other be able to see a great deal of you all. I am convinced however, that it would be better for Moo and me to see you at separate times. After all, you do belong to me more than to Moo – and Moo herself is apt to be very possessive at times! And I am sure I am right in making this arrangement. I have had Charman to drive me about once or twice lately, and it does simplify things a lot. Perhaps I am becoming independent in my old age – but that is better than being possessive! What do you think?'

It was certainly becoming easier to employ someone to drive her than to rely on Moo, who might make a fuss, or decide she could not face it. In the very next letter she described how on top of a 'bring and buy' sale and preparations for the 'Refugee Year Fête' they had Janet (her second sister) to a birthday lunch.

> Auntie Janet's birthday yesterday provided us with another opportunity for good works. She came to lunch, and after lunch expected to be taken into Farnham to spend the Boots token which you had given her! She had several other demands too, and was more than usually tiresome and Moo was practically hysterical by the time she took her home.

Although Janet had seemed a little lacking mentally she was remarkably gifted with figures and had held down a demanding job in a bank.

This was her seventieth birthday. Since her retirement she had lived in lodgings in Beacon Hill paid for by Frances. Yet another sister who came to live near Frances and depend on her. They all had the sense to realise that no one would be happy if she came to live with Moo and Frances. She made a pleasant life for herself apart from the tedious lunch weekly at Avalon. She had nothing in common with her sisters. Moo and Frances might quarrel but they did share interests and they both found Janet boring. She probably found them boring too. She would come to lunch, eat enormously and then fall asleep until she was taken home. Demanding to be taken shopping as a birthday treat was unusual, but clearly no more welcome for that!

Amid the frustrations of trying to run life for those who did not want their lives managed Frances had the satisfaction of knowing that at last the little museum in Llanystumdwy was complete. On February 16th 1960 she travelled up from Churt, beginning at 8.30 in the morning and failing to arrive until 7.45 in the evening due to snow in the Midlands. She wrote to Jennifer, ' the clouds lifted over the Barmouth Estuary just as the sun was setting and the light effect was simply beautiful over water and sky, which made the long journey really worth while.'

Although she was now seventy-one physical stresses did not dampen her capacity to appreciate beauty and enjoy it to the full. She was delighted with the new museum and called it 'real Clough'. A formal opening was planned for the 28th May just less than two weeks after their garden at Avalon was open for a day to raise money for the Church. They did this annually and it always entailed masses of work ensuring that the garden was at its perfect best for the day but she felt there was enough time to recover and enjoy the opening in Wales.

'We are sending out invitations to the family' she wrote on the 11th May,

> though I don't suppose any of them will come ... I go down on the 22nd and I can't go before because of Moo's birthday [on the 21st]. I tried to persuade her to come down too but she wont. It would have been nice if she could have driven me down, but as it is, I am getting Charman to drive ... The trouble is that Moo can't really leave Lulu [her dog].

On the 29th May she was able to report 'The opening ceremony yesterday ... was an unqualified success. We were fortunate in having a lovely day ... A very large crowd came ... Clough ... presenting the key was most amusing ... On June 1st she added, 'According to a letter just received from Ann Parry, the museum is attracting a lot of interest, and someone has written from Magdalen College offering a quantity of sketches [cartoons of LG] ...' But there was a ghastly interview with Olwen in the *Sunday Express* trying to explain why she and her sister did not come to the Opening Ceremony on Saturday. She said they 'would be letting the family down'. Muriel said . 'I always thought LG was their father. I wonder who their father was?'

The excitements continued. Less than a month later she received an invitation to attend the unveiling of the Memorial Statue to Lloyd George in Cathays Park, Cardiff due to be unveiled on July 8th. She had been wondering if she would receive an invitation as Megan had been on the Committee. She came to the conclusion that they obviously felt compelled to accept her, and she planned to accept. Afterwards she wrote

I had a wonderful day in Cardiff on Friday. I went down on the special train from Paddington on which were also the Prime Minister [Macmillan], Edna and Gwilym [Lloyd George], Jane Griffiths, M.P.s and other people. They were all very nice to me and we were met in great state at Cardiff with large cars and driven to a reception given by the Lord Mayor (a woman but still 'Lord Mayor' – her daughter was the 'Lady Mayoress'. Then we went on to the dais opposite the statue for the unveiling. I sat next to William George and looked after him. I forgot to say that Megan and Olwen were there also but of course did not know me. However Valerie [Dick's daughter] and Goronwy [her husband Goronwy Daniel], Owen and his wife [Dick's son and daughter in law] and even Robin Carey Evans [Olwen's son] were all very friendly.

The unveiling ceremony was very impressive, and so is the statue itself – though it isn't really Taid! ...

Then we went to the City Hall for a very grand lunch. I sat next the P.M. who was very nice and talkative. I got him to sign my place card for you. Don't lose it! He made a better speech than he had done for the unveiling. It was really a lovely occasion – with the Welsh Guards Band to play, exceedingly nice food and wine. I had Lady Plymouth on my other side, and she is very charming. I was really overwhelmed with everything and everyone – there were a lot of people there whom I knew, a lot of people were introduced to me. At one time I seemed to be surrounded by Mayors with gorgeous chains of office.

Gwilym and Edna both look awful. I think G must have had a slight stroke, as his speech seems to be affected and his face looks a bit odd. Edna has got very fat and heavy, and ugly having lost all her nice colour.

In her Wednesday letter she described the 'unholy row' going on in the House of Commons over the statue being made of Lloyd George. Macmillan had told her a bit about it at the lunch. Frances had said before, and now repeated her theory that Megan was holding things up deliberately in the hope that Frances would no longer be around 'to spoil things'. As a little aside she mentioned that Moo had pointed out a review in the *Telegraph* of a book by a young author, the reviewer ending up with the words 'Would any other author have given his hero two cats called Lady Megan and Lady Violet?' [presumably after Lady Violet Bonham Carter].

Dick had not been to any of these ceremonies. It is doubtful if he had even been invited. He had that year finally brought out his long planned book despite Frances's hopes of a change of heart. It was as critical and as sordid as had been feared. That it was so one sided and so clearly the attack made by an angry son ensured that it did not have the impact she had once feared. Frances found Lloyd George, far from being forgotten was being talked about more and more about as the centenary of his birth in 1863 was approaching. She would not be able to celebrate this with a great college opening but she was so busy she was less distressed about this than she had been.

Local concerns continued to fill every spare minute. The Twizzletwig fête was rainy but successful, and as Ruri-decanal representative (from 1954) she had a full day at the Diocesan Conference. She remained very concerned with International affairs in general and anything to do with Africa in particular. The P.C.C. asked her to give them a talk on Tanganiyka and the mission hospital they raised money for in Minaki.

On June 5th 1960 she wrote

Now K [Kruschev] is going to Cuba obviously with malicious intent towards the U.S.A. and he is behaving like a fish-wife in his speeches … I certainly think that his latest suggestion for complete disarmament should be examined and encouraged don't you? On June 19th she wrote

The talk on the BBC by Mary Goldring on nuclear armaments is in the *Listener* [one of the magazines she had sent out to Jennifer along with *Country Life* and the *Times* for Michael] so do look out for it. It is so clear and convincing but rather alarming! What worries me is that two Defence Ministers are Winston's sons-in-law and Winston is still behind the scenes, and I fear he would love a nuclear war before he dies. It seems a dreadful thing to say, but he once told L.G. that the only thing that really interested him – or that interested him above everything else was war!

In September she wrote that at the Trade Union Congress a large section wanted to vote for unilateral disarmament. She was anxious that the Americans should be prevented from using British bases for 'atomic practice'.

In addition to her concern about nuclear build up of weapons and an escalation into war, she was very anxious and disturbed by what was happening in Africa. She now read every article about Africa with the same passion she had once used for Lloyd George's projects and concerns. A typical comment from her in October of 1960 was,

> I see that the Congress people are already demanding a completely African civil service! I should have thought the Congo would have been a warning to them not to go too quickly ... 'Oh yes! I forgot S. Africa, which has decided to become a republic four-fifths of its people not having been allowed to vote ...

At the end of October Jennifer and Michael brought their family back to the rented cottage on Hayling Island and Frances met her newest grand-daughter Catherine Jane, for the first time. Catherine had arrived in the rainy season in Ifakara hospital. Even in good weather it was two hours journey from Mahenge in good weather. She had travelled home by canoe, lorry and in a basket on an African's head through the floods. Jennifer had malaria and the journey had been very challenging, but little Catherine was an easy going baby. Frances was very pleased, naturally, that her daughter was safely home with another gorgeous grand-daughter but she infuriated them by suggesting that they might be disappointed it was another girl. Frances still fundamentally felt that it was more important to have sons to carry on the name and to achieve great things and her faint reservations infuriated Catherine's proud parents.

Tensions were greatly eased by the distance between Hayling Island and Avalon this leave. Visits were frequent and Christmas was spent together but irritations did not build up in anything like the same way as when they all stayed together. Unfortunately the whirlwind of independence was moving at a rate no-one could have foreseen. The Longfords returned to Africa to find their future there was clearly going to be limited.

While they had been in England they had enjoyed a visit from a young Swiss attached to a Religious Order in Ifakara. Sister Olive was taking a long leave and trying to improve her English. Her stay with the family in Hayling Island was a marvellous help to Jennifer now coping with two young children in England without the domestic help she had become used to in Africa. As ever, Frances liked to meet Jennifer's friends and make them her own. As Olive would be staying on in London when Jennifer returned to Africa Frances invited her to stay at Avalon. Serene letters she wrote to Jennifer indicated how much she was enjoying Olive's company. On the 13th and 15th February she had written that they were weeding together in the garden and working together on English and that Frances was so much liking her that she felt she would miss her when she was gone. Muriel was away at the time, helping B sort out a house she had inherited in Gloucestershire. When she returned Frances's letters about Olive changed. From saying how much she would miss her she said that if she came down from London again she ought to stay with Nora Gardiner, as if she was a domestic help, because

> we don't really need anyone while Julie and Mathews are here ... she did quite a lot of weeding in the garden, but was chiefly occupied with her English studies. I think I was able to help her a good deal. But, Moo would, I think very much oppose her coming back here for any length of time.

Olive had assumed she was a guest and at no point seemed likely to want to spend a 'length of time' with them but she had assumed she was welcome and therefore suggested that she visit Frances and Muriel for a last visit over Easter before she left for Switzerland and Africa. Frances replied that they could not manage Easter as they were busy, but would be pleased if she came for a day or two later and wrote to Jennifer, 'We really could not have her over Easter, as though she is very nice and pleasant, we discovered that she demands more time than she gives'.

Time was limited it was true – on May 3rd she wrote that she had four committee meetings on Monday – but she was also usually hospitable and enjoyed entertaining. A neighbour's daughter wanted to paint in the orchards and Frances was happy that she should accompanied as she was by her three little boys. They played among the trees and when their mother had finished about midday she offered them all a drink. She gave the mother sherry, and the boys she gave what she thought was a coca cola, but relating the tale to Jennifer she said,

> I could not understand why they took such a long time to finish them. It turned out that I had given them beer by mistake! It is a great tribute to their manners that they finished the drinks and did not say a word. I only discovered later on.

Entertaining could be something of a strain. They did not manage to keep domestic help for very long and whenever Moo took over she made very heavy weather of it due to her anxiety that everything be perfect. Frances wrote on June 4th that Moo had cooked the lunch for some friends.

> It was very nice – chicken casserole and new potatoes and peas (frozen) and meringues, which were delicious with bits of ginger in the cream. With the electric mixer the meringues are so easy to do, and you can

make them beforehand. But Moo has been quite exhausted since, which means she has not been very good tempered.

Moo's temper was to be put to a more serious challenge in August when her chest was in such a bad way that the doctor told her she had to give up smoking. She had been a constant smoker, leaving a trail of ash in her wake, but the doctor made her realise that chronic bronchitis would result if she did not give up. B tried to support her by not smoking in her company and Frances noticed a dramatic drop in her cigarette bill. She had given up when expecting Jennifer but continued to keep a box of cigarettes available for visitors.

Whether from discomfort from her chest or withdrawal from smoking Muriel went into one of her periods of black depression. Frances suggested going to Devon for a holiday, but when in one of these moods she did not want to do anything. Frances sent for the doctor and when her sister did not respond to treatment sent for him again ten days later. The doctor told Frances afterwards that no one could help Moo, but that drugs might mitigate things a little. Frances wrote:

> From what he told me I realise that the conditions she experiences must be pretty terrible and now that I know more about it, I can be more tolerant at any rate. But what I must guard against is allowing myself to be dominated by what really amount to fits of despair, hatred and jealousy.

Gradually Muriel surfaced from the depths and life continued as before. Frances had so much concern in all things African that she was kept very busy in the winter of 1961. Independence was declared in Tanganyika. Frances went up to London especially on December 10th for the Thanksgiving Service for Independence in Westminster Abbey which she thought thrilling.

The new year was hectic. B was becoming very unwell indeed and could not be left on her own for long periods so the sisters brought her to stay with them at Avalon. Moo went down with flu and Frances had to cook for and look after two invalids. On top of this the telephone broke down. At first she had regarded this as a blessing 'as people could not ring up and ask if they could come! But now they come without ringing.' Some of those who turned up proved to be very welcome. One such was their cousin John Down who dropped in with his daughter and grand-daughter.

> They stayed to tea and we enjoyed their visit, especially as John, who is in retirement is an agent for wines and spirits, is going to arrange for us to

have all our drinks at trade prices, which means a considerable discount. He said he is glad to do something for me to repay me for getting him his first job when he came out of the army in 1919! He certainly made good of it, and one is touched when people do remember!

Jennifer was expecting her third child in January. On top of all the nursing and entertaining Frances fretted to hear how the delivery had gone and whether Jennifer was surviving the heat in Lindi that winter. Her confinement fell at a time of increased demands placed upon them by the historic momentum towards independence. On January 10th Frances heard that Michael had rescued a small boy swept out to sea with his friends while playing football on the beach. Frances always responded to heroism whatever the risk and wrote, 'how splendid of Michael! I do hope he wasn't too exhausted and distressed'.

On the 24th January the longed-for baby grandson was born.

I cannot tell you what joy I experienced when I got Michael's lovely message yesterday morning. I am afraid I did drop a few tears of joy when I put the receiver down and before I could recover myself sufficiently to go and tell Moo, who was also full of emotion! What a rich blessing for us all, my sweet! I am sure that you and Michael are filled with gladness at the arrival of your little son – though I feel bound to say that had it been a daughter I am sure she would have been greeted with equal love. But it is wonderful to have a grandson, and I think in my heart of hearts I must have wanted this, though I would not admit it to myself.

They called him Philip Michael. They thought that Frances and Muriel might like him to be called Paul after her brother killed in the First World War. Frances was touched that they should think of such a thing, but as she said, 'from superstitious reasons ... better not, especially as Grannie's brother, also Paul, and the only boy, died when he was 19.'

Anyway she loved the name Philip which she associated with some of her greatest friends: Philip Kerr, Philip Sasoon and others and she said, 'even its diminutive, Phil, is charming, I think.'

The next excitement was less than a month later when Jennifer's first book was published by Routledge and Kegan Paul. Servants made it possible for her to be both an attentive full-time mother and still find time to write. Her book was based on the research she had done in Bristol before she went to Africa. Frances was not sure if the material would not shock the vicar, but was nonetheless bursting with pride. 'It is beautifully written my darling and you have so cleverly avoided any comment of your own.' Later she enthused, 'we liked the presentation of the book very much: the only unnecessary thing we thought was the quotation right across the jacket "Hell with the lid off"[5] I expect they did that for sensation. The blurb is very good.'

She arranged for Durrants to send all the reviews and found that the book got universal praise. 'Moo and I are almost overwhelmed with pleasure and satisfaction at your success.' On April 1st she wrote to say that Jennifer's book had been reviewed on the radio on a programme, *World of Books* and that the review had been 'most eulogistic and enthusiastic, and so very nice about you personally'. Frances and Moo were particularly delighted because the other book reviewed was disparaged in comparison and it had been published by Gollancz who had turned Jennifer's book down.

Beaverbrook was writing his book on the last part of Taid's premiership and he wanted to go through it with Frances to check some points. Frances who was to lunch with him had mentioned in her letter that she might just tell him about the book. Jennifer sent an urgent telegram requesting her not to mention the book at any price. It was about real people and written under a pseudonym. The last thing she wanted was to be identified.

Tanganyika had now decided on a policy of Africanisation and the British civil servants were reaching the end of their employment there. Michael arranged to bring his young family back to England to work there. He would receive a small pension, but would need another job soon with three young children to support. Frances wrote saying they should make Avalon their headquarters. It made economic sense to go somewhere rent free while he got himself established. Churt was within relatively easy distance of London where work was likely to be. Frances had assured Jennifer that her tenants in the Farm Cottage would soon be leaving providing a separate roof for her household but this was wishful thinking. The tenants were not going immediately and Jennifer and Michael with three small children would take up their old quarters in the schoolroom wing. Frances wrote,

> Don't you really think it would be a good thing for you to have your headquarters here for a time? With Moo and me in the background to sit in -we promise that we wont interfere at all when you and Michael were here, but it would be glorious to see something of you all for a time.

It was not 'glorious'. It was a strain all round. The two ageing ladies found their routine completely disrupted and if they had found the

[5] Malcolm Muggeridge was quoted as saying that the descriptions were 'Hell with the lid off'.

clutter around one baby a bit much how much more so did they find the clutter around three! Michael loathed London and had never wanted to go into industry but he took one of the first jobs that offered, in order to start looking for a home of their own and get away. When the Cuban missile crisis seemed to bring the world to the edge of nuclear holocaust Jennifer found she regarded the possible end of the world in the light of a 'blessed release'. They spent every free minute looking for houses. Initially they had dreamed of a Tudor cottage, but Michael was six foot six inches tall and crashed into every beam. A tall Victorian house in Witley was bought. Although only nine miles away from Churt it enabled Jennifer to adjust to life in England looking after her children with all the additional domestic complications without comment or criticism.

Frances was enormously glad to have her daughter and grandchildren close again and quite appreciated that living together was impossible. It was so much better than having them living in Africa. She began by inviting them over at least once a week for lunch, but, as Moo said that cooking a big lunch was too exhausting, it was changed to tea every week. Frances had once written to Jennifer that Admiral James, their jovial and dearly loved friend, had decided to call Muriel 'the management' as she could never agree to any social engagement without first consulting her. Frances had thought this quite funny. She was adept at circumventing Muriel when it was necessary, but in time the routine of living with 'the Management' was not really very funny. Occasionally she would defy Muriel and the quarrels could be terrifying; for the most part she concealed plans of which she knew Moo would disapprove. In a way this was unfortunate because Muriel was much more careful with money and might have prevented some of Frances's excesses, but at the same time, Frances at least preserved her capacity to enjoy herself.

Financially things were going from bad to worse. She had the regular and substantial pension from the American Carnegie trust awarded to Lloyd George for his part in the First World War and bequeathed to his widow. At the same time the fruit farm was losing money and her generous presents and extravagances meant that she was going to have to make some cuts somewhere. Avalon was expensive to run. While it was plain that Jennifer would not be living there, it was tied up in a very secure trust for Jennifer and this made it impossible to make money from selling it. However, to save the running costs would be substantial and when the tenants of Farm Cottage had at last moved on they had an available alternative home. The bullet was bitten and the house she had built and the glorious gardens she had seen develop were sold to Americans. She and Muriel moved into Farm Cottage.

As Frances had always adored decorating and creating a beautiful home and garden she was not miserable about this. B had made a coup on some investments and she gave Muriel the money to build an extension. She gave it specifically to Muriel so that the house should be partly hers and Muriel would no longer be a lodger. The extension created a beautiful sunny study for Frances in which to relive her past while writing her autobiography.

1963 had shown there was substantial interest in Lloyd George. The centenary year had been filled with invitations to dinners and memorial services. She had been unable to attend the special broadcast service from Bangor University because she was ill with bronchitis, but when the Queen paid a visit to Llanystumdwy and the grave in August of that year she was delighted to attend.

Writing her book gave her great satisfaction. It took her some time as village commitments were still keeping her busy. She had been asked to be President of the Churt Over Sixties Association which she told Jennifer 'is a very prosperous and popular association and one of the most worthwhile in Churt and I feel very honoured to be the President. It is such a democratic and friendly institution.'

She continued to be invited regularly to social engagements, drinks parties and dinners and she enjoyed entertaining others, particularly when she had some sort of domestic help. It pleased her very much that she was still regarded as attractive or charming and that she received many compliments. On one occasion she was leaving a cocktail party and the host whispered to her that she had 'graced' the occasion, she was quite flustered by the intensity of the compliment and said she thought she was too old for that sort of thing.

Neither Jennifer nor Muriel really believed that the book would ever be complete. They regarded it as therapy, a useful distraction from present annoyances. But by 1967 she had not only completed it but secured Hutchinson to publish it for her. Muriel helped with the proof reading and the typing. After the hiccough of discovering she had 'sold' her auto-biography to Beaverbrook together with her other papers she managed to get an agreement with him whereby the royalties from this book did come to her in England, although he stipulated that any sales abroad should first be agreed to by him.

The book *The Years that Are Past* was not a long book, but it was well written and quite successful. All sorts of people she had not heard from in a while wrote congratulating her. It stimulated discussion and renewed historical correspondence. Jennifer says, 'nothing was as real to her, or as satisfying as thinking about, talking about and ultimately writing about LG.'

Spoiling her grandchildren came a close second. They were still young enough to enjoy spoiling without reservation. They did not worry that she was spending too much or interfering and they loved the beautiful rocking horse, the superb doll's pram and the treats. On Boxing Day she established a pattern of taking the grandchildren for marvellous outings, the ballet at Covent Garden, Billy Smarts circus, Humperdinck's *Hansel and Gretel* at Sadlers Wells and sometimes a pantomime. Ruth remembers being astonished by lunch at Simpsons when men in tall white hats cooked meat over flame by their table. She also organised that Ruth and Catherine should be taken to Trooping the Colour and bought them new pink coats. She also saw that Ruth and Jennifer should attend the State Opening of Parliament. In the gallery though which the Queen processed Ruth was brought to the front of the crowd and worried by a policeman who told her that if a beefeater stood in front of her she should stick a pin into him. As she was seven she took this literally and was most concerned that she did not have a pin and what would happen if she did. The child won a BBC essay competition describing this day and Frances was amused to see that the desire to write was passing on down the generations. She believed that all her grandchildren were exceptionally talented. Ruth was shocked when she was playing the piano to her grandmother one day as Frances suggested mildly that she should practise it a little more.

Frances telephoned Jennifer at least once a day and more often if she could think of an excuse. When Muriel decided that making tea for the family was too much Frances took to bringing a chocolate cake, raspberries, ice cream and some biscuits over to Jennifer's house for tea once a week. When she was not enjoying contact with historians or TV Documentary producers she equally enjoyed thinking of ways to please and interest her grandchildren. She heard that *The Sound of Music* was in nearby Barnstaple when the children were having their summer holiday in Devon and she wrote to Jennifer sending money and saying she had intended to take them to see it on their return but thought they might prefer it now. She asked her old friend Lord Boothby to give the children tea in the House of Lords and show them around the Houses of Parliament. It had given her enormous pleasure to introduce Jennifer to the theatre, art, and luxury, at every opportunity she tried to do the same for her grandchildren.

She began to grow rather deaf, something which made her social life less pleasant. She found it hard to follow conversation and she had to give up her committees. Conversing with individuals she could manage very well and her withdrawal from village affairs meant that she was more time available for writing to various historians who were in touch with her. She had admired A J P Taylor since his television lectures in 1962. At that time she had written to Jennifer,

> He is giving six lectures on 'the Twenties' but the first three have been of events which took place when Taid was P.M. and the article on the Peace Treaty is the first one I have known to do justice to Taid and his aims at that time. It is scrupulously fair and most interesting.

When he approached her with the idea that he should work with her to edit her letters and diaries in Beaverbrook's possession, she was delighted.

Meanwhile she was interviewed at length on television by Fyfe Robertson who asked her unexpectedly at the very end, if she had not minded never having children. The question took her by surprise and she did pause. It was now the late sixties and it might not have caused a scandal to admit that she had, but Jennifer had just told her to tell the whole truth in her autobiography or not to mention her at all. She could not bring herself to tell the whole truth so she gave the answer she had perfected over the years, 'Lloyd George was my child.' She recorded it before it went out and she did not mention this to Jennifer. When she came to watch it Jennifer knew this was only being consistent, but it made her feel obliterated – denied existence by her mother. She knew the feeling was not rational, but she did not like it. Frances remained unaware of her feelings: they did not discuss it.

In 1966 Megan died of cancer. Frances always believed deep down that the bitterness would be resolved some day, but Megan took her loathing to the grave. Frances went to her funeral – a seventy-eight year old lady, not welcome by the family and yet prepared to travel all the way from Churt to Criccieth, but it was important to Frances that she should make this gesture to her old adversary.

The battle did not die with Megan. In 1970 a memorial plaque was unveiled to Lloyd George in Westminster Abbey. By then Dick was dead and his son, Owen, the present earl arranged a champagne party after the ceremony in Dean's Yard. He invited Frances but would not allow her to bring Muriel who would, of course, be accompanying her and helping her now that she was eighty-two. Muriel was so offended that Frances did not feel she could possibly go to the party without her, but she still managed to enjoy the unveiling ceremony enormously.

Jennifer was on holiday in Devon and Frances wrote to her there on July 28th 1970.

Yesterday was a great experience. The service in the Abbey was just out of this world. The singing was heavenly and there were such lovely pieces of music. And then we had the Band of the Welsh Guards playing quite a lot. I am enclosing the Programme and perhaps you will return it to me when you come back, unless you would like to keep it.

Jeremy Thorpe's address was a wonderful performance, paying tributes to Taid all along the line and making him come to life. The stone is a beautiful piece of work, and you must see it when you come back. The elect stood round it when the Prince unveiled it, (he is a darling) and the Usher said to me, 'Will you stand just behind the Prime

Minister?' So I went and stood behind Harold Wilson, but the Usher said 'No, a little further along', by which I realised that he meant Heath (I can't get used to his being Prime Minister.)

The Abbey itself looked glorious with all its colour and light ... After the Service there was a champagne party in the Dean's Yard, by permission of the Head Master of Westminster School. I did not go as Owen would not give me permission to take Moo, so I strolled in the Cloisters with Sybil Stern, and we were joined by one of the Chapter, a most pleasant man who explained everything to us, and escorted us to the car in the Yard, very disappointed that we were not going to the Party. I had hired a car from Overton's for the day, and it was a great help ...

The blot on the proceedings was the Family, some of whom were revolting, especially Olwen who was throwing her weight about and looked awful. (Moo said I looked nicer than anyone else. I wore my black silk suit, which looks very smart, and my pretty blue hat. She looked very nice too, but she wasn't very happy with so many Lloyd Georges about, and she not being presented to the Prince.)

But the most unexpected performance was last night when there was a broadcast at 10 o'clock in which Olwen and Ann Parry played the top parts, supported by two Welshmen who I had never heard of. I must say Ann was quite good, but Olwen was revolting with a face like a Cheshire Cheese going mouldy, and full of giggles.

She finished by saying William Tenby had been there and had been very charming and was very good looking. She was not anti the family *per se*, and in fact she could also make critical comments about people she liked, but Olwen seems to have taken over Dame Margaret's place for especial vitriol. They had never been friends so the animosity was not tinged with the regret she had felt about Megan.

The ongoing bitterness did not seriously upset her in her declining years. It was just a fact of life. Her diary and letters were published to much acclaim and comment, in the United States as well as England. In 1971 she was approached by James Morris and asked to write publicly in protest about holiday developments that were planned on the Dwyfor. She wrote a letter to *The Times* and to the Prime Minister, the plans were scotched and she was told she had been a great help which pleased her.

In 1972, the historian Martin Gilbert asked her if she would like to join a party he was setting up to visit Israel for a month. She had been rather delicate since falling down the stairs leading to Jennifer's front door, but his itinerary for visiting Jerusalem, Bethlehem and Jericho before moving on to the coast was most appealing. Before committing herself she went to see the doctor to check that it would be alright. The doctor told her not to be silly. She was eighty-four now and would never be able to go abroad again now.

She died less than ten days later, on December 5th 1972. She began to feel very unwell about 9 p.m. and died in her own bed within an hour. Muriel had called the doctor from the house across the road, as she found when she tried to call from their own house that the telephone was out of order. The telephone played quite a large part in the drama. In the afternoon of her last day Frances had been expecting a friend to come to tea – Sister Carol Graham of the Farncombe Community, a small ecumenical Religious Community just outside Godalming. Frances had great liking and respect for her and was looking forward to her visit. Not absolutely sure that she had the day right, Sister Carol telephoned to make sure. She heard an ordinary ringing tone, but Frances heard nothing; Carol thought they were out and did not come, Frances waited and was very disappointed when they did not arrive. Had Frances and Muriel rung to find out why, they would presumably found out the telephone was out of order sooner; and the doctor would have been called more quickly; had Frances had not been disappointed over the travelling plans and her failed tea, she might not have had the heart attack that night.

Yet it was a good time to die. She had finished her writing and the collaboration with A J P Taylor had gone well. She loved her three grand-children and knew that Ruth planned to study history at university and would in due course write her story. Physically and mentally she was deteriorating, slowly, but irreversibly and she died while still retaining her dignity and a great deal of her beauty.

The quotations in the final chapter are taken from the collection of letters kept by Frances

Index